Pipe Dreams

One Teacher's Journey

By

A. R. Magaletta McClure

This book is a work of non-fiction. Names and places have been changed to protect the privacy of all individuals. The events and situations are true.

ISBN: 0-7596-9280-7

This book is printed on acid free paper.

1st Books - rev. 06/07/02

Acknowledgements

I'd like to thank the children, parents and many dedicated teachers who are too numerous to mention. Their love and guidance helped immeasurably in my formative years as a teacher. Without them there would be no story.

This book is dedicated to my forever friend and love
Dan McClure

Part I - Chapter 1

September 1973

"Didn't anybody tell you?" Mike's voice was breathy and sounded rushed. "We've decided to move your class next to our other special education classes," he announced. His eyes darted around, watching children and teachers pouring into the basement of Cherry Park School.

It was the first day back from summer vacation. My first as a teacher and Michael Donahue's first as a principal.

"Nobody told me anything," I stated flatly. "Only that I had a job teaching emotionally disturbed children."

He guided me through a maze of scattered children. Some were lost and crying, most had on nametags that identified them, their addresses and phone numbers. Others looked numb, resolved, having been through this in previous years. So this was public school. I could see seven and eight year olds directing their five-year-old siblings to kindergarten. The wisdom of the experienced, I thought.

I silently wished one of them would comfort me. I had a sinking feeling in my stomach that I suddenly remembered from my own early days of being in elementary school.

"Well, here it is." I could tell our nervous, new principal was anxious to be off on other matters concerning his school. He had deposited me at the door of an empty classroom. I had the strange feeling I wouldn't see him again. I wasn't far from wrong.

"We like to keep our 'special classes' together," he whispered the term as if it were sacred. I watched him move his fleshy body up the stairs, away from the bowels of the school, where I would spend most of that first year.

I opened the door and turned on the light. The room was dingy and depressing. Overhead steam pipes that covered most of the ceiling were rusty and snaked over and around each other. Thinner pipes circled the circumference of the floor. Concrete

1

walls, wooden floors and windows too high for small children to see out of.

If the kids did not have emotional problems to begin with this room would certainly help that little problem along. I walked over to the high, rectangular windows near the west side of the class.

If I stood on my tiptoes I could see outside. Yellow school buses were unloading hoards of happy, screaming kids. They were running across the front lawn of the school. Anxious and excited to see old friends again and exchange secrets on summer adventures.

I watched the old crossing guard at the corner of 5th and Buffalo St. waving small children to safety. He looked disoriented and I was more than a little surprised to see a small, blond, cherubic boy throwing up his middle finger, signifying the bird, directly in the old man's face. The boy ran, screaming with glee, into the safety of the building. The old man watched him run. Resolve and disgust etched on his face.

The school custodian had unceremoniously dumped five desks and chairs in my empty classroom. "Got no desk for you," he mumbled, "I'll see about a chair, though." He massaged his back with his hands. They looked old and knotted. Little did I know that he had attended this very school as a young boy. He left, grumbling about new teachers.

It was 9:30a.m and no one had shown up. Then I noticed it. The familiar yellow school bus. Only shorter, much shorter like a yellow block of cheese. It was a third the size of the regular buses. It was filled with young faces, staring blankly out the window.

An assistant gently coaxed three of the children from the bus onto the sidewalk. One, a chubby girl, about ten years old charged up the walkway to the school and began banging and slamming on the door. "Open up, open up, open up, open up," she chanted wildly, racing to the side window where I stood transfixed watching her. I knew she was one of mine. She stopped when she saw me at the window. "Come in?" I heard her mouth the words through the closed window. Her arm and hand were pointing toward the door she was unable to open.

I nodded yes and went to the door to let her and the other kids in. "You, teacher?" she questioned, as soon as I let her in. I nodded yes again, looking in the direction of the now agitated bus assistant.

One of the other kids stood outside the bus crying and pulling at pieces of his hair. The other stoically refused to move off the bus. "No school," he screamed at the bus assistant. "NNNoooooooo.."... I walked to where the bus was parked near the curb. My chubby, pigtailed friend trailing along with me.

"You be careful teacher," she whispered, "Alfie be mean." As I got closer to the bus I could hear the small, blond child crying mumbled words. "I am not a no-good son-of-a-bitch, I am not a no-good son-of-a-bitch, fucker, fucker, titty-fucker."

"Of course your not," I said to him. I tried to put my hand on his shoulder, but he shrank back.

I turned my attention to the other child on the bus. He was busy making faces at me. David was trying to repel the giant. "Give me a chance," I begged him, "I'm usually not this ugly so early in the morning." This brought howls of laughter from the other kids on the bus and a weak smile from the bus driver and her assistant.

He sprang to his feet suddenly and grabbed hold of my brown silk dress with his sticky little fists. I had just learned my first lesson as a teacher, but I'm not sure if I understood exactly what it was.

Another bus had pulled in as I stood in the "'No Parking School Bus Zone." It deposited two children and quickly drove off to its next destination. There were two more boys. One boy was tall, nervous and thin. The other boy was small, with long blond hair and had a red string that he had wrapped around his fingers.

I collected my small group around me and we went back to the pipe room. Alfie still clutching at my dress and occasionally growling in my direction. Robert was mumbling, swearing and

3

crying. Sophie was jumping about and shouting. John and Max were quiet and apprehensive.

"Where's the toys, teacher?" Sophie demanded as soon as we entered the class. "My last school had lotsa toys and candy too!" She looked at me hopefully.

We don't have any toys yet, I thought, or for that matter anything at all, except these old broken down desks and chairs lent to us by the school custodian.

Although I was a teacher in a public school I was hired by an organization called the Committee of Educational Services. COES for short. The COES contracted with most of the school districts in Oswego County, New York, to provide special education classes for children with disabilities.

My class was a new one and my kids came from all over the county. Fulton, Mexico, Central Square, APW, and Pulaski, as well as Oswego itself. Some of the kids rode the bus over one and half-hours just to get to school. Another one and a half-hours to get home again.

It was easy for the school not to claim responsibility. After all, weren't these kids from the county? Actually the responsibility of the COES.

Yes, these were COES kids. A name that, I would learn, became synonymous with special ed. and mental retardation.

The only thing was, these kids were not identified as mentally retarded. At least that was what most of their cumulative folders showed. Autistic, schizophrenic, hyperactive, brain-injured and developmentally delayed. Quite a tear sheet for kids all under the age of twelve.

That was another problem. The age span was incredible. Alfie and Max were six, Robert seven, Sophie ten, and John was nearly thirteen. A span of nearly seven years. Who had placed these totally unique children in one room together?

Emotionally disturbed was how they were described to me at my interview. The Director of Special Education was a rather unkempt man, who had the nervous habit of talking in short clipped phrases. Very well thought out.

4

"This is a pilot program," he explained, "the brain-child of the ARC and myself." The ARC was an acronym for the Association for Retarded Citizens. They, together with the Director of Special Education for the COES, had arranged to have these children form a class. A class for emotionally disturbed children.

They needed a certified teacher and I happened to be her. So we were off and running.

Mike Donahue's voice came booming over the P.A. system. "I'd like to welcome you all back to school and to remind you children to puuleese ... walk in the halls!" He sucked in some breath.

"I'd also like to remind you that banking is on Tuesdays only and that lunch money will absolutely, under no circumstances, be loaned to any child this year. That's all".

Daily dictums from our great white godfather. I came to expect them regularly. My kids always made a big fuss over Mike Donahue when he came down to our room, which wasn't often.

He usually had someone from the Board of Ed. with him or an influential parent or some ladies from the Women's League. He never came alone. He always stood by the door, and never came in. My kids would generally mob him at the door. Trying to shake his hand or pat his overly generous mid-section.

He always appeared indulgent, but he never stayed long. Neither did his companions. They always looked glad to leave.

"My God, how does she do it?" I would hear them whispering as they walked away. "It's a gift, a real gift, to be able to work with these children." Words I would hear often, along with dedicated and patient.

Most of these people were one big yawn to me and I found little time for their simplistic explanations of my use as a teacher. I preferred the company of the kids. They never needed to suck up to me. I never once in all the years I taught was called dedicated by anyone of them. If they loved me I always knew it was for myself.

"We'll just have to wait until all our supplies and toys have been ordered," I heard myself telling Sophie and the others.

I knew they wouldn't be in until Thanksgiving. I had heard the teacher next door talking about having to wait for her equipment when she started.

The other Special Education teachers were generous and shared what they had with us until our stuff finally arrived. It was like Christmas unwrapping all those boxes. We all survived those first days of school, although I gave up wearing silk dresses after Sophie had a violent outburst and ripped the skirt of one practically in half.

I took to wearing jeans and frequently found myself playing on the dusty wooden floor with the kids. I would spread out blankets, but they only kicked them aside.

Robert and John would build tall piles of plastic colored blocks. When the piles were about ready to topple over, one of them would push it and scream out "City! City!"

They were building large, glassed super structures. To me they were plastic blocks. To them, the world. I knew I had a lot to learn and that these kids could help teach me.

I decided to brighten up our room by painting the steam pipes. I had enough purple, blue, and green paint and we went to it with a vengeance. The kids had as much paint on them as the pipes did. It really helped. The room looked much better.

The looks of the other faculty members, however, were enough to make me give up painting forever. I never failed to notice the way they watched the kids in the cafeteria, or in the hall or the library. They seemed amazed, as if they had never watched an autistic child swaying back and forth before.

They almost all appeared wary of both the kids and me. This was an older faculty, I reminded myself. Many of these teachers had been here for years.

These were not teachers to be rushed. They took their time and did not give their acceptance easily. I could tell that immediately. We would all have to stay on our toes and try not to make waves.

My jeans, the painted pipes and the kids themselves, were objects of suspicion to a conservative, northern N.Y. community.

November 1973

We were all well acquainted by now. I knew all the kids very well and had made a point to visit with their parents or foster families. We often talked on the phone or relayed messages back and forth through the kids.

Sophie was living with a foster family in Oswego that seemed genuinely concerned about her. Her family had given her over to the State of NY when they found they could no longer manage this wild, unruly little girl. There was a strong suspicion of parental neglect and abuse.

Sophie had significant speech and language problems and often could not control either her behavior or her outbursts. She was on a powerful tranquilizer that was generally reserved for adults with intense mental and emotional problems.

She always slugged down her medication like a real trouper. I wondered what heavy doses of Vesperin could do to a child. Even her foster parents reported that only the Vesperin would calm her erratic behavior.

"I just don't know what gets into that child." Millie, Sophie's foster mother, was in her sixties and appeared to have a real desire to help this perplexing kid.

"The first week she came to live in our home I thought I'd go crazy. She threw boiling hot coffee on my legs over not getting her way!" Millie shook her head remembering the incident of a year ago.

"Ed rushed me to the emergency room at the Oswego Hospital." She wiped at her upper lip recalling the memory. "I wanted to send her back, right then and there."

"Something just kept telling me not to, maybe it was the good Lord, I really don't know." She smiled back at me.

"I certainly do feel grateful that Sophie has you for a teacher, so many others have not understood her."

I was not altogether as sure as Millie that I understood Sophie all that well myself. She could be impossible one minute and completely affectionate the next. Always remorseful over her unpredictable behavior.

The bus driver had reported to me, on more than one occasion, that she had been forced to pull her bus over to the side of the road. It seemed that Sophie would often pull the driver's hair when she could not get the favored seat in the front of the bus.

The driver recounted to me the shock of seeing passers-by watching this little girl pulling at her, the driver's, hair and clawing her face. Fortunately no mishap had occurred.

"I just couldn't believe it," she later told me, "she just grabbed right onto my hair and wouldn't let go for nothing. Finally I managed to pull over. I was never so scared in my whole life!"

When I questioned Sophie on this and other things she would invariably look at me sheepishly. "I sorry, Toni, I sorry. Don't do it again."

She always sounded so sincere, I found myself believing her nearly every time she offered these explanations. In the meantime I would work on helping Sophie find solutions to control her temper.

Robert was living at home with his mother, two brothers and one sister. The family lived in a compact, broken down trailer that was frequently without water.

Robert cried, swore and mumbled incoherent phrases to me until nearly Christmas. Much of his garbled speech centered on his family.

"Goddamn fuckin' bitch, shit on her ass, shit on her Goddamn ass. I will not, I will not, no, no, no, no, no. She's a pig cow. A fat pig cow. Fuck her. Fuck her!"

I quickly found out that Robert's mother was an outpatient from a mental health institution in New York. Robert had been placed in foster care soon after birth, but when his mother was released, he returned home again.

He was a small, passive boy who became the victim of his older brothers and his younger sister. They tormented him so much that at times I feared for his physical safety.

His swearing was one of the few outlets he had. I tried to encourage him to act out his feelings in play. He always seemed threatened. As if some invisible force would swoop down on him.

"Can't play this, no can't!" His small, thin, lips would tremble as I offered him a stuffed animal or toy.

"Show me with the toy," I would re-offer.

"Not now, later, later..." He would pee his pants if I pressed too hard or turn his anger on himself.

His mother called me frequently at home after school hours. She was a compulsive phone-a-holic and would often try to contact me explaining her own bizarre behavior.

"I just can't explain it," her words were often in a rush and ran together much the same way that Robert's speech did, "I try, I really do, but nothin' works. The damn Thorazine these damn doctors give doesn't do fuckin' nothin'. Just don't know what to do. Feel like killin' myself. Have tried it before you know. Don't think I won't do it. Don't think I won't!"

She would finish one phone conversation with me and then contact another faculty member to begin all over again. I got use to her 10:00 p.m. and 11:00 p.m. calls to my house. Robert's mother seemed to be at the mercy of the massive social service system in this country that somehow had caught both her and her kids in a nasty trap.

Robert's, natural, native intelligence would somehow show itself to me. I quickly picked up on his sharp wit and played it out to the hilt. I had him reading easily within weeks, even if he did cry through most of his old and ratty Dolch Readers.

Alfie was a tiny, but incredibly friendly kid right from the start. His initial fears were soon replaced with such hyperactivity that it made me tired just to watch him.

He seemed as if he never stopped moving. He frequently ate his lunch standing up and jiggled about constantly. He was not toilet trained at the age of six and had frequent 'accidents' for which he was always sorry and promised never to do again.

His mother, with whom he lived, was an enormous woman. As huge as Alfie was tiny. She had given birth to Alfie and was a single mother. Unfortunately, she succeeded in making both herself and him miserable.

"I get so mad with him, it makes me shake," her face would turn beet red recounting Alfie's adventures, or rather misadventures in her cramped apartment.

"He pees and sometimes he even craps in his toy box at home." She would look to me for confirmation or some sign of disapproval. "I just don't know why he acts this way. Sometimes I think he hates me."

"I ask him if he acts this way in school, but he just hangs his head. Someday I'm going to break his head."

She would often go on to tell me how when he messed his pants at home that she would plunge him into an icy tub of water..."Just to show him whose boss." Occasionally she would find a pair of soiled underpants or even an old, harden piece of excrement under his bed.

To curb his tendency toward hyperactivity a doctor had recommended that Alfie be placed on Ritalin. A drug that hopefully would help Alfie control his behavior.

However, I had read in his student folder that the drug had..."caused deleterious effects in a child that was already small and underdeveloped for his age."

During story time at school, Alfie would often lay his head on my leg and whisper, "Love me?" and without waiting for an answer close his eyes and try to find sleep and peace. There had been a good deal of speculation about suspected child abuse. He often came to school complaining of being punched, kicked or hit.

Although I always reported it to the school nurse and a record was made of it on health files, little if anything ever came of it. A hard, cold, taste of reality was being thrown back in my face. What could I, one teacher, do to help him?

Max never failed to make me laugh. Although I often suspected he inspired fear in most adults. His hair was long and blond, nearly to his shoulders. He stared off into space and would quietly mouth words. It was as if he were talking to some unseen person. Sometimes only his lips would move and no words would come out. At other times, Max would give out long, low sighs or groans.

"I feel like I want to choke you," he said to me early during the school year. His large blue eyes checked me with careful scrutiny, watching for signs of fear.

"I'd really prefer if we could manage to do our Peabody Language Lesson right now," I would usually summon a smart mouth answer back. He would laugh quietly and sometimes touch his long tongue to his nose or occasionally fall to the floor in mock agony.

He seemed to have the ability to operate each of his enormous eyes independently. One eye would be gazing at you while the other looked off in another direction.

Max lived at home with his mother, father and three older brothers. Max talked almost incessantly of death, dying, torture and catastrophic happenings.

"What would happen if I set you on fire, Toni?" He would look at me earnestly and wait for an answer.

"It would hurt and I wouldn't like it," his questions surprised and shocked me at first. Gradually I began to anticipate them. Many of the psychologists that I spoke with encouraged me to ignore his repetitive questions.

"It's merely a form of echolalia or perhaps a way to get your attention. The best thing to do is ignore it. Don't respond to any questions dealing with negative things." The school psychologists always seemed young, full of techniques for behavior management or operant conditioning, as they referred to it. Ring the bell and the doggie will come.

I had often wished they were right. However, they never saw Max drawing huge black clouds on white manila paper. He would color them in black, pressing hard on his no-roll crayolas. Talking to himself all the while. "It's going to rain and the clouds will come down to your head and squeeze you." He would shake his head affirming his statement.

"Yes, it's going to rain hard, rain hard." Then he would laugh and laugh and no sound would come out. "Right through the pipes its going to rain." He would then point to our purple and blue steam pipes. They would quietly hiss back.

He asked me to hang up the black clouds he drew. I hesitated. Thinking hard on the school psychologists and what they had told me. I hung the clouds anyway. We would talk about them. Make up stories about them. They were black hyenas in Max's mind. I showed Max Maurice Sendak's book... *Where the Wild Things Are*. He adored it. It gave vent and meaning to real feelings that I suspected he'd had for his six long, but short years.

John was, at nearly thirteen, the oldest child in my small group that first year. Tall, generally reserved, he seemed out of place with these younger children. His parents were fairly well to do and were very displeased that he had been placed in this class.

His mother complained bitterly to me that John's knees on his pants were worn out from playing and crawling on our wooden floor. She said she hadn't seen that since he had been a small child.

I agreed with her that John was too old for the class, but since I'd had nothing to do with placement she would have to take it up with the Director of Special Education at the COES.

I wondered myself, how these five unique children came to be placed in one class. Almost none of them had an initial psychological in their cumulative folders. Who then, had decided that they were in need of special education or a class for emotionally disturbed children?

I later found out that most had come from the ARC. They had been in a training class for the mentally retarded. The records were scanty and gave me little information.

Not one of the kids, with the exception of Sophie, was being seen by a child psychiatrist. Three out of the five were on drugs to control their behavior, although at one time all five had been medicated. More than half were from broken homes or homes that seemed ready to break.

I found myself feeling depressed. I was alone, without an educational support system to back me up. How could I help these kids? Kids who had been relegated to a room filled with crooked, rusty pipes.

January 1974

It was snowing like I had never dreamed possible. Thick, white sheets of snow layered on the sidewalk of the school. I tried to squint my eyes looking at houses that I knew were there, but couldn't see.

"We call it horizontal snow," I turned to see a white haired cafeteria worker, busy picking up mashed carrots from a long bench, filled with assorted bits of dropped or dumped food.

"Horizontal snow?" I wondered at the expression.

"You know," she continued, "when the wind is blowing so hard, it comes down this way." She moved her hands from west to east to show me what she meant. I smiled at the expression and turned back to the window fascinated by the endless billows of snow that seemed to pour out of the sky.

Winds, snow and icy cold weather were no strangers to this small northern community known as Oswego. Lake Ontario bordered it and the Canadian province of Ontario lay directly across the lake from us.

Lake Ontario at one hundred and ninety three miles long and fifty-three miles wide could be a vindictive body of water. Winter winds were known to go as high as fifty, sixty or even more miles an hour. It was a small wonder that it was known as horizontal snow.

"That's quite a group of youngsters you've got there." She was slopping up blobs of food into a stainless steel can. Her fingers pointed over to my group of five who sat huddled close together, eating their lunch as if vultures were about ready to snatch it away at any moment.

I smiled at her and watched Max suck down a long brownish-red hot dog as if it were a piece of spaghetti, grinning like a Cheshire cat with accomplishment at his feat.

We both watched as he sniffed at every item on his plate. Trying to decide which one to sample next. I would have to talk to him about not sniffing at his food. I had been told by one of the cafeteria workers that Max fingered and sniffed at much of the food before putting it on his plate.

"It's absolutely disgusting," she scolded me, "makes you wonder what their parents teach them." Or for that matter, their teachers either. I silently finished her unspoken sentence inside my own head.

I had grown accustomed to the stares of the other teachers by now. The looks of undisguised curiosity followed us throughout the school. This was no ordinary special ed. class. I could tell that they thought these kids were strange, unusual and different.

Fortunately, the kids seemed oblivious to the attention they generated. I would occasionally catch other kids laughing at or mocking them, but most of it was an act of derision performed in secrecy. At most, I would see a few students or even faculty nervously giggling in our direction.

As we walked down the hall to our classroom I wondered what made many of us so frightened of those who appeared different. All of my students were basically gentle souls who would do nothing to hurt anyone, not on a conscious level, at least.

My thoughts turned to my husband. We had been married the previous spring and he was now a student at the State University College at Oswego.

14

At the age of nineteen, about four years before I met him, he had been in a motorcycle accident that nearly cost him his life. Instead he had lost a leg. After two amputations and a good deal of rehabilitation he faced the world minus his right leg.

I recalled the times I had seen people stare at him as if he were an alien. Having to explain to the curious why he was the way he was. Never being allowed the simple freedom to just be. People with any difference have always had to explain themselves to others. "Are you a freak, are you on your way to the circus?" I can still remember the young boy, hardly fourteen, screaming out to Dan, only days before.

Dan calmly crutched over to where the boy was standing. Wanting to explain that no, he was not a freak. Only a person, like the boy. But, he had run away, probably surprised when he saw Dan making his way toward him.

Max interrupted my thoughts and brought me back to the present. His blue eyes were dark and cloudy.

"They called me a re-da-tard," he announced quietly. Sophie nodded her head, confirming his statement. I looked at both of them. Max's hands were touching the concrete walls of our class, as if, he were trying to learn to Braille them. Seeking soundless assurance on the validity of his words. Sophie was jumping around, very excited, the Vesperin tended to make her gait unsteady and off balance.

I looked at him; surprised he knew the word.

"They called me a re-da-tard," he said again, "and I don't like that."

"It's retard, Max," I volunteered, "and who called you that, anyway?" Not knowing if I should correct his mispronunciation of a word that I was already learning to hate.

"Them kids, back there." Max's hand pointed out the class down the hall, to the cafeteria.

"They call us re-da-tard," he continued with eyes full of accusation, "they say, you're the re-da-tard teacher." His hands moved silently, up and down the concrete, hands searching, scanning for answers.

Robert's eyes were filled with tears already. Lips trembling and white with anger. He began touching his small, fragile body with his thin fingers.

"Billy, calls me that too!" His tears dripped into his tight mouth. "I'm going to tell Mom on him!" He ran over to the stuffed animals in a corner of our classroom.

"You big, fat, cow, I'm not gonna let you call me that anymore." He was totally involved with beating and punching a koala bear that I had purchased from a school catalogue only weeks before.

"Yeah," agreed Sophie, "they call me that at Marcy too." She was referring to the psychiatric institution she had lived at in her younger years.

"They say, I am retard cause I can't read or tie shoes or nothin'. But, I want to be teacher, like you!" She came close to me and grabbed my waist, squeezing hard.

We had all joined Robert in the corner. Surrounded by mounds of furry animals and dolls. I found myself listening, more than talking to them.

It was still snowing hard by 1:30 and I suggested we take a walk in the snow. Getting dressed could be a major production. Everyone needed help with boots, buttons and zippers. I tried to get them to help each other.

Out in the snow, they seemed renewed and invigorated. The snow nearly buried little Alfie and I had to pick him up and carry him, he was so scared.

John, Robert and Sophie had busied themselves with constructing a snowman, while Alfie and I watched. Max was wandering about, still talking about the incident in the cafeteria.

Snow had settled on Max's hair and eyelashes. I thought he was beautiful. He looked far away and in deep thought. "Your a re-da-tard," I could barely hear him whispering to himself, "No, your not!" He would answer his own statement back to himself. The eternal struggle to find out, for himself, who he really was.

I wanted to comfort and protect them all that snowy afternoon, but I knew that the world and some of the people in it had other ideas.

The warmth of the school felt good as we piled into the building from the snowstorm that was raging outside. I could hear Mike Donahue's voice coming over the PA system, but the kids were making so much noise I couldn't hear what he was saying.

"We've just got word that school will be dismissed early today." A roar of approval from kids on the second and third floor came down to us in the basement. "Please listen carefully now or you may not hear when your buses have arrived." His voice sounded impatient and excited.

He proceeded to rattle off bus routes and numbers that had been previously assigned in September. I heard teachers out in the hall grumbling and complaining about early dismissal and the stupidity of sending kids home in a snowstorm that was nearly a whiteout.

This was a common occurrence in Oswego. The sun would be shining at 9:00a.m. and by 11:00a.m. winds that reached up to sixty miles an hour and hard, driving snow would be blaring across the lake. I quickly learned how deceptive Lake Ontario could be.

I had heard tales of the blizzard that had hit the town in 1966, seven years earlier. One hundred and ten inches of snow had fallen in seventy-two hours. School was closed for a week and many people were left stranded and without food.

I bundled the kids up carefully and walked each of them to their buses. Waving goodbye to them, I managed to read Max's lips as he was saying the word… "re-da-tard, re-da-tard" over and over to himself, through the windows of the bus.

I slowly trudged back up the walk to the school. The custodian let me in the already locked doors and I sat in my darkened class, looking up at pipes that we had painted in an impetuous moment only months earlier. The falling snow created an eerie effect that cast shadows of tiny, moving dots on the walls. It reminded me of a kaleidoscope, one of my favorite toys, as a kid. I moved the chair I was sitting in to get a better look at the patterns on the wall.

I had to wait for Dan to finish class at the college before I went home. He had our only vehicle, a green Dodge Van. I put my feet up on my wide teacher's desk that had finally arrived and flicked on the tape recorder, thinking I'd listen to some music while I waited.

Instead, I heard Robert's unmistakable voice. It was high and sounded strained and halting. "This is the tape recorder, ladies and gentlemen. It's me...Robert Alan Greene. And I am coming to you here from this room. (Lots of giggling, coughing and moving around the microphone) "Uh, hmmm... uh, uh ... how'd you like to hear a song?" I could hear him putting a record on the record player, getting ready to tape it. Elvis Presley's voice came across, scratched and barely discernible.

"Comma' on an be my teddy bear, comma' on an be my teddy bear"... I could hear Presley croon and Robert yelling with delight in the background.

"I'm gonna be a singer, like Elvis Presley!" I heard Robert say into the tape recorder. "Just like Elvis."

"And nobody is gonna tell me I am a no good fucker, anymore after that. Not Mom or Billy, or Scott, or Barbara... not nobody says that to me anymore, no never!"

His voice was stronger now, clearer than it had been months earlier. "And you will not take my things anymore and break 'em. And not hide 'em either. Or I will smash in your face Billy Greene! I will smash it in for you good and Mom will blister your behind for you!"

The tape recorder clicked off and I was left alone in my class with silence and Robert's words still ringing in my head. Thinking of him in a trailer alone with a mother who had intense emotional problems of her own. She had admitted to me that she kept Robert confined to a playpen until he was nearly four years old. It was a small wonder he felt such fury and helplessness.

I hoped that his brothers and sisters would not torment him with their incessant demands for favors or endlessly punch him, as his mother told me they often did.

I sat alone, in my class, and thought of the kids that had come to this room since September.

March 1974

"My God, I just can't take this kid anymore!" I was listening to the special ed. teachers whose rooms were next door to mine, talking.

"He just stands there," Pat said, "he won't move, he won't come in. He stands there or even lays down in the hall."

I knew that they were talking about Fred. He was in Pat's class. I had seen him fling his lunch pail across the cafeteria a week earlier because he didn't like what his mother had prepared for lunch.

Pat had been having a difficult time trying to control his outbursts all year, but lately Fred wouldn't even make a small attempt to cooperate.

I would see Fred's large thirteen-year-old body sprawled out in the corridor many times during the day. If he refused to get up Pat would not let him eat his lunch.

Other teachers in the school, feeling sorry for him, would feed him leftovers from their own lunch. You could frequently find Fred munching on marshmallows, fritos or chips while lounging in the hall.

The school psychologist for Cherry Park reevaluated Fred and decided that he might be better off with my group. There he would, hopefully, get the attention he needed.

Pat had nearly fifteen kids in her group. All of varying skill and ability levels. Her class was known as an EMR class. Educable mentally retarded. I was quickly figuring out, that abbreviations were very common in the world of special children.

Although most of my kids were much smaller and younger than Fred, he loved them immediately. The school psychologist had told me that Fred was paranoid schizophrenic.

Fred's language development was poor and he frequently gestured with his hands to get what he wanted to say across. He had an unmistakable look of friendliness and was immediately accepted by all the kids, particularly John. Now, the two older boys had found some companionship with each other.

I was happy for them and for the way my small, but somehow heterogeneous group was beginning to pull together. Fred's behavior was unpredictable, and it took us all some time to get use to.

One day, he came to school with a black eye. The school nurse called home. Fred had told both the nurse and myself that he had walked into a door. His mother's story was different.

Fred was becoming increasingly more difficult to manage at home. At thirteen, he still wanted to ride tricycles, play games that were meant for pre-schoolers and purposefully talk like a much younger child.

She told the nurse that she knew it was wrong, that she hadn't meant to, but that she had hit him. His black eye was the result.

That afternoon, I could hear Fred crying. I looked around my class. All present and accounted for, except for Fred... but where was he? I could hear him, but he was nowhere in sight.

I found him out in the hall. He had somehow managed to stuff his long body into one of the hall lockers. It took me sometime to find out which one his crying was coming from.

Finally, I opened up the right one. "Fred," I said, "come back in the room, whatever it is, maybe we can help you." By then most of the kids had collected in the hall beside us. Fred still stuffed in the locker and me kneeling beside him, talking and trying to coax him out.

"Come on Fred, buddy, we'll fix it up." Little Alfie told him.
"I'll let you listen to my Elvis records," Robert offered.

"If you come outta there, Fred," Sophie suggested, "I'll let you have one of my peppermint candies."

"Get out of there now," John ordered, "or I'll bash in your face for you." Max slowly wandered around whispering... "Fred's in the locker, Fred's in the locker."

Finally, after we had all said something, Fred put out one leg, then another. I helped ease him out slowly and the whole group walked the fifteen feet back into the pipe room.

June 1974

The year had slipped by so fast that I hardly believed it. The kids had all made incredible progress. I had managed to get them all on a work schedule that proved productive as well as fun.

I was using what I called a modified behavior management program. I rewarded the kids with checkmarks for the work that they produced in school. These were later traded in for free time, cookies or some other desired activity. I was never really convinced this was effective. I kept thinking of something I'd heard that Maria Montessori said. The quickest way to get a child to stop doing an activity they enjoyed was to reward them for it.

Things were running smoothly and although some of the faculty members were less than friendly to my kids, I chalked it up to personality rather than outright prejudice. Many, including the art and gym teachers, had been helpful and had even offered to take the kids by themselves for extra classes or special projects.

I remember thinking how good things looked when I was suddenly called to the office to accept a phone call. It was the Department of Social Services for the county of Oswego. They were calling about Sophie and the news was not good.

"Mrs. McClure?" I heard the voice on the other end saying...this is Mrs. Hunter from child protective services, I'm calling about Sophie."

"What can I do for you, Mrs. Hunter?" I asked. Somehow I knew that this was not exactly a social call. I wondered why I was being called from my class during school hours.

"How is she doing in school?" she asked, "Her parents have been inquiring about her."

"Her parents?" I said, repeating her words. I had barely heard a word about Sophie's parents all year.

"They want her back," she said quietly, "I'm afraid that they have the right to pursue custody."

I couldn't believe my ears. After all I had read in Sophie's file about the abusive and neglectful treatment she had received in her home, I was amazed to even think they would consider returning her. I thought of Millie and Ed, Sophie's foster parents.

"What do Millie and Ed think?" I found myself thinking aloud, already knowing the answer to my question.

"Well," she responded, "naturally their upset about the whole thing. You know how fond they are of Sophie. It was very difficult to find people like them to even consider taking in a child like Sophie. She's been very frustrating to handle."

I finished the rest of the school day in a blur. When I returned home, the phone was ringing. I knew who it was before I even picked it up.

"Toni?" Millie's voice sounded strained, on the verge of tears, "They want to take Sophie away from me and Ed," she rushed on, "what can we do? Can you help us, Toni?"

I assured her that I would do everything in my power to keep Sophie with them. "She doesn't want to go," Millie continued, "she wants to stay with us."

For the next three weeks, Maureen Hunter and I met and talked about Sophie, her parents and her foster parents. It seemed liked we went round and round in circles. Running fast, but getting nowhere. I was beginning to know what people meant when they talked of the 'revolving door' in the social service system.

"I thought," wondering aloud, "that if a child was placed in foster care, their parents gave up custody rights."

"A common assumption," Maureen shrugged, "but, incorrect."

Although, I had nearly completed my first year of teaching, I still had a long way to go. I was still very naive and had yet to acquire the experience that would come over years of teaching.

"If the placement is a voluntary one," Maureen sighed, "then the parents have every right to regain custody." She lit a thin, dark colored cigarette and exhaled some smoke before going on.

"This particular placement was a voluntary one on the part of her parents." She raised her eyebrows, as if in resignation, I felt she had been in this spot before.

"You mean," I asked, "they gave her up... wanted her placed in foster care?"

"That's right," she agreed, "and now, they want her back."

"It's not fair," I said, "Sophie loves her grandparents." I was referring to Millie and Ed. Sophie had always affectionately called them grandma and grandpa.

"If its fair your looking for," Maureen eyed me sharply, "you're in the wrong profession." She snuffed out her cigarette and picked up her briefcase. "I'll do what I can," she said on her way to the door, "but, fair is not a word for people in this line of work."

I thought about her words the rest of the week. Just what kind of work had I become involved in, anyway? Sophie was sullen and explosive, sensing, I think that her world was about to become unraveled once again.

The kids and I packed away our small class for the summer. Everyone was tired and in need of a break. Maureen came to school with a worn, blue suitcase, a day before the end of school.

"Come on Sophie," she coaxed, "want to go for a ride with me? I'll buy you an ice-cream on the way." Sophie's eyes lit up, forgetting about the troubles of the preceding week.

"I'll call you," she nodded her head to me, as Sophie half pulled, half dragged her out the door.

At the time, I thought Maureen was taking Sophie back to the home of her parents, but this was not the case at all. She, or rather, the Department of Social Services, had decided that in the best interests of all concerned, that Sophie should be returned to the Marcy Psychiatric Center. There she would live and go to school.

I later heard that she told Sophie they were going to..."Visit grandma and grandpa"... so that the long ride to Marcy would seem more enjoyable to her. When Sophie realized where Maureen was taking her, she refused to move from the car. She remembered her previous stay at the Center and had often spoke of it to me, during the year, with loathing.

I wrote to Sophie during her fourteen-month stay at the Marcy Psychiatric Center, but only once did I receive a response. It was written in precise, delicate long hand. Thanking me for my letters and gifts. I thought it very strange that a child, who could barely write her own name, could suddenly compose such eloquent letters.

But I would live to see Sophie again. What a different kid she would be by then. Older, wiser and more tuned to the harsh realities of her life.

Ed died of a massive coronary only weeks after Sophie left their home. Millie recounted the story to me tearfully, one afternoon, on a street corner downtown.

"He died of a broken heart," she shook her head sadly, "they told me it was a coronary, but he died broken hearted." She looked up at me, eyes full of pain ..."He loved that child like his own, like his own baby..."

I walked home slowly, thinking of Sophie and of all the other Sophie's I had yet to meet.

Part I - Chapter 2

September 1974

I could hear the screaming from inside my classroom, even with the door closed. I put down the green construction paper that I was using to cover an old bulletin board. Walking over to the door, I had the sinking feeling that I had become accustomed to so many times before.

I looked down the hall and two men were carrying a tiny child that was so hysterical he appeared rigid with fright.

"Where should I put him?" asked the boy's bus driver, "He's been carrying on like this since I picked him up at his house. God, I hope he doesn't do this every morning." I pointed to an old blanket near the toys and the two men quickly put him on it. "Good luck." one of them said, on the way out, "She'll need more than that." I heard his companion laughingly answer.

I looked back at the small boy who was still screaming so much that his face had turned completely red. He opened his mouth wide and bit with viciousness into his thin arm.

"I'm crying," he screamed through his tears, "I'm crying." I went over to him and sat down on the blanket.

"Hi, A. J." I cheerfully volunteered, "my name is Toni and I'm going to be your teacher this year." He was still screaming and crying, but he was looking at me now.

I went on oblivious to his non-response. "Want to see where your desk is? I've got one ready for you." I walked over and stood by a cream colored desk that seemed absurdly big for this little boy.

"Do you like it?" I pushed on, waiting for an opening, "Want to try it out?" To my surprise, he jumped up and ran over to the chair that I offered. When he sat down his head nearly disappeared behind the top of the desk. The whole scene was so ridiculous that I burst out laughing. He looked at me for a moment and forgot his tears and hysteria. His eyes locked into mine.

"Are you a girl?" He asked in a musical, singsong voice, "Am I a boy?" His tiny little hands flapped over and over in front of his face. He looked as if he were about to take off ... the flight of the bumblebee.

He laughed hysterically and slid to the floor from his chair, his face still smeared wet with tears. I picked him up. "Are you a girl?" He asked again, "Am I a boy?" His face was contorted and I sat fascinated by him. He was still cackling and flapping his hands.

"Mom, makes me ravioli, ravioli," he called out and then dropped to the floor again, laughing and still flapping. I looked up to find Alfie and Robert standing by the door, as fascinated as I was.

"Whose that?" asked Alfie, "He sure is weird, whoever he is," I smiled at Alfie and introduced the two boys to their new classmate. "Aren't you going to give your old teacher a hug?" I asked the boys, "I haven't seen you all summer." Alfie came sailing into my waiting arms. It was like homecoming day. Robert hung back, but I could tell he was glad to be back in school again.

"Toni," I heard my name being called, "where did you go? I couldn't find you." It was Max, he had grown taller over the summer and his long blond hair had been cut short, nearly shaved. I gasped, but recovered my composure quickly. His shaved head made his already huge eyes practically enormous.

"We were on summer vacation Max," I said, "and now it's over and we're all back in school again." He walked over to the periphery of the class. Reaching with his hands to touch the walls. "Summer vacation," I could hear him whispering to himself, over and over, "we were on summer vacation."

My group had grown smaller over the summer months. John had been placed in a class for the trainable mentally retarded. His parents had not been pleased with that placement either. At thirteen he was just too old to be placed in this class any longer.

Sophie was living at the Marcy Psychiatric Center and attending school there. Fred had been given another chance in his old classroom, but with a new teacher. I hoped all would work out for him.

The opening of the new school year seemed easier for us this time. Robert, Max and Alfie were calmer, more at ease with themselves and with school. It would leave me with greater opportunity to learn more about A.J., who he was and where he had come from.

Like most of the other children, A.J. had attended a pre-school class run by the ARC. They had referred him to the Oswego County COES, who had then placed him in my class.

A.J. had just turned six and was extremely small for his age. His folder talked of possible dwarfism, autism and signs of intense emotional problems.

Between the ages of two to three A.J. had managed to ingest enough wall paint to lead poison himself. His mother reported that he had been born perfectly normal and had no major illnesses or problems at all until these incidents.

She had left him, in the care of a young baby sitter, while she went to work, earning money to support her growing family. By the time she and her husband realized what was happening the damage had already been done.

A.J. frequently talked of the events in very explicit terms. His vocabulary and use of the English language was nothing short of incredible. "I ate paint," he would often tell me, "that's how come I'm brain-damaged." He would flap his hands in front of his face, laughing and managing to shock even those who were more than willing to listen.

He would stop unsuspecting children or teachers in the hall. His questions, statements and announcements seemed to escape no one. Over and over again, he would assail us with his questions.

"Are you a girl? Am I a boy? I ate paint, didn't I? How tall are you?" The questions seemed endless and he seldom waited for a response or reply.

If you were with him long enough, you soon got the feeling that your participation with him was not only unnecessary, but also unwanted. All he really needed was your undivided attention.

A.J. had a tendency toward abusive behavior that I hadn't seen in any of the other kids. He bit his arm frequently and would occasionally bang his head on the floor.

"A.J." I would ask, "would you like to play with the chalkboard?" He would flap his hands in response.

"Then go over to my desk," I would add, "and get some chalk." He usually followed directions very well, if I could manage to get his attention.

"What do you want to draw?" I probed, "A boy?" He would look at me, his head moving in circles and look upward.

"A boy, biting his arm," he would respond, "a boy eating lead paint." He would draw loose, free form figures of boys that always had large, ugly marks on their wrists.

"See," he would reply, "like mine." He would then show me his arm that had already, at the age of six, become callused from his bites. His frustration level was so low, that if he happened to drop the chalk on the floor while he was drawing, he would lunge into his arm, screaming and crying.

The other kids tended to stay clear of him in the early weeks. Curious, but yet afraid. Later they would befriend him when they saw how vulnerable he really was, but for now, he was on his own.

His obsessions and fears became the focal point for all of us that year. The pipes in our class became living, breathing things to him. He talked of them incessantly, so much so that one of the teachers in the school began to call him Pipalini.

"Those pipes will not hurt me, Mrs. Gallo," he would remind one of the teachers, "Toni says the walls and the pipes are not going to hurt me." He would look back into our class, from the hallway, listening to the pipes hissing and grunting. Believing and yet, not believing his own words. Wanting to trust and yet not being able to.

"How is the little Pipalini doing?" Gina Gallo would ask me, "Any progress?" Gina had taught special children herself, for nearly ten years before switching over to early childhood education. She always had something nice to say to one of the kids and I really appreciated it.

"Just pipe dreams," I would answer, "only pipe dreams, so far." We would both break up laughing. A.J. was Gina's favorite. With some time I felt I could help A.J. understand things better. To be able to live in and enjoy the world without being so terribly afraid of the things in it. It would take time, that was for sure.

October 1974
Our days didn't seem long enough for all the lessons and activities I always planned for my little group. Language Arts, writing, reading, math and physical activities were only a few of the things that I managed to teach every day.

The kids really seemed to enjoy working and learning with each other. I had studied art in college before deciding to teach and many of my projects and designs in the class centered around the arts, whether it was music, theater or painting. I encouraged them to pretend, to play, and to make believe! Some of the school psychologists suggested that it was inappropriate to have these children of make believe, play and pretend even more than they already did.

The kids loved school and fortunately I was slowly learning to trust my instincts rather than the pronouncements of my sometimes-disapproving colleagues.

I encouraged the kids to role-play and set up real play situations where I would involve all of us. "I'll be the kid," I would offer Max, "and you be the teacher." I would pretend to be him and sit at his desk. He loved it; it seemed to bring out the best in him.

He would sit at my large teacher's desk and pretend to read a manual, sensing that somehow, he was gaining both knowledge and importance. "Do I hear you talking, young lady?" He would look up from the desk at me accusingly, "Get over in the corner right now!" His voice was angry, "I said right this minute!"

He would get up and take me off to a corner of the room where he would put an abacus in front of me.

"There," he would gloat, "now you are in jail and can never come out! Never." He would laugh with delight over his newfound game.

Over and over again I would experiment with them, trying new ideas. So many of the professionals who worked with these kids had concentrated only on their problems. I wanted to find something in them that was funny and real.

I brought in old clothes, hats, purses, gloves, and jewelry. Anything that I thought would encourage them to identify and understand their own feelings. "Do you really think it's appropriate," I once heard a counselor sniffing, "that you encourage 'these' children to play-act in such an odd manner?"

"Do you really think it's appropriate," I said, "that you don't?" Creative play and imagination was not in vogue with the theory behind which we educated our 'special children', and I was keenly aware of the counselor's attitudes and opinions. It was shared by some in our profession.

Management and control were bywords in classes for emotionally disturbed children at the time. Interaction, communication, sensitivity... these were words for psychiatrists, not teachers. The truth was that the kids rarely, if ever, saw a psychologist or psychiatrist or even a counselor. Once a placement was made, that was that. The cost of psychotherapy was very high, up to ninety dollars an hour, and few, if any, parents, could afford such extravagant expenses. Even if it was for their own child.

Psychotherapy was thought of as a lavish and imprudent extra in 1974 for an already burdened school budget. Once, every three years, all children in special classes were administered a battery of psychological tests. Mostly to reassess placement and establish general intelligence.

Outside of those triennial visits, they never saw a psychologist, except in dire emergencies. I did what I could for the kids, but I needed supportive help in dealing with their problems myself.

Regardless, play became a major activity in school. They were hungry for it. I always tried to involve myself in their play, or at least, be a silent observer to it.

"I am an old, old man," Robert would moan, while walking around our class, during playtime, "I take lots of pills." He would be using the large tinker toys, which I kept near the housekeeping corner, for crutches.

"Yes," Max would agree, "and you're going to die very soon." He would lie down on the floor, simulating death, for Robert. I would watch, fascinated and intrigued. The play of children is such an amazing affair, I could hardly imagine adults who were uninterested or even worse, afraid of it.

Their play often led them into exploring other unseen, but real parts of their psyche. All four boys often drew me powerful pictures that helped show me the way their minds and hearts worked. Alfie once handed me a drawing he had completed of his mother. She had huge teeth and appeared to be holding a very small object in her left hand. When I questioned him about it, he answered in a very matter of fact manner that "she's got me in her hand, that's so I won't get away."

I hung most of their drawings, paintings and other art projects around the room. I brought in my own work from home and encouraged them to look at my artistic attempts as well as their own.

I invited my husband, Dan, to come to school and take photographs of them. He made eight by ten black and whites of them for us and we all had the pleasure of seeing ourselves become larger than life.

The kids were thrilled with the results of seeing their faces looking back at them from the wall. I often noticed more than one of the boys talking to the photographs.

31

"See," A.J. would say to his picture, "I don't bite my arm anymore." He would hold up his arm, which was still heavily callused, from constant biting, proudly, to the unseeing photo.

The weather was rapidly turning colder now. The autumn leaves were at their peak and I found myself busy scattering pumpkins, gourds and dried sheaves of cornhusks around our class. Thanks to the generosity of the local farmers in the area, we always had an abundance of all these things.

The boys were anxiously looking forward to Halloween and I was just as excited as they were to usher in the holiday. Little did I know that we would be getting another surprise before long.

November 1974

It was nearly time for the buses to arrive and take the boys home. They had started to pick things up. Chucking toys into boxes and putting away books, pencils and the number lines we used for math.

I was standing on A.J.'s desk, stretching up to reach the pipes and take down the orange pumpkins that we hung for our Halloween party only a week before. I smiled to myself, remembering how funny they had all looked in their Halloween costumes.

Max had been dressed as a cat, one of his favorite animals. It had been a home made costume and he had been drawing pictures of cats for a week afterward.

Cats with long furry tails that stretched out and seemed to yawn their way across his sketchpad. Cats with prolonged tongues and distended bellies. Stuffed full, he had told me with, "mice and a lot of candy."

Little A.J. and Alfie had both been terrified of the whole thing and had refused to participate in this holiday of pretension.

Instead, Alfie hid in the bathroom for most of the party and A.J quizzed Max endlessly on the number of teeth in a cat's mouth. They both ate their ice cream and cupcakes under their desks, peering at us as if we'd gone crazy.

Suddenly, I looked down from my vantage point, on A.J.'s desk, to see one of the girls from the class next door. She was visibly shaken. "Toni, come quick," she said, "Miss Kent needs you." I jumped off the desk and dashed next door, knowing that something was very wrong.

Inside the room, Jane Kent's class was watching the scene, which even I could not believe. On her back was a chunky, dark haired boy. Screaming obscenities at her and clutching at her clothing. He refused to budge and Jane could not shake him off her back.

She looked tired and desperate from fighting. "Please," she whispered, "get him off my back, I can't move him."

I came closer to the pair and tried to regain my composure. "She can kiss my father's balls," he snarled at no one in particular, "you can get out of here now, you faggot," he said, practically spitting in my face.

I recognized the boy as Donald. I had seen him standing outside my own class many times during the previous weeks. He was new to the school and Jane had been having a hard time dealing with his behavior. He frequently left class and even the school building. Running the school halls, much to the embarrassment, of our image conscious principal.

I had seen Donald and the principal locked in what looked like mortal combat, on the fire escape, on the side of the school. Donald had bolted from his classroom and Jane notified the office.

"Come down from there, right now, young man!" I saw the Principal's face turning purple, his usually cool composure, turning sour. "Try and make me" yelled back Donald, he turned and ran into the gymnasium door, that led out to the fire escape. He had been going on this way for weeks, until finally, he exploded, and attacked his own teacher.

"Donny," I said, "why don't you come over to my class and we can talk this thing out." I was looking for a way to smooth over the whole situation.

"My name is Donald," he pressed his lips together, "not Donny!" O.K. then," I offered, "Donald." I waited a moment, seeing what his response would be, he was still clawing at Jane's back. On impulse, I lightly touched his back and to my amazement he let go and strutted out of the class and into mine.

Fortunately, all the boys, except Robert, had gone home. Robert, sensing something was very wrong, sat motionless. He was mumbling and had started crying, his lips shaking and big eyes brimming with unspilled tears. I put my hand on his head, but he shook it off and walked toward the door muttering.

Donald, was casually walking around the room, picking up toys and dropping them on the floor. He gingerly picked up Robert's prized Elvis Presley album. I could hear Robert's sobs becoming louder. Donald and I both looked in his direction. "Baby," I heard Donald say to him, with disgust.

He spotted a compass on a workbench and snatched it up, eyeing both it and me at the same time. All the boys frequently used the compasses to draw circles. Donald touched the edge of the instrument, testing its sharpness.

Before I could stop him, he ran over to a large yellow, plastic igloo that I had just that morning inflated with air. The boys had enjoyed doing their reading in it and I had found that I could just manage to squeeze inside the cozy hiding place with them.

Pop, pop, ssssssssttt... Pop ssssssssttt... I could hear Donald puncturing the plastic panels of the igloo with the compass. I walked over to where he was standing and grabbed the compass from his hands.

"Just what do you think your doing?" I demanded, "That doesn't belong to you." I was angry, mostly because I knew I would have to inflate and repair the igloo. The hand pump the gym teacher had loaned me to fill the igloo with air had not been working, so I blew it up with my breath.

It had taken me an hour, but I wanted to have it ready and waiting for the boys when they came in that morning. Now, it looked like a shriveled, used lemon.

"Just what do you think your doing?" Donald pranced around the room, mocking my words, "That doesn't belong to you." He flung the compass to the floor, near my feet; I picked it up and put it in my pocket.

He laughed at me. "You're just like the rest," he said, looking directly in my eyes, "plain, old, chicken shit."

"Chicken-shit?" I said, repeating his own words back to him. He looked at me, taken unaware, I suppose, hearing me say words that teachers weren't supposed to.

"You're going home," I announced to myself as well as Donald, "right now." The short bus that carried Robert and Donald home had arrived and was waiting for them.

"Oh, no, I'm not!" he said, and made a mad dash for the ladder that was in the back of the class. It was to be used for fire drills or emergencies. He perched himself on the top of the ladder and crowed at me, "Come and get me, chicken shit teacher!"

My patience, which had been so loudly praised, by so many who were not teachers, was drying up quickly. With a show of strength, that I didn't know I had, I picked Donald up by the shirt collar and hauled him out to the bus.

Tucking him under my arm, I managed to get him to the door of the school bus. He screamed and kicked at my legs while we struggled down the sidewalk. I lost one of my shoes in the process, but I never even stopped for it. I knew I was on a mission that had no return.

The driver, who we all affectionately called, 'Cowboy' was placidly waiting for us at the bus door. He spit out a long stream of brown tobacco juice and smiled his toothless grin at me. "All in a day's work, eh, teach?" he chewed on the horrible smelling stuff, "All in a day's work." He looked at Donald sternly, "Looks like you've met your match, bronco."

He laughed and scratched at his head, pointing to the assigned seat that Donald was to sit in.

I limped back up the now familiar path, stopping for my shoe and greeting some parents who looked at me suspiciously. I banged on the locked doors, waiting for some kind-hearted person to let me back in. It was starting to rain and I was exhausted from the struggle.

From inside the school, I saw Donald standing at the back of the bus. His hands pressed up against the windows, staring at me. I walked down the steps to my basement classroom and dropped into my chair, drained and suddenly sleepy. I knew that this boy would be transferred to my group and that it would take all of my still limited teaching experience to understand him.

December 1974

Winter had set in on us once again and I was prepared for it this year. I had purchased a long maroon coat with a fur collar, gloves and a wool hat that I could pull down over my ears. A.J. told me that I looked like his dog, 'Bootsy' when I wore the coat, and would love to pat and stroke the shaggy fur collar.

Donald Conners, or D.C. as I liked to call him, had been with us about a month. He was still hostile and aggressive, but he had a sharp, biting wit about him that I came to love.

He was much more alert, tuned in, and aware than the other boys, but he seemed happy to be with us and I spent a lot of time teaching him individually. Time that, unfortunately, other teachers didn't have. For now, this placement would have to do.

"Good morning," I cheerfully greeted the boys, as they came in, ready for another day of school.

"Go squat on an open fire," D.C. replied, flopping his round, compact body into his seat.

"Well," I said, speaking to no one in particular, "business as usual." Donald's face was angry and I knew he was in a potentially dangerous mood.

"The kids on the bus were calling Donald, fatso," Alfie impulsively told me, "that's why he's mad."

"Is that right, D.C?" I gently asked, "Are they calling you fatso?" He looked at me and defiantly put his chubby legs up on his desk. Waiting for a reaction. Not getting any.

"Yeah," he finally replied, "they call me that all the time," his brown eyes looked sad, depressed, "but I don't care!" I looked at him hard, wondering what I could do.

"Well," I added, going slowly, "we could both stand to lose a few pounds." I patted my own bottom and A.J. began to laugh hysterically.

"Toni's going on a diet!" laughed Max. The kids really seemed to enjoy this piece of news; it even made D.C. smile. I would call Donald's mother and see if I could get her to cooperate. An enormous woman herself, I guessed she weighed close to 300 pounds.

Donald's lunches were starchy and with little, or no, fruits and vegetables, he was fast becoming very obese. He had forgotten his lunch at home one day and his mother made a quick stop to the supermarket to pick up something. She purchased nearly a pound of bologna and brought it to him in the school cafeteria.

"Here," she said, handing the still wrapped package to him, "don't eat it too fast." He gobbled up the sliced sandwich meat before she even left. Leaving only the empty, smelly wrapper. Other teachers, looking on in shock.

Donald's mother tended to indulge him. He was her only child and she wanted him desperately. She had nearly a half a dozen miscarriages before giving birth to Donald and a twin brother that died shortly after delivery.

Donald was her salvation and although his behavior perplexed and angered her she wanted the best for him. I often heard her talk of his being alive, as a miracle.

Shortly after Donald was placed in my class, I called her to school for a parent conference. Hoping to learn more about this child who seemed to infuriate so many of the people who had worked with him.

"I don't know what's wrong with that one," she said, "sometimes I think he wonders if he's going to die like the rest of my children." She shook her head and went on.

"I've tried to give him religion," she told me, "but, it don't seem to do no good. His father should spend more time with him. Not drink so much." Her eyes filled up with tears as I tried to console her.

"If only Frank didn't drink so much," she said, talking to no one in particular, but looking at me. "The Salvation Army," she explained, "has helped us all a lot. I don't know what I'd do without them."

I thanked her for coming and she got up to leave. I promised I would do everything possible to help Donald make a more successful adjustment to school. She was having trouble getting out of the chair she was sitting in and I offered my help. Embarrassed, she ignored my futile attempts. Finally, she wiggled herself out of the chair. Her massive torso had been lodged between the arms of the seat she was sitting in. Relieved and still confused she had rushed from my class, anxious to be on her way.

After school, I called Donald's mother, hoping to catch her before he arrived home. She agreed that Donald was putting on too much weight. She said that he often comforted himself with food; that was all he had.

"He eats so much," she off handedly remarked, "I'm afraid he's going to get as big as me." We concluded that we would both try to monitor his eating. I agreed that I would try to reward him with things other than food. Trips to the library, movies or special activities rather than food.

Although we all tried, Donald seemed to put on more and more weight as the days went by. He attacked his food with something that looked like it was close to hatred. I had to watch him carefully in the cafeteria, or he would dip into the lunches of other kids. Once he was caught stuffing cookies into his pockets, by one of the cafeteria workers. He tried to plead innocent, but they fell out of his pockets through holes in his pants. Ashamed and contrite he burst into tears and told me about his dog, who had died. His parents had not let him see the dog after death and D.C. had always wondered about it. Once again, I had been given a lesson in teaching. I took him back to our class and he sat in my lap, thinking that I had never seen him cry before. As he fell asleep, I could hardly believe this was the same kid who had made us all so angry weeks before. I once read that tears were a river that took you somewhere. I hoped D.C. would find his 'somewhere.'

At our Christmas party that year he brought me a lumpy, used, paper napkin. There was something in it.

"Open it up, Toni," D.C. said excitedly, "it's for you." I looked deep into his dark, mysterious eyes. He watched me carefully as I unwrapped the gooey package. Inside was a mashed, half-eaten cupcake.

"I thought you might get hungry tonight," he said.

"It's the best present I ever had," I hugged him and found myself wishing that Christmas would be a good one for him this year.

February 1975

We were in the midst of deep winter and I wasn't feeling any too happy about that to begin with. I walked down the hall with my empty coffee mug, on my way to the teacher's room.

We shared the basement of the school with the other special education classes, the library, cafeteria and the teacher's room. The teacher's room was generally filled with cigarette smoke and more gossip than I could handle so I tended to stay clear of the place unless I really had to go in.

This cold, February morning, I had decided to grab a quick cup of coffee before the boys arrived. I knelt down to tie my shoe before I opened the door to the room; hearing the voices of teacher's laughing and joking. Trying to squeeze out a few more minutes until they had to meet the day's challenge.

"It's unbelievable," I heard one of the voices say, "their all so weird. They give me the creeps." The laughing and chatter made it hard for me to hear.

"That little one," I heard a woman's voice, "the one who flaps his hands in front of his face. God, why does he do that anyway? She should wipe his nose more. It's disgusting."

I stood up and tried to look through the smoky windows of the teacher's room. All I could see were shadowy figures, talking, smoking and drinking coffee. I was hurt, surprised and angry. I knew they were talking about the kids.

Two teachers passed by and I leaned back against the walls, pretending to be engrossed in my plan book. I stared at the blank page while I listened to their mindless talk.

"That big one gets me," it was a man's voice, deep and gruff, "he's always hiding underneath the steps, talking to himself." They were talking about Fred. He had not made it in his special ed. class this year and he was back with me again. Fred, who had become increasingly nonverbal, talked basically with his hands. Or, to himself, when he was alone.

"She's the real winner though," it was the woman's voice again, "looks like a left over from Haight-Ashbury!" That last comment broke them both up and I listened to them have a laugh on me.

I walked back to my class feeling bad and with no one to talk to. I sat at my desk and thought about the words that I had just heard. To laugh at me was one thing, but kids who were totally blameless was another. I couldn't believe other teachers could be like that.

I knew my class was uncommon. Classes for children with emotional problems were new to the school, but this was dishing that was mean-spirited. The other special classes in the school had children whose problems were much less severe. They were kids who needed intense remedial work.

One on one instruction, good teaching and they would be able to make it on their own. My students, would need all the teaching, love, guidance and support I could give them. I knew many of them would need it, not just as kids, but as adults too.

I spent an angry day with the kids, taking out on them my own frustrations. They were distracted and bewildered at my behavior. I was usually relaxed and at ease, I could tell they were all walking on eggshells, trying to avoid my mood. "Robert," I barked, "what kind of work do you call this?" I held up a sheet of light green paper that held his spelling words for the week. The words were written so lightly that I could barely read them. Probably reflecting his tense feelings.

"I need x-ray vision to read this stuff," I ran on unable to control myself, "do it over!" Robert sat at his desk stunned at my words and I watched his eyes fill with tears. Alfie walked over to his desk and put his hand on Robert's shoulder.

"Don't cry, buddy," he said, "Toni don't mean it." He looked over at me and I was at once, filled with guilt, remorse and shame.

I went over to Robert and knelt down next to him. "I'm sorry, Robert," the words came spilling out, "I'm not angry at you." I looked around at all of them. "I'm not angry at any of you, really I'm not."

Silence. The kids had once again been hurt and by someone they trusted. I felt terrible about the way I had acted. I was no better than those merciless teachers I had heard earlier that morning.

"Look," I suggested, "why don't we all have some hot chocolate. We finished our work. We can turn out the lights and watch the snow fall while we're drinking it."

No answer. They just stared back at me, wondering if I was back to normal. I could have kicked myself for the way I had been acting all day. Just as I was about to give up, I heard Donald break the ice.

"Hell," I heard him say, "long as I'm not paying for it." I breathe a sigh of relief and thanked God for his smart mouth answers.

"Good," I announced, "D.C., you get the cups, I'll make the hot water." Slowly the six boys got up and began to move around, I prayed I had not done too much damage and promised myself that I would never again take out my problems on them.

As I waved goodbye to them at the door that afternoon, I was grateful that the day was over. From inside my darkening classroom I watched their buses move off toward home.

A.J., slipped and fell on the snow and ice. He lay there on the ground crying and biting his arm through his blue snowsuit. I looked on, from inside the class, while a teacher on bus duty, walked over to him. She picked him up and brushed the snow off his pants. I watched her wave his bus goodbye and couldn't help thinking that some of the teachers in the school wanted us here.

April 1975

Spring, at long last, had returned. After a hard winter, we were all glad to feel the fresh cool air and warm breezes that we knew were right around the corner. The boys were anxious for a change and I decided that we needed to explore the community surrounding the school.

At first, I took them for long walks in the neighborhood. They tended to group together as they walked, seeking shelter and safety in each other's company. Gradually, they split up, walking in twos or by themselves. I watched their reactions very carefully. A.J. collected rocks and put them in his pockets. He talked constantly of breaking the pipes in the classroom, walls or telephone wires with his treasured rocks. Max stopped to smell the new crocus. Although he seemed obsessed with death he loved living things. Flowers, plants, animals and small babies seemed to delight him.

D.C., still sullen and angry, banged and punched at all the stop signs, garbage cans and cars we passed. He seemed wise beyond his young years to me.

I would try to slip his hand into mine, but he was disgusted by all my attempts at friendliness. Robert never left my side during our walks. Staying close to me, he would mutter and mumble, his speech had become more intelligible and we could carry on a conversation now.

"Look at those Canadian geese!" I would exclaim to him, pointing over our heads, to a stream of birds flying in a vee.

"Wow, wow," he would respond, "there's a billion of 'em. Careful they don't crap on our heads now." He would get so excited at seeing the beautiful, migrating birds, that his little body and face would twitch with pleasure and joy. I was thrilled to see him so happy.

Fred and little Alfie always walked hand in hand. They made a comical pair. Alfie at seven was still tiny and extremely hyperactive. He always played the macho, dauntless role. Fred was childish and still preferred nursery games, puzzles and gesturing with his hands at fourteen.

I made a mental note to explore other classroom alternatives for Fred. Surely there was something more appropriate for him. It hardly seemed fair to place Fred with such young children. He needed to be with other boys and girls his own age. With other adolescents, perhaps, he would give up his yearning for childish things.

As we walked back to the school, I decided it was time for a few field trips. I knew that the school budget was very tight so rather than have a school bus we would use the public transportation that was available to the community.

I had the boys take home permission slips for their parents to sign. Each one would bring twenty cents. This money would pay for bus fare. I promised that I would spring for cokes at Ho Jo's or a nearby restaurant after the trip.

Our first trip was to the local P&C Supermarket. They were all so excited and happy to be leaving schoolwork and familiarity behind. The feeling was contagious and I found myself as giddy as they all were.

We waited on the corner for the bus to arrive. It was a beautiful, sunny day and we all had huge, brown bag lunches with us. Everybody was talking all at once; excited about the whole experience. They greeted strangers who walked by them and I couldn't help but think we all had a lot to learn from these kids. I saw the blue and silver bus slowly moving down the street. The kids jumped up and down when they spotted it and I checked to make sure everyone had their own bus fare. The huge bus stopped in front of us and opened its doors. D.C., Alfie, A.J. and Max seemed to squeeze up to each other, almost pushing each other on board. They scrambled to the back of the bus, still greeting people and exchanging jokes and small talk with each other.

Fred dropped to the grass we were standing on and Robert began to cry seeing Fred's distress. The bus driver looked on, impatient and wanting to get going.

"I can't get on," Fred whispered to me, "the man in the black suit is going to hurt me." His arm was pointing to an elderly gentleman, sitting in a window seat, watching us with unabashed curiosity.

"He's just another passenger on the bus," I offered, "he's probably a very nice man." I looked at the white haired man who now had a quizzical look on his face. We had managed to attract the attention of many of the other riders.

"Come on, lady," the bus driver said, "I don't have time for 'Days of Our Lives', lets go." He was referring to the popular afternoon soap opera and I started to panic, thinking that field trips were not such a good idea after all.

On a hunch, I looked back at the old gentleman. He was smiling at us, helping me with his eyes and I felt his support. "Watch," I said to Fred, and waved to the old man. He waved back and smiled at Fred and myself. Fred looked at me and just as suddenly as he had flopped down on the ground; he got up and waved back at the man profusely.

The two boys boarded the bus and I breathe a sigh of relief. As we walked down the aisle to join the others, the man tipped his hat to me and Fred grabbed my hand, pulling me along. "Don't ever talk to strangers," he hissed at me, "don't you know anything?"

I smiled at the man and soundlessly thanked him for his help. The other passengers seemed solemn and unmoved compared to my noisy band of kids. What a difference! I was glad I was with the boys and not part of the silent, unspeaking majority of adults who probably rode this bus daily.

The tour of the supermarket was fantastic. The boys seldom went out on excursions, even with their parents, and I was glad we had decided to come. The staff of the grocery store was friendly and responsive.

They showed us the fruit and vegetable section, pointing out seasonal fruits and vegetables. Each kid received a bag of fruit and a handful of balloons to take home with them.

The area where they butchered the meat proved to be one of their favorites. The gruesome, red-brown carcasses provoked many questions and admiring comments.

"Are these dead?" demanded Max, "Were they alive once?" The cold, still, meat hung in long slabs and obviously awed and impressed them all.

"Of course they were alive once, you dummy!" D.C. added, "Don't you know cows are alive?" The thought made Max think and I could hear him whispering to himself, "they were alive, they were alive."

We walked up and down the aisles and I pointed out the various sections of food. Frozen foods, dairy products, breads and cereals, and best of all cakes and pies!

I was amazed at how well behaved they were. The only mishap we had was when Max and D.C. decided to sample some flour that lay in an opened package. The shelf was wobbly and the flour fell, covering their shoes with the white, dusty stuff.

Later, we ate our lunches in a local hamburger greasy spoon, drinking orange sodas and cokes. They all agreed that this was the most wonderful restaurant they had ever been in. Max tried to read the stained menu that the waitress left and Alfie and D.C. occupied themselves with attempting to sample the sugar, catsup and salt that was on the table.

"I wish my mother would cook like that," complained D.C., "all she ever makes is stew and bread." He was busy watching a young man stuffing himself with greasy fries, burgers and a milkshake.

"Let's eat here sometime," suggested Alfie, "can we, Toni?" I said that we could, but we would have to head back to school for now. They all reluctantly left and I was secretly glad to be outside in the fresh air again. The smell of frying burgers had made me sick.

Our trip into the outside world, beyond the boundaries of school grounds, had proved exciting, challenging and fun. I promised myself that I would take them on many more. Our class and school itself could only teach these kids so much. The rest of the world had so much to offer and I was willing to help them find it for themselves.

June 1975

It was the last day of school and we were all anxious to tie up loose ends and go home. I had already seen my class list for the following year and Fred wasn't on it.

Mixed emotions flooded me as I looked at him. There was no class for children his age and he would have to be sent to a private school. At fourteen he was much older and bigger than my other boys. I wished a miracle for him, but none came.

With the advent of P.L.94-142, The Education For All Handicapped Children Act, the public schools would have to assume more responsibility for their disabled children. No longer, would they be able to push our kids aside and pretend they didn't exist. The fact remained; however, my own class was too restrictive for him and the kids too young.

The school district, because there was not a suitable class for Fred, would be forced to provide a taxi to take him to and from school every day. The school was in Syracuse and was more than an hour away from his home.

I made a note to speak with the Director of Special Education. If there were an extension to my class then Fred wouldn't have to go to school so far from home. Besides, I thought, none of the kids were getting any younger. What would happen to them eventually?

These unpleasant thoughts interrupted my last day with the boys. I had planned a small birthday party for Alfie. He was eight years old and it was hard to believe that I had taught him for almost two years. He was still as tiny as ever.

As we ate our cake and ice cream I thought of the times, both good and bad, that we had all shared together. We were really a family and families helped each other, through thick and through thin.

"This is the best party I ever had," Alfie told me later, "do you think I can live with you and Dan?" His eyes were downcast and he ran off before I could answer. Probably not wanting to hear the "no" that he knew would come.

I wondered what the summers were like for the kids. Hot, long and heavy with empty hours. I thought that I would try and change that for them this year.

Summer 1975

I had decided to teach summer school. Much of my decision was based on the fact that the district had money to spend and lots of it. We could take the kids on field trips, swimming and plan activities previously denied to us.

None of us knew where the money was coming from, but I thought that it had something to do with the new public laws for the handicapped that Congress had recently enacted.

Jane Kent and I taught the special education classes that summer. We were still in the basement, but we had a lot more kids. They came from all over, children from all kinds of special education classes. Each one had their own personality, temperament and background. And what a summer we gave them!

I planned most of the field trips and they were time consuming and costly. The kids had a ball as we took them to the Corning Glassware Center, the zoo, the Watkins Glen Gorge and every state park we could find. We stuffed them full of watermelon and hotdogs. I knew that all of this couldn't even begin to make up for all the years that they had spent neglected within our huge and impersonal educational system.

Our final trip was a campout at Niagara Falls. We had been planning the trip for weeks and now it had arrived. The twenty or so children showed up excited and eager to be off. We managed to get lots of extra supervisory help so that was no problem.

We loaded up the bus with sleeping bags, tents, enough food to feed seventy five people and a ton of clothes, games, balls and anything we thought we might need in case of emergency. It was a wonder that the bus could move with all the things we had packed.

Max and Robert sat near me on our way to the Falls and we grew to know each other better through the experience. I was enjoying their company and happy that they were getting such a fantastic opportunity. Max had become preoccupied with water recently. He wanted to draw pictures of waves and of people drowning in them. All the way to Niagara Falls he drew curvy lines across sheets of cheap newsprint that I had brought along.

"This man is going to drown," he would matter of factly tell me, pointing to a small stick figure engulfed by the waves.

"Maybe we can save him?" I would cheerfully suggest.

"No, Toni," his voice was forceful, "he's going to drown."

I watched him go through this ritualistic ordeal over and over again that summer and for many years after.

His drawings were tight, controlled and precise. He would whisper in his faraway voice, "he's going to drown, he's going to drown."

I was beginning to wonder if seeing the magnificent sight of Niagara Falls was more than he could handle right now. I was confused when we arrived at the Falls and he barely looked up.

"That's nice," was about all he managed to say.

I didn't realize then that the vivid pictures in his own mind were far more real to him than even something as powerful and intense as Niagara Falls. I was learning, as we all were, and Max was helping me find the way.

We pitched our tents in a run down, off the road, trailer site and headed off to catch a better look at the waterfalls. Robert was beside himself with excitement and wet his pants even though I hadn't seen him do that in months. We had planned a trip on the Maid of the Mist, a large boat that went right up to meet the raging waterfall. We donned black, rubber raincoats that were long and hot. Without them, the Falls would drench us. We would be that close to the awesome sight. A boat filled with people in black raincoats. I remember thinking how absurd we all must look.

I had never learned to swim and was not very fond of the water. Being so close to the Falls made me queasy and I wished I had never suggested the idea.

I turned away from the Falls feeling my stomach coming up into my mouth. I felt like pulling my rubber raincoat up over my head. How had I ever gotten into this situation?

Max was standing next to me. I could feel him watching me. He was laughing hard and the Falls were so loud, I could just about hear him talking.

"Are you afraid, Toni?" he was near hysterics, "This won't hurt you." I looked at him through the water and mist that was pouring on the boat. I had been afraid for him, and here he was taking care of me.

I'm sure I didn't sleep that entire night but it all seemed worth it the next morning. Max and Robert came running over to me, each with an immense bundle of weeds that they had picked.

"Here," Robert held out the wilting bunch of weeds to me, "these are for you." I took them from him, loving them both more than ever at that very moment.

"Do you think their poison ivy?" Max asked. He ran off laughing and I thought that maybe he half hoped they were. I put the weeds in a coke bottle filled with water and began to take down my tent in preparation for our return home.

Kids, teachers, a couple of psychologists, the bus drivers and a few assorted people were running all over the camp grounds packing and eating breakfast cereal at the same time. It was one big mess and the kids loved it.

We were all tired and happy on the way home. Most of them slept on the way back and fortunately no one decided to throw up. A pretty good track record considering some of our other excursions.

We all congratulated each other for surviving after we returned home and I'm reasonably certain I slept for twelve hours straight through. I was tired but it was worth it just to see the expressions on the faces of the kids.

Max brought his sleeping bag to school with him many times that next year. Hoping, I think, that I would get the point and take them camping again.

He would spread out his bag and pretend to roast hotdogs near a make believe fire. Never seeming to tire of the same thing over and over.

I knew how important the summer and its trips had been to the kids. Without it they would never have had the experiences that so many of them desperately needed. It had been an expensive summer and the money had been well spent.

Part I - Chapter 3

September 1975

I had heard rumors and a lot of speculation, but now I was certain. Mike Donahue was walking in the basement of the school with two men that I had never seen before. I saw them stop at the front of my door.

"Those will have to go, of course," said Mike and his voice drifted off. He was pointing to the pipes on the ceiling in my class and I knew instantly what they were talking about. Cherry Park School was going to be renovated. There was a lot of talk that we would all be moved during the renovation. Nobody knew where, but one thing was for sure, it wasn't going to be any picnic.

The Board of Education had approved a million-dollar budget and the renovation would start at the end of the current school year. It would take a year, maybe more.

Secretly, I was very happy. Even though I had tried to make the room as colorful and bright as possible, it was still just a square box of concrete, wood and overhead steam pipes.

A young girl I saw walking down the steps to my basement classroom interrupted my thoughts. It was Sophie! I put aside my thoughts of the coming renovation and our eventual exodus from the school.

"Sophie!" I was so happy to see her again, "How are you?" I was standing near the steps leaning on the wooden banister. She walked by me and hardly glanced in my direction, she had grown taller, slimmer and appeared to have an air of shrewdness about her that I hadn't noticed before.

It had been over a year since we had last seen each other and she was behaving as if it were a day or two.

"O.K." she said, answering my question, "Where is everybody?" I was still in shock over her cool behavior. She was usually so forward, I would have to get use to this new Sophie.

I had been informed that Sophie would be returning to school this year so I was not totally surprised to see her.

She was at home now, living with her parents and brother, after spending over a year at the Marcy Psychiatric Institution. I could see that it had not been easy for her.

"Would you like to pick out a new desk?" I asked. She was looking around the room, probably remembering old times and trying to sort out new feelings.

She slipped into the closest seat. "Are Robert and Max still here?" I heard her asking. I nodded my head yes and the two boys magically came running in.

"Here they are now," I said, and the three old friends stared at each other. Disbelief was thick in the air, I could actually feel it.

"Hi," she said to them, "I'm back." She was starting to loosen up a little at seeing them and I felt a bit more at ease. I'd heard terrible stories of her yearlong stay at the upstate institution. She often refused to get out of bed and had become insolent and even more difficult to manage than before. She'd been on a ward with adolescent girls and had picked up many undesirable habits. One of which was hiding matches and cigarettes in her socks. She was still on medication, more than before she had left.

I wondered if she knew about the death of her foster father and I found myself praying she wouldn't ask me about Millie or Ed. I felt badly for this little girl who at the age of only twelve, had already been in and out of institutions, foster homes and was now again with her natural parents.

How could anyone expect her to behave any differently than she did?

Alfie, D.C. and A.J. arrived and I introduced Sophie to the latter two. She knew Alfie from her first year with us. Looking at my group, I realized how much they all needed each other and how much work we would all have to do. Getting to know others was not the easiest thing for them.

That fall proved to be a difficult and trying one for all of us. Sophie and D.C. frequently were at odds with each other. Fights, temper tantrums and sulky moods became the norm.

"Why does she have to be here?" D.C. would ask me, "She's dumb, anybody can see that. I betcha she can't even read." Furious with his words, Sophie would attempt to read the first grade primers that I had casually scattered on some shelves.

"Dan -- had--a-fat--cat," the words came laboriously and I found myself straining with her," the cat - ccccannnn--sit--on - a -- b-b-bat." She would look up at me and I would nod my head approvingly, hoping to give her some encouragement.

Reading, writing and all the other skills that most people take for granted came hard and slow to many of the kids. To some like A.J., they would come not at all. I always found myself rushing headlong into a vigorous days work with the kids. I wanted them to feel the satisfaction that came with learning something new. I felt as if I was walking a dangerous tightrope with them. If I pushed too much, explosions, property destruction or self abuse could be expected. I was learning to be a master at reading their feelings and mine too.

With the advent of the new public laws, the kids also began to receive art, gym and music classes on a regular basis. Once a day they would have a special class in one of these areas.

The different teachers who worked with them had various approaches of handling the kids. The best were firm, organized and loving. The worst were militant, rigid, and authoritarian. Needless to say, the first type was much more successful.

One of the best was Andy, the art teacher for grades K-6 and all the special classes. Many of my colleagues seemed to love his easy going, relaxed manner. He was inventive, creative and seemed willing to take chances in experimenting with ideas, projects and schemes. Something was always brewing in his class.

That fall, he helped the 6th grades construct a small log cabin. Children could actually walk into the fresh, pine smelling house. Some of the other teachers, however, seemed unimpressed, almost jealous. The kids loved him.

He was crazy about my kids and they responded in kind. Seeing him in the hall, they would run up to him and practically knock him off his feet.

"Mr. Spano!" they would yell, "Is it art today? Can we come down to your class today?"

"Of course, you can come," he would usually answer them, "I'll see you later." Many times, he would give up his own planning periods or free time to work with the kids. In him, I felt as if I had a comrade, an ally. He frequently complained to me about the lack of cooperation among some of the faculty.

"Your kids are fantastic," he would often tell me, "its some of the faculty that I could do without."

One day, as autumn was moving along, an incident happened that I wouldn't soon forget. The kids had been working on an art project in his class, he had sent them back to my class to finish up, they seemed totally engrossed and I didn't want to disrupt them. I sent them into the bathroom, across the hall from my room, to clean up. We were without sinks or water in our own class.

We were busy admiring the papier-mâché projects they had just finished painting. Everyone was pleased with the results and I was already planning on hanging them as mobiles.

Suddenly, our thoughts were interrupted, it was the school custodian and he was livid. The kids and I watched in shock as he ranted on about spilled paint in the bathroom. How he knew that my kids were the culprits I never found out.

"Are you stupid?" He was way past angry and I was incensed that he would talk to the kids in such a mean way.

"How can you talk to them like this?" I finally responded, "The kids didn't mean to spill paint on the floor." I was sure they hadn't done it on purpose, but even if they did I felt they deserved better treatment than this.

He walked away in a huff as another teacher tried to calm the kids down. She had seen the entire scene. I was mad and some of the kids were starting to cry. Robert's white lips were beginning to shake and I could hear him swearing and muttering to himself. I sent D.C. and some of the other boys into the bathroom to clean up the mess they had made.

"Shouldn't talk to me... shouldn't, shouldn't, fat pig cow..." Robert was beside himself and I was furious that my kids had been made to feel half-witted.

I spoke with the principal immediately after school and then I drove out to see the Director of Special Education. I wanted the matter dealt with. Fast letters flew back and forth, between the two administrators.

Finally, I went to my school mailbox; a letter was in it from the principal. He was indignant and resentful that I had told my supervisor about the incident. He said, in his letter, that he "felt capable of handling these incidents without outside interference." It was short, clipped and terse.

I couldn't believe that an impersonal letter in my mailbox was supposed to settle the whole thing. Nothing further was ever mentioned to me, but I was wary of the custodian and made sure that the kids stayed out of his way.

What nobody, except the kids and I knew, was that Robert messed his pants for days afterward. He simply refused to go into the bathroom. Nothing I said or did seemed to make a difference. I found myself looking forward to the school renovation and wondered where we would be.

November 1975

Thanksgiving was approaching and the air was turning colder as the days slipped by. The trees had long since been emptied of their leaves. Their black and brown branches seemed so elegant and long, like they were reaching out to us with their beauty. We were busy doing a unit on the Pilgrims and the Indians. I wanted the children to get an appreciation for Indian life, customs and attitudes. I had long respected their fortitude and ingenuity. We discussed sharing and love.

"We should have a big dinner like the Pilgrims and the Indians!" D.C. was excited, his brown eyes glowing with the thoughts of all that hot, piping food.

"Let's do it," Sophie agreed with D.C, "I can make a turkey!" I smiled at her and wondered if it was possible and how much it would cost. Inflation was hitting all of us hard and the price of food was sky high.

"Turkey, turkey," little A.J. yelled, his hands fluttering in front of his face, "is a real turkey gonna come here?"

"We should do it," I found myself saying to them, "and we'll invite some other classes to join us. Like the Pilgrims and the Indians did."

I wasn't at all sure that was what had happened given the Europeans track record with indigenous peoples, but I started making mental plans immediately. I knew that the Wampanoag tribe covered Massachusetts and Rhode Island and that they had celebrated Thanksgiving ceremonies for thousands of years before the Pilgrims arrived. But I didn't know much more than that.

The other two special education teachers thought I was crazy, but they agreed it would be fun and would help the kids to learn more about cooperation.

So it was settled, and the preparations for the big day began. We would have the feast the day before Thanksgiving and all the kids would help in preparation, cooking, setting the table and so on. We would be feeding about twenty-five kids and a half dozen or more teachers. The list seemed to grow bigger as we moved closer and closer to the actual day.

The COES and some local supermarkets were more than generous in helping us with the expenses. A twenty-pound turkey was donated and COES gave us the much-needed cash for all the trimmings.

The days revolved around preparing for the big meal. The kids made up language charts listing all the food that we would eat. I was glad to see that the up coming holiday was carrying over into their other thoughts. They seemed active and industrious. It was hard to believe they all had such intense emotional and developmental problems.

I wanted to give them as many of these well-timed opportunities as I possibly could.

"Robert," Sophie would beg, "help me make up a list of the food we're gonna eat." Nervous, but anxious to please, Robert would help her with the list. He could read and write very well by now despite his apprehensive ways.

"O.K.," he would reply, his eyes blinking, and pick up a magic marker. They made dozens of long lists and I was impressed with his spelling and her undivided attention. Two years ago neither one could have managed this.

POTATOES   SALIDCORN   TURKEYSQUASHSIDER GRAVYCRAMBERRYMUSHROOMS   NUTS   WHITE MEETBEETS MILK DARK MEET STUFFING   PUMPKINS SWEET POTATOES PI

"Look at this," Robert was so excited by his accomplishment, "I did it myself!" He was running around the room showing his charts to anyone who would look.

Max drew pictures of food while A.J. and D.C. pretended to purchase the food at the store. "Howsamuchisathem turkeys?" little A.J. looked hilarious, dressed up in a gray, felt hat I had brought from home, "It's too darn much," he would continue, not waiting for an answer. "It's $2.00 for the whole bird," D.C. looked like he drove a hard bargain. "I'll take it, anyway," A.J. would say. They were so funny.

Alfie stayed close to me during those months. His mother had remarried and she was having a hard time with him at home. He often came to school complaining of being hit. Sometimes he had black and blue marks.

"Can we eat anything we want, Toni?" He would ask, "All I want?" He was so small and thin. "We'll eat ourselves into a stupor!" I promised him, thinking that maybe we could send him home with the leftovers, if there were any. His mother confided in me, that lately he had been stealing all the knives from the kitchen cupboards, I couldn't imagine what he wanted with them.

He really wasn't that aggressive at least not in school. At last, the day had arrived. We all sat down to eat, thankful that we were happy and together. The amount of food was ridiculous. The table was piled high with turkey, stuffing, potatoes, corn, peas, cranberries and pumpkin pie. There looked like enough to feed an army.

We had decided to invite some of our favorite teachers from the school to feast with us. As it turned out, anyone who happened to be passing by was welcome to grab something to eat.

I was glad that we had all gone to the time, trouble and effort to prepare this feast. I knew that some of the kids would not have all this tomorrow at their own Thanksgiving Day tables.

"Do I have to eat all this?" It was Alfie, he looked green from having eaten so much. "Of course not," I laughingly told him,

"I'll eat his!" yelled D.C. He was in his glory with all this food around. "Don't get sick," I tried to warn them, but we all stuffed ourselves anyway.

They walked to the bus slowly that afternoon, belching and bellies crammed full with food.

December 1975

This was to be our last Christmas in the school before the renovation took place and I wanted it to be a happy one. With the Thanksgiving Day preparations hardly over, we began to get ready for the coming festive event.

I had learned to play a little guitar in college and I taught the kids all the Christmas songs I could remember. They loved to sing and it became the thing of choice to do.

"Dashin true the snow, in a bunhorse open sleigh," A.J. would sing, mixing up the words and I would smile and play on. My playing was comparable to their singing! I encouraged them to sing loud, hoping no one would heard my out of tune guitar and off beat chord playing.

"Let's go caroling," I suggested to them one afternoon, it was already starting to get a little dark out and many of the houses that surrounded the school had already turned on their Christmas lights. I bundled them all up and watched A.J. put on his black rubber boots. He hated the snow and cold.

"I can't, I can't put them boots on," he would scream and bite into his arm. If he managed to get them on his feet, he would scream some more and kick them off, "I hate it, I hate it, go away snow!" Getting him dressed and undressed, in the winter, was not the most pleasurable thing I could think of.

I wondered if my guitar strings would pop outside in this biting cold. We made a quick dash around the neighborhood, singing to anyone who would listen. People seemed friendly and smiled their thanks.

The kids began to eat icicles and pieces of the pure white snow that lay everywhere. There were mounds of the stuff already.

"Don't eat yellow snow," D.C. yelled and ran off, sliding on the slippery pavement.

"Silent night," they sang, "holy night, all is gum, all is beer... round young virgin, mother and bile, holy infant so tender and smile." I hoped no one was listening as well as I was. The days rolled on and I decided to take them ice-skating. There was a big rink in back of the school and it seemed like a waste to pass this chance up. Those who had skates brought them in, the rest we managed to borrow.

I had never been ice skating before and the experience was just as new to me as it was to the kids. The rink was huge and we had arranged to have it all to ourselves. As soon as we had laced everyone's skates we wobbled our way over to the ice. This was not as easy as it looked.

"Hold me up," Sophie yelled, she was clutching at me and we both fell to the ice laughing. Her heavy doses of the medication she was still on made her equilibrium none too steady. We lurched across the length of the rink. It was incredibly hard just to stand up. I felt new admiration for the young ice skaters that I had seen on television.

Robert and A.J. spent a lot of time crying in the stands that were attached to the rink. A.J. bit his arm and screamed on about the ice hurting him. Sometimes it seemed like there were so many needs to fulfill in the kids and not nearly enough time, or people. Many times I found myself choosing between whose needs to answer first. Of course, this was ridiculous since they all needed so much attention.

"The ice will hurt me, the ice will hurt me"... he would scream on endlessly. He was so small and everything seemed a terrible threat to him. He was afraid of rooms, walls, and the pipes in our class, anything that overwhelmed him. It seemed like there were plenty of those things. A.J.'s mother told me that his younger brother tormented him at home. He talked every day at school about "Fat Frankie" his younger brother. How he would get a big collection of rocks and smash "Fat Frankie" to pieces.

"You're just a fat cow andiwillnotgooutonnaice. Youhearmeyouse a fatcow... goddamnyou fortakin me outhere onthis ice..." the tears would drip off Robert's face as he watched us from the stands with A.J. howling, alongside him.

We must have looked like quite a group to the man who ran the ice rink. I could barely handle standing up, never mind skating and the kids were either flinging themselves around the rink or screaming and crying in the stands.

"Hey," Sophie yelled, "Look at me!" She had managed to propel herself along the ice dragging D.C, Alfie and Max along with her. They all landed near my feet. I fell down myself just from laughing at them, the least little thing threw me off balance.

"Let's go back," I suggested to them, ice hockey players had started to fill up the rink and I didn't want the kids or myself to get in the middle of their practice sessions. We were exhausted and sweaty from the whole thing. They enjoyed it so much, I thought it was worth going through the entire hassle. Even Robert and A.J. had stopped crying long enough to watch us falling all over ourselves. I reserved the ice rink for us for every Friday until winter was over. Look out Olympics, here we come.

I had purchased a small, but well proportioned evergreen tree for the Christmas holidays. We spent a little time every afternoon decorating it. Paper chains of red, green and white hung in lopsided circles on our little tree. It reminded me of the Christmas tree that I had seen in the 'Peanuts' comic strip.

I brought in a needle, thread, cranberries, and popcorn. I wanted to show the kids how to make strands of popcorn and berries.

"I can't do this!" D.C. yelled, he had flung his needle and a fistful of corn to the floor. Stringing corn required a good deal of patience, which he often seemed short on.

"I'll help him," Sophie volunteered," watch me do it, D.C." It was amazing, but somehow she had mastered the art of stringing popcorn. Even though Sophie's coordination and motoric problems often interfered she kept with it and had strung about two feet of the crumbly stuff. We all took pleasure in her accomplishment; even small victories were monumental ones to us.

"Your mother eats pig grease!" yelled D.C. and ran out of the room. He had bolted out of sight before I even reached the door. He was angry, seeing Sophie succeed in doing what he could not. He had not run far, crouched behind the swinging doors that led from the basement to the stairway below the first floor, he sat sullen and looking violent.

"Why don't you go play Annie Sullivan?" D.C. hissed at me as I came closer to him. I wondered who had told him about

Helen Keller and her teacher Ann Sullivan, but I decided now was not the time to find out.

"Come back with me," I said, "we'll try it one more time." We could both hear other classes singing Christmas carols and having a good time laughing and partying. He looked so sad and small sitting there in his worn, lumpy looking flannel shirt.

I thought he was going to leave the building, as he sometimes did, but he stood up and took my hand. I wanted to talk to him some more, but he had that 'let's not push our luck look' in his eye so I dropped it.

We drifted on toward Christmas and the start of the New Year in much the same way. Problems and solutions, problems and more problems. I thought of how many times I had tried to help the kids come to grips with their own special and personal realities.

Often, there were no solutions to the problems. Only what I called 'Band-Aid Therapy,' that is, therapy that is only a small Band-Aid on an open sore. There were times that I felt frustrated and overwhelmed with the problems that confronted me daily. Dysfunctional families, malnutrition, and unbelievable neglect were typical things that I encountered every day. The lack of consultant services was compounded by the lack of administrative and parental interest.

It was beginning to seem to me that if you chose to teach special children as a career, you also chose isolation, disinterest and apathy with it. After less than three years I had seen many excellent teachers leave the profession because of the profound malaise that sets in when they suddenly realized they were in this alone.

My Christmas wish that year was for all teachers to realize that we were each part of the other. No public law could legislate that feeling into existence. Only time and effort could produce that desired change and I was growing weary with wanting it.

The Christmas party was quiet and uneventful compared to the Thanksgiving feast of only a month ago. We sat around our little Christmas tree and watched the blue and green lights blinking on and off. The kids opened the gifts I bought them and I drank cherry Kool-Aid, thankful for the upcoming vacation.

As we were about ready to go home, Robert handed me a gray, cardboard egg carton. On it he had written, in purple chalk, To Toni-my best Teacher. There was dried egg yolk on it and it looked like it had been bashed in. I opened it and inside were some moldy grapes and what looked like the remains of a dead goldfish. "He looked hungry," Robert explained, "I knew you wouldn't care if I gave the goldfish some of your grapes." I closed my eyes and thought that even without all of the consultant and psychiatric services I felt Robert and the others needed that these kids were very, very special indeed.

March 1976

The year had rolled along in the gray-white mush that I had come to know as winter in upstate N.Y. Colds, flu and other assorted winter ailments had kept many of the kids from attending school. I still had a lingering cough that I couldn't seem to shake. It seemed that everyone had the winter blahs.

One day, A.J. was the only one who came to school. He walked in angry at the blizzard that was beginning to rage outside. "Am I the only one in this place?" he asked me, while he threw his hat, mittens and jacket in a heap on the floor. He punched himself in the chest and keeled over landing hard on the wooden floor

He laid flat on his back, flapping his hands in front of his eyes, and screaming about snow sticking to the classroom pipes.

Mike Donahue and a small group of parents peeked into my class. Mike, seeing A.J. lying on the floor, tried to quietly usher the parents from my room. I always felt that Mike became unraveled at watching one of my kids in a 'crisis', but some of the parents were more interested in watching us.

"Let's hang up your coat now A.J.," I said to him firmly, "maybe we'll make pizza pie later since we're all alone." He jumped up from the floor and ran screaming to the visitor who stood transfixed by our door. The poor man looked like he was in shock.

"Pizza pie, pizza pie," he yelled at the man, "ya wanna have some pizza pie?" He flapped his hands wildly; they seemed to vibrate between his stomach and the top of his head. He was laughing hysterically and I tried to place myself between him and the man at the door. I knew how the strange and unpredictable behavior of the kids could affect those who were not comfortable being with them. The man smiled a sickly look back at me and said to A.J. "I'm not hungry right now."

"Not hungry right now, not hungry right now," A.J. ran shouting towards me, collapsing in my arms. I picked him up and held him for awhile. Even at nearly eight years old he was no bigger than a four year-old and a tiny one at that.

His nose was running so hard that mucus was dripping off the end of it. I couldn't believe he was in school so sick and without even a lousy Kleenex. After he calmed himself down we went to the library and I read him a few of his favorite books. He loved stories about giants and monsters.

He fell asleep after fifteen minutes and I carried him back to our room, he was grunting, sneezing and coughing. I heard him talking about 'Fat Frankie' in his sleep. The younger, but much feared brother.

"Smashyou wid a big rock, Fat Frankie," A.J. mumbled in his sleep, "you are a fatpiggy." He looked so fragile in his sleep, I found myself wanting to smash all the Fat Frankies that were bothering him and all of the other kids too.

"Did you eat my pizza?" he said, he was awake and rubbing his eyes. He looked cranky and his nose was red and puffy from running. His hand was on his penis and he was rubbing it hard.

"Do you have to go to the bathroom?" I asked him. I looked at him and his face contorted in a grimace. "I'm afraid in there," he said to me, "take me in there."

We walked across the hall to the dilapidated bathroom. He was mumbling and whining about being afraid to go in. He had managed to get to the point where he could go in by himself. I always stood outside the door, talking to and encouraging him.

"How you doing A.J.?" I called into him. He was talking to himself and I could hear what sounded like a roll of paper towels tumble on the floor. He was laughing and I almost went in after him to see what was going on.

"I picked 'em up," he called back to me.

"Good," I said, "now flush the toilet and don't drink any of the toilet water. That's what the fountains are for." Just as I finished saying that my visitor friend of earlier that morning appeared. He looked at me as if he were convinced that I was truly crazy. A.J. and I walked back to our class with as much dignity as possible.

"Can I have a drink now?" A.J. asked and I filled up a paper cup with water for him. The sinks and fountains in our school were too high for him. It had been some time before I realized he was quenching his thirst in our school toilets.

I watched him drink down the water and refilled his cup. Thinking that he should be home in bed with his baby aspirin and orange juice.

We spent the rest of the day making gooey pizza from a cardboard mix. It tasted terrible, but he loved it. Slopping cheese, tomato sauce and gummy flour dough all over the table, he looked sick, but contented. It had been wonderful to spend the whole morning with just one child. I felt relaxed, and in no need to rush around. Answering questions, taking time, this was how teaching should be.

School closed before lunch that day. The blizzard was in full swing and I would not see A.J. for the rest of the week. I was glad he had some time to recuperate and nurse his cold. I hoped 'Fat Frankie' would not torment him too much.

May 1976

It was just about time for 'group' and I was waiting for all the buses to arrive. The month of May was nearly over and I was thinking with renewed interest of where they would put the special education classes during the renovation of our school.

'Group' was the term that I called our sessions that we had been having for well over a year. They were a sharing of personal things and experiences. Sometimes wild things happened in 'group' and I was very cautious about sharing these with outsiders. Feelings came out in 'group' and I wanted the experience to be as relaxed as possible.

Some of the more nonverbal kids would act things out with toys or anything else that happened to be lying around. Some of them talked during 'group', some said nothing.

I had just finished setting up our chairs in a circle. The boys came running in the room with Sophie hot on their tails. "She's crazy!" yelled D.C, and ran off to one corner of the room. Max, Robert and Alfie looked pale and shaken. I looked over at Sophie and knew we were in for trouble. Her hair was wild and seemed to match the look in her eyes.

Suddenly, without any warning, she pounced on Max and began to pull his hair. They were rolling and tumbling on the floor and she was screaming loud obscenities at him. Finally, I ripped the two of them apart. Everyone, with the exception of D.C. was crying and absolutely beside themselves. I wondered what had set Sophie off. I had never seen her this out of control before.

I bent over to touch Max's head and see if he was O.K. My hair was very long and I didn't realize it was within her reach. She latched onto it and flung me around. I tried to talk her out of it, but she was beyond that point already. Picking my glasses off my face, she threw them across the room.

"You goddamn bitch, I'll get you for sending me to Marcy." She was talking about the institution that she had lived at several different times in her young life. I knew this was no time for explanations. Her strength was incredible and I fought her off as hard as I could.

She threw me back against the pipes that lay near the floor of the room. I was unconscious for minutes and when I opened my eyes all the kids were standing around me, some were crying. I was shaken and dizzy. I tried to get help, but she jumped on my back screaming and swearing at me.

I lay there with her pulling my hair and punching me in my ribs. Finally, I started to yell for help. The kids were so frozen with fear that they all stood just watching the two of us.

"Hey," I yelled, "hey you, come in here and help me... help me, help me!" I was yelling the words out as loud as I could to anybody who could hear.

"Don't you hear me ... I need help!" I was yelling so loud I thought the walls would collapse. Fortunately, the door to our class was open and the library was directly across the hall. The librarian came to the door, amazement and fear showing plainly on her face. "Please help me," I said to her, "I can't get her off my back."

Sophie was still pulling my hair, but she was crying now and refused to let go. My hair felt like it was being pulled out by the roots.

"Please let go, Sophie," I whispered to her, "please let go of my hair." She was crying loudly and her grip seemed even tighter. The librarian came closer.

"Let go of Toni's hair," she said to Sophie. I could tell she was afraid.

"If I let go of Toni's hair," Sophie cried, "she won't be my friend anymore." She was growing calmer now and I sensed an opening.

"Let go Sophie," I said again, I could feel the librarian gently and cautiously pulling her hands away from my head. My head ached and I was seeing stars. I went out of the room to ask one of the other special education teachers to call for help at our administrative offices.

They came to pick up Sophie and brought her to the local mental health facility. She had calmed down considerably and I could tell she was ashamed and afraid.

"They gonna take me back to Marcy?" she kept asking me over and over. "It's O.K. Sophie," I told her, "everythings going to be fine." I knew that her parents had been having a hard time dealing with her at home. They couldn't keep track of her and she wandered around their apartment complex bothering neighbors and friends. I wondered if they regretted their decision to take her back into their home.

At the mental health facility they recommended that Sophie's medication be changed. I was glad that no one mentioned sending her back to the state facility. Whatever she had done, sending her away was certainly not going to help.

I had a head x-ray performed at the local hospital that afternoon. They warned me to watch for signs of concussion, but thankfully none came. I was grateful that the kids and I had escaped with no harm done.

The kids talked about Sophie's outburst for the rest of the month. I could tell that it had even awed D.C. I tried to down play the whole thing, but it was obvious that it had deeply affected them.

Because she was now twelve years old, Sophie had been slated for a new class in the fall. There were still no other classes for children with emotional and developmental problems. Like John and Fred before her, she would be placed in another group. It was decided that a class for trainable retarded children would be the best alternative. Sophie's cognitive and social skills were at the level of a six or seven year old child. I hoped that she would be happy in this new placement. She had a reasonably productive and placid year with us, outside of her final outburst. I was sorry it all had to end that way. Sophie, with her unpredictable moods and ways, had gone out in a flash of fury. I still don't know what it was over or if the school librarian ever recovered from her shock.

June 1976

Our classroom was in a mess and there was more dust being kicked up than I dreamed possible. Even the red spiders came out to wish us farewell. We were leaving Cherry Park School and none of us knew when we would be back.

The boys were beside themselves. They would be leaving all that was safe and familiar. For them this would be a brand new adventure. Max wandered around the room, touching walls, windowsills, broken toys. I wished that I could read his mind.

Brown cardboard boxes were strewn over most of the room. We were all in the mist of packing and boxing the contents of our class. Everything had to go, books, language charts, our yellow igloo, games, puzzles, toys, and many other precious items that the boys refused to give up. A.J.' s collection of rocks, Robert's records and albums, Max's drawings; all these were necessary things that they wanted in our new school. The boys were having mixed emotions about leaving and I shared those feelings.

It seemed like the entire school was filled with dust and the gritty feeling that comes from moving. All the teachers, from grades K-6, were busy packing and storing their supplies. The desks, chairs and other pieces of major equipment would also be shipped with us. It all had to be packed and moved, all of it. Most of us spent our time praying that the boxes would eventually reach us.

We had heard some wild stories about the crew that was to move us out during the summer months. They were a young group of men; hopefully they wouldn't heave too many boxes down the stairs. I found myself wishing that I hadn't packed the tape recorder and some of the other breakables.

We would all be placed in different schools, vacant buildings or spare rooms until the renovation was completed. We would not be moving as a whole school to occupy another building. This came as a surprise to some of the other teachers and there was a good deal of sadness and disgust with the way the whole matter was being handled.

It was fairly common knowledge, that the renovation would be completed in a year's time. After that, we could come back to a school that would be a totally different place. I could not begin to fathom what Cherry Park would be like newly renovated. I had become accustomed to the oldness of the school and so had the kids.

The thin slated wooden floors, the lack of carpeting throughout the school, the ancient classroom pipes, the boiler room, the aging cafeteria and auditorium, the water fountains that were too high for the kids were all part of the building that I had taught in for three years. Cherry Park School with carpeting was equivalent to an oxymoron. Although my class, was one of the ugliest classes in the school, I wanted the million dollars in renovation money spent on the kids rather than the building. I'm sure they would have appreciated better books, supplies and equipment more than hand blow dryers for the bathroom and wall to wall carpeting.

"Are we gonna take the pipes with us?" A.J. asked me, he was staring at them and flapping his little hands furiously. I think he was the only one who was not sorry to leave the pipes. They had begun to peel and crumble with the paint that we had put on them years earlier. They looked like long, slithering snakes that were in the process of shedding their skins. He had always hated and despised the pipes. They must have loomed large and ugly in his fearful mind.

"Nope," I answered him, "the pipes stay here and when we come back they'll be gone." Looking at the faded colored pipes brought back a flood of memories. We were all three years older. My little class had survived and now there was talk at the COES of creating another class to follow mine. A class that would be for kids over the age of ten with both emotional and developmental problems.

"The pipes will be gone," Max whispered to himself as he walked around the room, "the pipes will all be gone." He took the change very hard and seemed anxious about the move. I decided to give all of them something to hang on to.

"Guess where we'll be going to school next year?" I said to all of them. They all looked so sad and depressed.

"Where?" Max ran up to me and grabbed my arm, "Where are we going?" His eyes lit up with expectation.

"We're going to the Campus School!" I was so excited myself that I could barely spit out the words.

"Ya mean we're goin' to college?" Robert asked me, "That's where all the big kids go." He was jumping up and down, his hands covering the entire length of his slim body. He was so excited I thought he would burst.

"In a way," I told them, "the Campus School is at the college." I looked around at them. They were all so excited with the news that I was glad I had told them.

"I'm goin' to college," A.J. shouted, he was jumping up and down with Robert, "I'm goin' to college."

The Campus School, or Swetman Learning Center, was located at the State University College at Oswego. The SUNY campus was started in 1861 and had enrolled over six thousand undergraduate students on six hundred and ninety acres of land. The Campus School was in its fifteenth year of existence on the campus. It had been started as an alternative to the public schools and for the benefit of the education majors at the college. Student praticums and observations were very common at the Campus School. I knew that the experience would be a very different one for the kids, much different than the public school they had been in for three years.

"We're goin' to college!" A.J. and Robert were still shouting, "I'm gonna play rock music and eat subs!" They laughed and carried on about the new adventure. Alfie, D.C. and Max took a much quieter approach, absorbing the information slowly into their minds.

As I watched them help me pack our things those last few weeks I thought about all the good times that I had come to know through them for the last three years. These were kids whose parents had been told, that they would never be able to function in a school, at home or in society. We had proven the specialists wrong and I was bound and determined that our new odyssey would be equally as enjoyable. New horizons were just around the corner and we all looked forward to meeting the challenge.

Summer 1976

The Campus School was sticky and hot. It had acquired the gummy, boarded up feeling that schools get in the summer without children or activity to fill the halls. I was in the basement of the school where the primary cluster held its sessions during the school year. The sounds of the ARC pre-school class drifted toward me as I walked down the hall. I was on my way to a class to observe a little girl that was to be placed in my group in the fall. I hoped the screaming I could hear was not coming from that room or from that particular child.

I slipped into the long, narrow observation room that was attached to the ARC pre-school class. This particular group of children was the class that Alfie, Robert, A.J. and Max had come from. The observation room was dim and had a rectangular window that I could watch the children through.

A small, rotund little girl with bright red pigtails was underneath one of the tables screaming at the top of her lungs. Her face was beginning to match the color of her hair. Her lung capacity was amazing, she could scream A.J. under the rug. The other children in the room seemed oblivious to the noise, they just kept on playing with their plastic blocks and trucks. I watched her scream on hysterically for a good five minutes. At last, she got up from under the table, dried her eyes with her hands and sat down.

She looked at her teacher and pointed to another child's toy. I could see the teacher shake her head 'no' and hand the chubby little girl another toy. She took it, threw it on the floor and began screaming and crying all over again.

This was my first introduction to Roxanne. I couldn't take my eyes off her. She was, without a doubt, the most resistant, stubborn child I had ever seen. She was strutting around the room, directing other children and manipulating her teachers to the point of absurdity. She seemed to have almost total control of what was going on inside the classroom.

I tapped on the door to the class and peeked my head through, looking around for the teacher. She was busy with another child so I sat at a table near Roxanne and watched her for awhile. She was intent and her attention seemed good. She put together a ten piece puzzle quickly and went in search of another. I offered to help and she seemed friendly.

"Can I take her for a walk?" I asked Maria, the pre-school teacher, "Maybe I can get to know her better."

"If you want," Maria said, "she hasn't been out of the room much this year. I just can't manage her and the other kids too, but if you want to take her, be my guest!" Roxanne jumped up and began tugging at my arm. Her receptive language was so good that she had understood my conversation with Maria.

We were out in the hall within a matter of minutes. I was anxious to walk around the school and see my new classroom for the coming year. Roxanne was in no mood to wait for me and began to run headlong down the hall.

"Wait!" I yelled out to her, she was practically out the door that led to the exterior of the Campus School. She turned to look at me once and just ignored my instruction. She looked like a newly freed convict. I ran after her and finally caught up to her near one of the student dormitories.

"You will wait for me," I told her when I got ahead of her, "and you will also hold my hand." I was determined that this kid and I both would learn something on this, our first walk together. She looked at me and started to scream and cry again hysterically. Dropping to the ground, I watched what I assumed to be a full-blown temper tantrum.

"NOT, NOT, NOT, NOT, NOT... NOT, NOT, NOT, NOT, NOT NOT, NOT, NOT, NOT, NOT, NOT, NOT... NOT, NOT!" she screamed the word over and over at me, it was the first one that I had heard her say. I couldn't believe what I was seeing. Apparently, neither could the college professor and his class, who sat watching us on the lawn of the campus.

The young, bearded teacher sat mesmerized along with the rest of his students, watching Roxanne scream and carry on like she had taken leave of her senses. I smiled at them and waved. Oh God, I thought, get me out of this situation.

"Get up, Roxanne," I whispered close to her ear, "or I'll make sure that one of the other kids in school eats your Twinkies." I didn't know if she even had a Twinkie back in her classroom. It was a dirty trick to play on her, but her rules weren't always the fairest. She jumped up and started to run ahead. I could hear her yelling, "Twinkie, Twinkie" over and over.

I stood my ground and motioned for her to come back to where I was standing. I held out my hand and she reluctantly took it. We trotted by the professor and his students; Roxanne waved to them gregariously. I listened to him begin his lecture on the philosophy of education. I thought that his students could probably learn more about that topic by watching Roxanne.

We made a few other stops in the Campus School before I returned Roxanne to her classroom. She wanted to go to the bathroom and play the piano in the school cafeteria. A repeat performance of the scene near the dormitory happened in both these spots. She seemed to possess no self control whatsoever. By the time we reached the ARC pre school class I was as exhausted as if I had run a 26K race. No wonder this kid's teacher seemed listless and distant, she was probably weary from monitoring the tireless energy of this red-haired little girl.

"It'll be a relief," Maria told me at the room, "to have her gone. None of us can take it anymore." I smiled at her and dragged myself down the hall and out of the school. I was too tired to even stop at my new class on the second floor. The fast approaching school year would hold many things for all of us, and I just knew that Roxie would not be the least of them.

Part II - Chapter 4

September 1976

Our new classroom at the Campus School was a startling contrast to the room we had been in for three years at the Cherry Park Elementary School. It was large, spacious and had a teacher's office connected to the main room. The light that poured in through the windows was somewhat dazzling after the dimness that we had all become accustomed to in our other school. Even the kids seemed different to me.

They were, after all, three years older than they had been when I first met them three Septembers ago. It was hard to believe that time had passed by so quickly almost slipping through my fingers. The relationship that I developed with them was not the usual teacher-student one. It was special and I knew that when the time came for us to each go our separate ways it would be a difficult transition. We each knew and understood each other. For the most part, it was casual, easy, and I was both amused and intrigued when other adults had a rough time dealing with them.

"Where's Cherry Park School?" Max asked me, he had barely come in the door. He was taller and had on new jeans and a brightly colored shirt. "What happened to the pipes?" he was looking up at the ceiling and seemed to be stunned not to find any overhead paraphernalia hanging from above.

"Where are the pipes?" I asked his question back at him. I had found over the years that Max knew most of the answers to the repetitive questions he asked. Rather than ignoring him, or turning him off, as the school psychologists suggested, I began asking him back his same questions. He almost always answered me and in that way sort of reinforced himself with his own answers.

"The pipes are at Cherry Park School," he told me, "and Cherry Park is being remenovated."

"Renovated" I corrected, "Kind of like a face lift." He smiled at me and I wondered if he knew what I meant.

Carlos and Simone appeared at the door, holding onto each other's hand. They both looked scared to death.

I had been to each of their previous classes the year before. They were both being transferred to my group. Carlos had been in Kindergarten for two years, the last year had been a bad one for him and his teachers. He was an imaginative, inventive little boy and I liked him immediately. His previous teacher complained that he seemed flaky, out of touch and removed from the other children. He didn't respond to directions and his attention span was minimal. He was very dark and had deep brown eyes and hair. His complexion was the color of coffee and I learned that he was of Mexican descent.

I remembered how he had played with me when I visited him in his Kindergarten class, less than four months earlier. He was completely absorbed by his magical, mysterious toys and the way he seemed to breathe life into them.

"Wanna play with me?" he asked, "Your pretty." He spoke the words to me, but never once looked in my direction.

"Sure," I said to him, "what do you want to play?"

He didn't answer my question, but proceeded to set a lavish table in front of me. Plastic plates, forks and spoons sat side by side with colored plastic fruits and vegetables. He was as busy as any homemaker I've ever seen.

"Here," he said, handing me a plastic plate filled with the laces that were used to string colored beads on. The laces had purple beads on top of them.

"Mmmmmm..." I said, playing along with him, "looks good, what is it?" I had a suspicion of what it was he was serving me, but I wanted it confirmed.

"Spaghetti and meatballs," he said, somewhat annoyed with me, "whadaya think it is?" He was busy mixing up more string spaghetti in his aluminum pot. Pouring on more colored meatballs. He was beautiful and I fell in love with him instantly.

"The purple meatballs are my favorite," I told him, pretending to shove a whole one in my mouth, "what's yours?"

"I never eat the stuff," he said and continued his meal time preparations until his teacher called him for a nap he didn't want to take. We said goodbye reluctantly and I watched him wander off looking for his lost sleeping mat.

He seemed disoriented and I wondered if his learning difficulties weren't due more to a learning disability rather than emotional problems. At any rate, he had been placed in my group and he was standing at the door frightened and trembling.

Simone was standing with him, babbling disconnected words and waving her hands and fingers in front of her face. She was so much taller than Carlos and had managed to grip him tightly around the neck. Carlos's eyes were starting to bulge out of his head. He was trying to pry her fingers from his throat.

"Choking me..." were the only words I heard Carlos utter, "let go of my neck!" I really don't think she meant to hurt Carlos, but Simone had squeezed his neck so hard he dropped his brown bag lunch.

"What's inna your bag?" she nearly sang the words out to Carlos, "Is it roast-a-beefa!" She laughed out loud and dashed over to the windows yelling at the top of her lungs.

"Lulululululululululu... lulululu ... lululu!" The sing song words sounded like the strange sound of the loons that I heard when I was camping the previous summer. Simone reminded me of an exotic, rare bird. I wanted very much to get to know her, but when she was not singing her words or talking about food she became passive and faraway. She stood by the window rocking back and forth saying the names of foods.

"Do you like roast-a-beefa?" I heard her say to herself, "Do you like buttermilka?" She rocked and rocked and her hands fluttered endlessly in front of her eyes. It seemed like she was trying to filter the light through her thin fingers. Her listing of foods seemed to go on and on.

"Macaroooooooooniiiii... lulululululu," she crowed, "peachy pie, I eat in on the davenport!" She took delight in her own words and was ranting on while Robert, A.J. and Alfie watched in fascination. "Do ya' like a pizzzzzzzaaa pie?" she ran over to the boys and stood swaying in front of them. She put her hands on little A.J.'s neck and squeezed hard. I could hear his breath leave his throat. "Do ya like pizzzzzzzzzza pie?" she asked him again. I saw him nod his head as I pulled her hands away and guided her toward an empty desk with her name on it. She took it passively and sat rocking and reciting her food list. We all stood watching her and I noticed Max had begun to rock back and forth with her. They seemed to keep time with each other perfectly.

I was glad that I had recommended another class for D.C. this year. He had already spent two years with us and I felt it was time to move on for him. He was placed in a class for children who were educably mentally retarded. He had been angry with me for suggesting the move, but he needed to be with other boys and girls with whom he could work and relate to. He would not get a chance to do a lot of that if he stayed with my withdrawn or explosive bunch. I just hoped he could hold his sharp temper and tongue to make it through the school year.

Robert and Alfie were still staring at Simone when Roxanne came charging through the door with her mother. Roxanne's hair was soft, smooth and still in the pigtails that I had seen only two months earlier. Her mother had the same red hair and was a small, slim woman. She looked exhausted and I had a strong hunch why. Roxanne was busy eyeing all the toys, games and books.

"She won't be happy until she's touched everything in this class," Roxie's mother said, looking around. Roxanne looked like she was preparing to examine every last scrap of paper that I had placed casually around the room.

I recalled our meeting with Roxanne's psychiatrist last month in Syracuse. Roxanne had been seeing the therapist for only a few weeks, but she had spent most of her time in the bathroom screaming hysterically. Her mother told me she could hear the screams through several closed doors.

"I strongly recommend psychotropic drugs," he told both of us, in his upstate medical office. Roxanne had been left at home in the care of her grandmother.

"Ritalin or some similar type drug might reduce her intense hyperactivity and increase her attention span," his lips twitched while he was talking, but he seemed business like and anxious to convince us of the necessity of medication, particularly in school.

"She doesn't act right when she's on drugs," Roxanne's mother meekly suggested, "as a matter of fact she's worse." I heard the words, but I couldn't believe my ears. Worse? I decided right then and there that we should proceed with caution on the drug issue. Besides, I had heard about the side effects of using drugs on young, hyperactive children. Alfie's doctor had implied that his growth had been stunted due to their indiscriminate use.

"Please call me if she still seems excitable after a week or two of school," he said to me, as we were leaving, "we can decide then which drug to use." I smiled at him, thanking him for his time.

Roxie's mom left her with me after I introduced the other kids to Roxie and told me to call if there were any problems, but she was gone before I could even answer. Roxanne ran to the back of the room where I had placed five or six boxes of toys and playtime activities. She dumped all the toys in a huge pile and perched her round little body on top of them; gloating and looking like a royal queen. It was really quite comical.

"Come on Roxanne," I said to her, "it's time to come and sit down." She looked in my direction, but ignored my instructions. I motioned to my brand new teaching assistant to give me a hand. We walked over to Roxanne and with one of us on either side of her we hauled her to her feet and dragged her over to her seat.

I was generally not one to manipulate or pull children around, but this kid needed to see where I was coming from right off the bat.

79

I knew that talking, coaxing or cajoling her would get both of us nowhere. I wanted her to see immediately that I was in control of my classroom and that I expected her to operate within the limits that I established.

She shrieked in her high pitched voice so loudly that the teacher next door came over to see if everything was O.K. Roxanne was sitting at her desk pounding the top of it with her little fists. Her face was twisted into an ugly grimace and even Simone had stopped her chanting litany of foods to watch.

"NOT, NOT, NOT, NOT, NOT, NOT... NOT, NOT, NOT, NOT... NOT, NOT, NOT, NOT, NOT,...NOT,NOT,NOT!" She was still beating the top of her desk and squirming to get away from Rose, my teaching assistant, who sat straddling her from behind.

I hired Rose myself that past summer. She was a mature, older woman with three children of her own at home. I was impressed with her calm, thoughtful attitude and was pleased when she accepted the position as teacher assistant. Now she looked as if she wished she had stayed at home with her own kids.

Although she was inexperienced, I sensed her strength and hoped that Roxanne's shrieking wouldn't scare her off. We saluted the flag and sang 'My Country Tis Of Thee' while Roxanne screamed on and on. Finally, she exhausted herself and put her pigtailed head on her desk and cried herself into a semi-sleep.

The kids and I were tired just from watching this incredible show. I wondered if any controls had been put on this kid before. She seemed like she did not know or understand the meaning of the word 'no.' I learned from her pre-school teacher that she had been on a strict behavior management program. If Roxie misbehaved or was uncooperative they ignored it. They reinforced only 'appropriate' behavior. How they could ignore her yelling, screaming and carrying on was beyond me.

"Up, up, up?" she woke up and was pointing to the toys in the corner of the room, where they still lay in a big heap, "Up, up, up?" She looked at me hopefully, her big, green eyes still wet with tears.

"No," I said to her firmly, "we have work to do now. We'll play later." A repeat performance of earlier that morning started again. I dragged myself through the morning's work with the kids. We were all exhausted and tired from hearing Roxanne's constant whining and crying. I had to remind myself that it had taken her six years to get to this point and it certainly wasn't going to change overnight.

I tried to explain that to the kids, but they looked at me in a blank way. "Will you just shut your yap," A.J. finally burst out to her; "shut--your--mouth." He said the words distinctly and I could tell he was at the breaking point himself.

Rose rode shot gun on Roxanne from behind her desk for a solid two weeks. It seemed like the two were bound together magnetically. But she didn't resign and I knew we would all make it together that year.

October 1976

I stood at the window of my class sharpening pencils and watching hundreds of college students strolling on the campus of the State University. They seemed youthful, vital and full of unrestrained exuberance. It was late afternoon and the kids had been gone for about an hour, I stayed to prepare some plans and to clean up.

It was Friday and the weekend seemed to stretch long, and lazy in front of me. The kids had all had a good week, they seemed to adjust daily to their new surroundings and I was very pleased. Even Simone and Roxanne were beginning to accept direction a little better. Things had calmed down and we were getting into a routine.

Being on the campus was still very intoxicating compared to the relative seclusion of public school life. The Campus School seemed noisy and full of different people.

At the Cherry Park School teachers and children were basically the only ones around. Here, college professors, students, parents and hordes of professionals mingled together. Talking, fraternizing and exchanging miscellaneous ideas on education and teaching. I found the entire experience liberating and somewhat cosmopolitan.

I had confided my feelings of amazement to the principal of my new school. He was very reassuring and told me that many public school teachers often felt relief at the unconventional and unceremonious ways of the Campus School. After being treated like a tall child it was refreshing to be asked my opinions on the education of children.

Even the other kids in the school seemed to relate more openly to my kids. They often spoke to them in the halls, calling them and myself by name. Frequently, they would ask me questions about my kids. I found it thrilling, at last, to come out of the closet and talk. No longer a captive in the basement, I felt like I'd been freed. As I looked out at the young college students I remembered my own days on campus. I had been part of the sixties generation. The tumultuous decade had ushered in the Vietnam War, civil rights, demonstrations and a host of urgent concerns that had led us to extremes. I participated in the two major demonstrations against the Vietnam War in Washington D.C. The first took place in November of 1969 and the second in March of 1970. I joined VISTA in 1969 and took a leave of absence from college. I worked with the welfare rights organization in Richmond, Virginia.

I chose to work with children that most of us have been taught to fear or avoid. It seemed that the majority of the attention we paid to the disabled in our communities was at the yearly telethon or walkathon or fund raising events. The rest of the time, we banished them to invisibility. Regardless, I had elected to work within the system, hoping to better the situation. After all, as the 1960's slogan goes, 'if your not part of the solution your part of the problem.'

Bob Morgan, the principal of the Campus School, interrupted my thoughts. He frequently made visits to our class to say hello and see if things were running smoothly.

"Are you still here?" he popped his head in the door, "It's way past quittin' time lady, go home!" He was always so friendly and helpful; I smiled at his amiable bantering.

"What do you think these look like?" I said to him, holding up an art project that the kids had just completed. They were caterpillars made from vertical strips of discarded egg cartons.

"Uh," he raised his eyebrows, "a multi-breasted woman?" We both laughed at his ridiculous analogy.

"How're things movin'?" he asked, "Easier this week?"

"Better," I told him, "I still feel like a newly released inmate."

"I know how you feel," he sympathized, "I used to teach in public school myself. When I first came here I felt like asking permission just to go wash my hands." I nodded at him emphatically; his words had echoed my very thoughts.

"I gotta go," he said, looking at his watch, "heavy date with the head of the Ed. Department." I watched him walk down the hall, talking to various people and waving to others. It was still very odd to see so much of a principal. I had become accustomed to leading a relatively secluded existence in the basement; I felt like I had been asked to rejoin the world.

Not all of the teachers from Cherry Park School shared my enthusiasm for our new building. Many of them thought the Campus School was a licentious breeding ground for spoiled brats, who were creative but illiterate. They complained bitterly of roaming children, a lack of discipline and above all, a complete disregard for organization. What most of them meant by this was that the kids were not asked to sit in rows, stand quietly in straight lines, march like commando units down the halls or participate in boring, characterless busy work. Because of this they were labeled ill mannered, unrefined juveniles.

I found most of the kids and the teachers at the Campus School refreshingly open and inquisitive. Many of the teachers worked long and hard. I found myself respecting them for that.

"Hi ya' sweetie," it was Mark, one of the kids from across the hall. He was talking to Simone who had missed her bus and was waiting for another. He watched her sway back and forth, following her with his eyes. She was bending and rocking so deeply that I thought she would touch the floor.

"You must feel like you need a Dramamine after a day of that," he said to me. I could barely understand him because he had on those red wax lips that I used to buy as a kid.

He looked at me intensely and pulled me to one side. "Is she... uh," and then he made the sign for 'crazy' by pointing to his head and making small, fast circles.

"Losing her hair?" I said to him, "Oh, no, Simone's hair is very thick." I patted the top of her head and she smiled back at me and squeezed my arm. I think some of D.C.'s smart mouth had rubbed off on me.

"Very funny," he said, he was chewing the waxy lips into a gummy ball, "see ya' Simone. Watch out for your teacher. I think she popped her wing nuts this morning."

In this way, I managed to get to know a lot of the kids and teachers I shared my new school with. They seemed unafraid of either the kids or myself. They frequently stopped in my class just to talk or see how things were going. My kids really seemed to enjoy all the attention they were getting and I loved the open atmosphere. It invigorated me and I found myself working harder than ever. New ideas and projects seemed to present themselves to me daily. The productive, fertile imagination of the school was beginning to influence my teaching. Best of all, I was receiving encouragement for all my efforts. The campus was beginning to thin out now. Shadows seemed to be growing longer and I noticed Dan walking toward the Campus School with a friend. They were laughing and joking, oblivious of the brilliant orange and red leaves that were falling all around them.

A sudden enormous gust of wind made Dan stop dead in his tracks. He held onto his friend while his prosthesis stuck out straight in front of him, flapping in the wind, with a mind of it's own. I saw him laugh and wait for the wind to subside.

After nearly four years on the campus, he would be graduating with a degree in industrial arts this coming summer. I knew how hard he had worked for his education and how much he wanted to teach kids himself. He often came to my class to visit the kids.

'How tall are you, Dan?" Max would charge over to him, anxious for a chance to be near him. Not waiting for an answer, he would rush on with a countless list of questions.

"Hi,... hi... hi, Dan," Simone would stand near him, not looking in his direction, "can I touch your beard?" I was delighted that she would ask. Usually she paid little attention to visitors, preferring the enjoyment of herself to other people. He would let her touch his brown, curly beard and she would bite her hand between the index finger and her thumb with sheer excitement. She adored being close to people but tended to get over zealous and squeeze or hug them to the point of actually hurting them.

"Dan," A.J. would say to him, "you kiss your wife now!" And all the kids would watch while Dan gave me a big, wet one right on the lips.

One day he watched while I struggled with Roxanne outside the Campus School. It was time to go home and she had sprawled her chunky little body on the cement sidewalk, refusing to either get up or board the bus.

College students walked by us and looked at me as if I were an ogre, she was crying and screaming at them hysterically.

"Help me, help me, help me, help me... help me, help me, help, help, help, help me, HELP ME, HELP ME!" Her screams were piteous and many of the students would actually try to lend her a hand to get up, but I refused them.

She was perfectly capable of getting off the sidewalk herself, but insisted on using anyone who happened by.

She often went into the halls of the Campus School, after coming out of the bathroom, with her pants down, hoping someone would pull them up for her.

I leaned down next to her and softly whispered in her ear with a technique that I'd perfected since our first meeting. "Get up, Roxie," my mouth was right next to her ear, "or I'll smash your Mickey Mouse thermos into smithereens." I wasn't even sure she had a Mickey Mouse thermos, but it never failed. She would jump up yelling, "Mickey Mouse, Mickey Mouse!" and get on the bus. I was never quite sure if Roxie understood my words. Her expressive language abilities were extremely limited. One thing was for sure though; she never mistook my intent. Roxanne knew I meant business from our very first meeting.

Although my tactics and procedures for handling Roxanne were unconventional, and I was sure they would never be documented as a textbook management program, I was getting amazing results. Her parents and ex-teachers were astonished at how well she responded to me. Meanwhile, she continued to run things at home and at church school like a miniature version of General Patton.

I would recount the daily incidences to Dan every day over dinner and he would shake his head and laugh. No child could cry as much as I told him Roxanne could. But it was true, her mother told me that she would break into tears just hearing the theme song from 'Lassie' when she was a baby.

"What are you looking at?" Dan said, he had just come in the school and was watching me staring out the window.

"I was just watching you walk across the campus," I told him, "God, it's really windy out." His long hair and beard were a disheveled mess.

"Let's get something to eat," he suggested, "I'm starving."

"No argument there," I agreed with him and we left the school to go to our favorite Chinese restaurant.

Dinner consisted of egg rolls, won-ton soup, fried chicken livers and a steaming plate of chicken with snow peas, water chestnuts and broccoli.

"We should take a drive to the Adirondack State Park this weekend," Dan said through a mouthful of chicken liver, "I bet the leaves are at their peak."

"I bet their past peak," I told him, "the kids were collecting tons of them this afternoon."

We took a long, luxurious ride that weekend. The Adirondacks seemed alive with color and I was filled with happiness. We camped in one of the state parks that was still open to the public, and made love while we froze in our blue sleeping bags, listening to the Beatles, Dylan and the Moody Blues. The next day we hiked up to one of the fire towers that are scattered throughout the area. Standing at the top of the shaky, wind blasted tower I looked out over the immensity of the beautiful forests below. I knew I was walking down a good road.

December 1976

The kids were once again nervously awaiting the coming Christmas holiday and all the excitement that it would bring. I had made plans to have a spectacular Christmas party, but in the meantime, I wanted to do something unusual. I had scouted the campus pretty thoroughly and found two swimming pools available to us. Rather than taking them ice skating again this year, I thought swimming might provide a pleasant change.

I had decided to take them to the indoor swimming pool at the women's physical education building. Lee Hall, was not that far from the Campus School and it seemed like an ideal location. I had instructed the parents to send in bathing suits, towels and a comb or brush with their children. I had arranged to have the pool reserved for us every Thursday afternoon for the entire winter season.

There were a number of children in my group who had some very unusual fears or phobias about the water, so I managed to locate some generous college students to donate their time and expertise in helping them become more accustomed to the water. Each child had an individual student-instructor, many of whom were certified lifeguards. I felt confident and sure that this would be a positive experience and I tried to quell my own apprehensions about the water. Perhaps, I would learn to swim myself, ...someday. Dan had tried, unsuccessfully, to teach me to swim. He loved the water and claimed he could swim blindfolded and with his hands and foot bound. Since I really preferred not to witness this incredible feat, I avoided pools, the ocean and water in general, like the plague. My morning shower was about the extent of my water experiences. I was determined, however, not to pass on my water phobia to the kids. The days before our first swimming session were filled with talk and speculation about the water and swimming. I had the student-lifeguards visit the kids at the Campus School before we even met at the pool.

Max had become almost totally possessed with a water preoccupation. During a recent psychological testing session with a school psychologist, he had been asked to draw a picture of himself. He drew the same picture that I had seen him draw for over a year now. That of a drowning person. Only now, he was asking questions about water depth, temperature and allowing babies or animals to be dropped in what he called, "the deep end."

One afternoon, one of the lifeguards stopped by my class for a short visit with my kids. She had some color photographs with her of children and adults swimming and enjoying the water. Max was absorbed by these photographs and persisted in quizzing her about them. I forewarned the college students about the kids and their water difficulties, but how do you prepare a person for an assault?

Max went right up to the young, blonde, co-ed and put both his hands on her shoulders. It surprised me, he was normally very cool and reserved with strangers. I think he thought of her as an expert on the water and swimming.

"How deep is the deep end?" he asked her, she looked at me and then back to Max.

"How deep is it?" she said, looking at him, "Well, it's very deep. Over 6 feet." He was hanging onto her every word, desperate for information.

He jumped up on the nearest chair and raised his hand as high as he could over his head. He was standing on his tiptoes and straining to the point of bursting.

"Is it this deep?" he said, Rose and the other kids were watching him with utter fascination. The young lifeguard was in shock over his behavior.

"It's very deep," she replied, "you shouldn't go in the deep end, unless you know how to swim."

"What will happen?" he said the words, practically choking on them and already knowing the answer.

"What will happen, Max?" I interjected, I knew that he knew the answer to his own question, as he so often did. He walked away from us and began whispering in his soft, strange voice... "you will drown, you will drown, you will drown."

The lifeguard looked at me for support and I patted her arm. She talked to the other kids about how good the water felt and how much fun we were all going to have in it. None of them looked any too convinced. Especially with Max talking about drowning and being dragged under.

Just as she was about to leave, Max ran over to her.

"You do not throw babies or animals into the deep end," he informed her, still gripping at her arms. She smiled at me and left the room. I could almost hear her thoughts as she walked down the hall. I laughed and Rose and I made bets on whether or not she would return. Max spent all his spare time drawing pictures of drowning people and erasing my pictures of lifeguards that I sent to help.

Lee Hall was only a short distance from the Campus School and we made a quick dash over, there was not much snow on the ground, and the kids were excited and talked to every other college student they passed. It was extremely amusing to watch the reactions of the college kids. Some pretended not to hear the kids and walked by them, others waved back and smiled.

The pool was Olympic size and it had bleachers that were attached to it for spectators. The lifeguards were already there and waiting for us. We all helped the kids change into their swimsuits. I sent one of the male lifeguards into the room marked, 'Men' with Carlos, Robert, Alfie, A.J. and Max. Rose and I took Simone and Roxanne.

Simone was deathly afraid of the water and I promised her mother that I would not force her to go in. As it was, Rose had quite a time getting her suit on her. Simone had very little use of her hands and refused to cooperate,

She broke away from Rose and dashed into the showers that were in the locker room. Two young girls were showering and chatting with each other about afternoon classes.

Simone barged right up to them, with the top part of her bathing suit falling to her waist. She managed to squeeze her tall body under the shower with them.

"Do you eat meat-a-balls?" she babbled at them. They looked stunned beyond words. "Do you like tuna-fishy, fishy, fishy?" I had no choice, but to go in after her. I knew she would not come out if I called to her. Fully clothe, I stepped into the shower and snatched her away from them, excusing the both of us.

By the time I got back to Rose and Roxanne, they were involved in the middle of a tussle. Rose was trying to wrestle a black purse from Roxanne, who was busy examining its contents. It probably belonged to one of the girls in the shower. All I could think of was to get them both out of there as quietly as possible.

I hoped the other lifeguard with the boys wasn't having too much trouble with them. I didn't have to wonder for long, he came up to me as soon as I brought the girls down to the pool.

"He told me this is his swimming suit," he said to me, holding up a pair of filthy, gray underwear. I saw the fruit-of-the-loom label shredded on the back of the shorts and looked over at Robert who sat crying and swearing near the bleachers.

"Goddamn pigcowmom... you bigfatcow," he swore, "I'll get you for this." Words I'd heard many times before. I looked at the jockey shorts. There were so many holes in them, I wondered which ones were for his legs.

The other boys were dressed and already in the pool with their pretty, talkative lifeguards. Most of them were crying, but the situation seemed under control. Max was out of the water and standing near the far end of the pool. I could tell he was checking the water depth. The lifeguard who visited us the other day was with him. She seemed more relaxed with him and answered his questions over and over.

"Why," he asked her, "shouldn't I throw Duckie in the pool?"

"Who's Duckie?" I heard her ask him.

"The cat," he replied. He was still checking the water depth. He had his hands around his throat and he looked like he was simulating choking or drowning. I wasn't sure which.

"Should you throw Duckie in the sewer?" he asked her. The poor cat, I thought, wondering if he actually did those things. I knew he frequently threw Duckie off his front porch. I would have to ask his mother if he had included the sewer in with the porch.

"Let's go in the pool," I heard her suggest. "In the deep end?" Max asked her, full of excitement over the danger. They had become fast friends within minutes.

"Yes," she said, "but, only because I'm with you. Never go in the deep end until you can swim." He hung on her every word and was whispering to himself..."deep end, deep end, deep end" as she guided him into the water.

I went over to Robert and promised him that I would find him a suitable bathing suit. I kicked myself for not checking them before we came to the pool.

Simone sat down near Robert, she looked white from fright at being so close to such a large pool. Her mother told me that she loved the water until a year ago. She suddenly refused to go in after a bad experience in a summer school class. I remembered how she had run under the showers with the college students only minutes ago, why wouldn't she go in the pool?

"Simone," I said, "let's put our feet in the pool." Even I could manage that without much problem.

"No" she replied, "I don't want to." She was starting to rock back and forth, twisting her fingers into strange shapes. She had spent so many years manipulating her fingers and hands that she was able to touch her thumbs back to her thin, white wrists. I put my arm around her shoulders.

"It's O.K.," I reassured her, "I've got an idea." I walked over to a small waste paper basket that I spotted near the office next to the bleachers. Dumping out the few scraps of paper that were in it, I brought it back to where she and Robert were sitting.

I dipped the pail into the pool and came up with some of the clear, warm pool water. I put the pail down in front of her.

"Put your feet in it," I tried to tempt her, "it feels good." She looked at me suspiciously, but slowly dipped in one foot and then the other. She was so delighted with herself that she bit into her hand between the thumb and index finger. Her favorite spot to bite. I had long since learned that like A.J. she bit herself if she was either upset or overly excited. I took her hand from her mouth and held it in my own.

"Doesn't that feel nice?" I said to her, "Pretty soon you'll be swimming in the pool like a fish."

"Fishy, fishy, fishy!" Simone crowed at Robert and me, "Simone's a fishy!" She was very pleased with my analogy.

"Yeah," Robert told her, "your a fish." I'm not really sure why or how the name stuck, but from that moment on Simone's nickname became Fish. We all called her that. I suspect it was to her liking because it was the name of a food. Her favorite topic of conversation.

The other boys were getting along very well with their lifeguards and all but A.J. had stopped crying. Carlos was using a small, square float that we had brought with us. He splashed around thoroughly enjoying the whole experience. Just watching him made the trip worthwhile.

Roxanne was trying hard to escape from the firm grip of the male lifeguard that I had assigned to her. They were involved in a struggle that looked like she was going to win. Finally, she slipped away from his grasp and started to paddle over to the deeper end of the pool near Max.

Since she couldn't swim, she started going under. He pulled her up, but she continued to squirm out of his reach. Her sheer physical strength, will power and ego were nothing short of phenomenal. She put her fist in his face and shoved it under the water. When he came up I noticed that she had raked the side of his face with her nails.

"I wan water, I wan water, water, water... I wan water!" she screamed, as I helped him pull her out of the pool. She had absolutely no self-control. I brought her back to the locker room to change. If she could not control her behavior she would not be allowed to participate. I knew I couldn't back up one inch with her. I had been the first person to ever set limits with her and although it was exhausting, it was beginning to have an effect. She dressed herself while she cried hysterically.

"Sorry," she mumbled softly to me, "sorry, sorry." I had heard the word many times during the past four months. Slowly I had learned to ignore it. I had seen her use it on too many people to get her way with them. I was determined to have her learn that her manipulative outbursts would have consequences attached to them. The days of her getting her own way were over. Roxie spent the rest of the pool time with Robert, Simone and myself on the bench.

Although our first session at the pool had been somewhat less than ideal, the kids all looked forward to our weekly visits. I salvaged a pair of swimming trunks from the Campus School's lost and found box for Robert. Simone was sitting at the pool's edge by Christmas time. It all seemed worth it to me.

As the Christmas party and celebrations came closer and closer, I found it hard to believe that this was the fourth year I would be preparing for the festivities with the kids. We had all come so far. I hoped that Sophie, Fred, D.C. and John were well and happy.

I had persuaded one of the local drugstores to donate some Christmas presents to the kids for our party. The manager of the store, in a moment of Yuletide generosity, gave me seven view-masters and the colorful reels that went with them.

As I watched them silently clicking their new Christmas present that year, I thought of the peace that this school had brought us.

January 1977

I had seen three other Oswego winters before this, but they were nothing compared to the one that we all found ourselves involved in now. The snow seemed literally to pour out of the sky. Being so close to Lake Ontario made the winter seem twice as ominous.

The lake seemed dark and forbidding, whitecap waves rolled across the horizon, while tons of the white, flaky snow drifted steadily from the sky. I was sitting in my office reading the new state regulations from Albany. I was drinking hot coffee and wondering what would happen to the educational bureaucracy if their paper supply were suddenly cut off.

The kids had all been sent home earlier that morning. The blizzard that was raging outside promised to be a big one. I was warming my hands on my coffee mug and contemplating putting on my mittens when the school secretary appeared at my door.

"You have a phone call, Toni," she said, "I think it's Dr. Gramm." As I walked down the hall, my sixth sense told me this was not a social call. The Director of Special Education for the Oswego County COES was a small man with eyes that darted back and forth, sizing up any situation, teachers and all the administrivia that went with the job. He reminded me of 'Columbo', the private detective that I had seen on t.v. reruns. When he visited my classroom, which was next to never, he usually stood by the door, smiling nervously and pulling at his beige raincoat. He never taught and it seemed incomprehensible to me that he should be involved with so many special children and their teachers.

However, like 'Columbo', Dr. Gramm was a cagey man, with a shrewd way of getting answers, finding out information and remaining on top of the administrative pile. He often played the unsophisticated innocent, but in reality, was a reasonably good judge of his teacher's and their competency level.

I picked up the phone in the secretary's office and sat down on the green plastic chair that was next to it.

"Hello, Dr. Gramm," I said into the receiver, "this is Toni." It always made me jittery and tense to talk to him. I was usually very cautious of what I said to him, measuring every word.

"Hello, Toni," he answered back, "some storm we're having. What are you still doing in the school?"

"Oh," I replied, "I'm just reading the new state reg's from Albany on disabled children." There were so many new guidelines and laws that seemed to change daily, it was very important for us to keep up with policy changes.

"Lots of changes going on," he said, "listen, we have to make a switch in classes." He paused for a minute to see if I would respond, when I didn't he continued.

"We have to move your class, one of the other special education teachers in the Campus School is unhappy with her class size. She wants a bigger room and she does have more kids than you do." I knew who he was talking about. Two of the other teacher's from Cherry Park decided to share a classroom here in the Campus School, they felt that team teaching might be a good idea.

I knew things weren't working out for them when I noticed that they had barricaded the middle of the room with filing cabinets, closets and storage bins. I had never team taught myself, but I thought that cooperation, not isolation, was an essential ingredient in the success of such a program.

"We have a really nice class for you, just down the hall from the room you're in now," his voice was flustered and he was trying to read my reaction over the phone. I was upset, the kids had just adjusted to this new room and now he was asking us to move again and in the middle of the school year.

"Why can't the other teacher move?" I asked, "She's the one who's unhappy with her room. Not me." Already my mind was filling with thoughts of brown cardboard boxes, jumpy kids and the inevitable frustration that moving brings. I couldn't believe it was happening all over again.

"She has more kids than you do," he said, "they need a larger class. The one you're in now is perfect." I knew there was no sense arguing, his mind was made up.

"When?" I asked him. I knew how difficult changes were for my kids.

"Tomorrow," he replied, "I'll send down some men to help you." I could hear his breathing, it was hard and fast.

"By the way," he continued, "you're getting a new student."

"But I've already got seven," I said. I stood up and began to fidget with the black phone cord.

"Well," he stated with no emotion, "we're going to make it eight." I listened to his words and wondered how Rose and I were going to manage eight kids. We were barely able to deal with seven of them, so many needed individualized attention.

"How old is the student?" I asked. He paused for a second.

"She's five years old."

"Five," I said, "that's ridiculous. Simone is eleven." The age span would, once again, be six years between the youngest and oldest.

"You teach a low incidence child," he said, "there's not many children who are both emotionally disturbed and have other developmental problems."

"Just to get the record straight," he continued, "let me remind you that I don't work for you, you work for me."

After I hung up the phone, I walked down to the main entrance of the Campus School and stood staring out at the mid January storm that seemed to be running wild. My own emotions seemed to be close to the eye of that unforgiving winter storm.

I thought about the words that Dr. Gramm and I had just exchanged. He was wrong; I did not work for him. I worked for the kids that had been entrusted to my care. I was their teacher and I would not be satisfied with anything less than being a good one. I didn't care that their problems were as he had put it, 'low incidence', to me they were significant. The children that I taught were larger than life. I was convinced that no one was going to put them in a back closet.

I wandered back to my class and went into my office. The room along with my coffee had grown cold and I felt an acute alienation from the educational system that I'd chosen to work within. I could hear the voices of college students walking through the halls of the Campus School.

"I can't wait to be a teacher," I heard their voices drifting into the office, "imagine your own classroom." If you can keep it long enough to make it real, I thought to myself.

I picked up the state regulations for disabled children that I left on my desk. They were covered with brown stains from my coffee mug. I thought about the state regs that mandated no more than a three-year age span between the youngest and the oldest child in any special education classroom. What a joke! I could still see six year old A.J. playing with fourteen year old Fred just a few short years ago. I tossed the state regs in the garbage and went out for a walk in the truth of the blizzard that was surrounding us.

February 1977

One of my favorite holidays had just passed and remnants of it were still visible in our new classroom. Bright red valentines were strewn on the walls, windows and the door. Making them had turned out to be a sought after activity during the past two weeks. The kids wanted to make them endlessly.

Sunlight streamed in the windows and I basked in the sensation of feeling the sun on my face. It was seldom that we saw the sun in mid-winter upstate N.Y. I took a few minutes to luxuriate in it before the kids arrived.

Our new classroom was much different than our old one down the hall. It had three rooms to it and was smaller. One room we used for the work area, it had the children's desks, chairs, cabinets and the like. The room to the right of the work area was the playroom, complete with large tinkertoys, wagons and anything else I could cram in. What I couldn't fit in wound up in the room to the left of the workroom. My own large teacher's desk, supplies and the software that I didn't want disturbed, landed in there. Max had made a sign for the room... 'Toni's Office. Keep Out.'... It was a huge sign in bright red letters. Max had drawn a skull and bones underneath it to emphasis the message. I always smiled when I looked at it, because most of them spent of good deal of time in there. They loved to sit at my desk and pretend to be teacher. Even A.J. would scribble gibberish on paper I gave him.

"These are my lesson plans," he would tell me, his little hands flapping away, "now do not disturb them." His vocabulary was growing daily and I never ceased to marvel at the limitless extent of it. His arm biting had decreased somewhat and in turn, his self-concept seemed to be a little better. The screaming tantrums of two years ago were nearly gone.

I watched Carlos get off his bus, little Patty was right behind him. They held hands and walked together up the steps to our classroom. Patty had arrived right on schedule, just as Dr. Gramm had informed me she would. Like Carlos, she was dark haired and had come from Kindergarten, where she had been having a very difficult time.

Although I realized Patty had learning disabilities, I really wasn't convinced that this was an appropriate placement for her. Apparently, neither did her parents. They were against it from the start. I watched her mother's face weeks before as she observed A.J. Simone, Roxanne, and the others rocking, swaying and flapping their hands. Her look of shock was unmistakable. She knew her child was having problems, but nothing like these children were experiencing.

It made me wonder about criteria for placement, not only in my class, but in all special education classes. No one seemed certain about screening, testing or evaluation procedures. It all seemed like a game of chance, and I found myself thinking about the various drugs that different doctors and psychiatrists had wanted to 'try' on Roxanne.

I took some consolation in the fact that at least Carlos had found someone to talk to in my group. He and Patty became friends very quickly; they seemed to be the only children in my class who did not flit in and out of reality. They learned quickly in a small group and Carlos took a great deal of pride in showing Patty his first reader.

Max came charging up the steps and into the classroom. His face was red and beads of perspiration had formed on his forehead.

"There's a polar bear outside," he said, his voice was shaky and frightened, "it's bleeding all over the ground." I looked over at Rose who was standing near the sink, watering our sweet potato plants. We exchanged looks, wondering what he was talking about.

"Where is it?" I said to him, "Show me." He went over to the window and pointed down to a small mound of snow that seemed to have red juice or maybe catsup splattered on it.

I looked at Rose and then at Max. I knew there was no use explaining to him from up here that what he was seeing was his mind playing tricks on him. In a flash of recognition, I felt I knew what it was like to have a perceptual or neurological problem. I wondered how much of Max's life was made up of his fantasies or illusions.

It took some doing, but I managed to coax him down the steps and out the door to his imagined 'polar bear.'

Later that afternoon, I went to the public library and took out a few books on role-playing. I had become reasonably proficient at the art of it years ago during a two month training session to become a VISTA volunteer.

I felt that playing or acting out different situations and feelings would give the kids more of a grasp of the world they lived in. I knew it was worth a try. The only thing we stood to lose were imagined 'polar bears' and things that go bump in the night.

Rose and I role played in front of the kids every morning for 'group.' At first, she was stiff and clearly uncomfortable. No one had ever asked her to pretend that she was something other than what she was. But gradually, she loosened up. She became the perfect 'straight man' for our morning vignettes. The kids loved seeing us ham it up, only Simone, still kept the whole role playing experience, at arms length. She cried and bit her hand just watching us.

Finally, I decided that the kids had watched us long enough. I wanted them to try their hand at the art of make believe. As I suspected, they turned out to be pros at the art of pretension.

I would set up a situation that Rose and I would act out informally in front of the kids, then we would give them each a turn. We had to guide and encourage them along, especially in the beginning, but eventually some of them became expert actors.

"O.K.," I would suggest, "today Rose and I are going to role play… eating lunch in the cafeteria" --then she and I would do a short, impromptu rendition of the noon scene that we both witnessed daily. I told them that we would either play it the 'right way' or the 'wrong way.' I hated to get so square-toed with such an experimental art form, but I wanted to clearly express to the kids that there were different ways to behave. I wanted to concrete things up for them a little more, take away the uncertainty and abstractness that so many of them did not understand.

Everyday we role-played a different situation that I would make up off the top of my head. It was one of the few times during the day when I didn't have to strain for their attention. They had their eyes glued on us. Role playing--"eating lunch in the cafeteria"--went something like this:

ME: BOY, I'M STARVING. GIVE ME SOME OF YOUR COOKIES...

ROSE: NO, I WANT THEM FOR MYSELF.

ME: COME ON, GIVE ME JUST ONE LITTLE COOKIE - -(I would then reach over to Rose's plate and grab a couple of cookies that we had set out.)

ROSE: HEY! GIVE ME BACK MY COOKIES, THEY'RE MINE! (We might pretend to start a physical fight or push each other.)

Needless to say, this was the 'wrong way' of eating lunch in the cafeteria. My aim was basically to teach simple social rules, respect for self and others and identification of feelings, both positive and negative. I wanted to teach them not to run from uncomfortable feelings or to jump to conclusions, as in the case of Max and his 'polar bear.'

We would always give them a more suitable code of behavior after we had role played it the 'wrong way.' The 'right way' of "eating lunch in the cafeteria" might go something like this:

ME: THOSE COOKIES LOOK GOOD, CAN I HAVE ONE?

ROSE: NOPE, THEY'RE MINE AND I WANT THEM.

ME: PLEASE CAN I HAVE ONE - I'LL TRADE YOU SOME GRAPES FOR THEM.

ROSE: NO, MAYBE TOMORROW.

We would always discuss the role play situations directly after we finished playing with them and I tried to remain conscious not to resolve or settle everything. I didn't want them to think problems in life always turned out smoothly.

I tried to come up with role playing situations that paralleled their own lives. For example, we might role-play fears of the night, physical abuse, aggressive behavior, stealing, fear of water, dogs, or new situations. I always gave the kids a choice on whether or not they wanted to role-play.

The 'wrong way' was an extremely popular one and I let them play it that way as often as not. I felt that they could learn just as much, if not more, if they were permitted and even encouraged to express angry, negative and even hostile feelings. I was not afraid of the kids and watching them play act seemed to bring us closer together. I had long since learned that the repression of feelings or the confusion of them was not a healthy thing. Our role-playing became a focal point of observation in the Campus School that winter. One of the college professors was very intrigued and sent his education students to observe us at our play acting every morning.

The kids were growing accustomed to the freer atmosphere of the Campus School and I was beginning to notice a change in their ability to cope with new people. I found myself secretly wishing that we could remain in this school even after the renovation was completed.

April 1977

My new student teacher had been with us nearly a month. She was an energetic girl who seemed genuinely concerned with learning how to teach children. She seemed competent at instruction and most of the kids were cooperative with her. Except Roxanne and Simone.

I had never had a student teacher before and it was very hard for me not to interfere if things seemed to be going poorly. Roxanne and Simone, sensing a ripe opportunity, took advantage of her inexperience daily.

"It's time for work, Roxanne," she would meekly suggest, "Do you want to come over to the table and sit down?" Roxanne would sprawl under the table in the playroom and scream... "NOT, NOT, NOT, NOT, NOT, NOT!" She would jump up and open one of the windows in the play room and scream out to the college students who were walking by,"NOT, NOT, NOT, NOT!" I often wondered what they thought of the strange yelling. Still, I refused to interfere. If this student teacher wanted to teach kids it was best that she learn now how difficult it could be.

It was not easy watching Roxie go through the very tantrums that she had tried with me only months earlier. She and I had developed a working relationship that was extremely compatible. Everyone, including myself, was more than pleased with her cooperative behavior. Unfortunately, this behavior did not yet carry over to other people who dealt with her. With every new person, she tried her old ways of behaving. I found that most people let her have her own way, it was the rare individual who would not cave into her outbursts.

Roxanne had learned at a very early age how to control people. She knew that most adults were afraid of her behavior and she played it up to the hilt. Gradually, I realized that at least half of Roxanne's difficulties lay with the expectations that other people had of her. She adjusted her behavior according to the way others responded. If they let her, she would take complete charge of most situations. Of course, this was an unreasonable spot for a child who was not yet seven years old to be placed in. Few people realized how insecure and over anxious she really was. All most of them ever saw was a youngster who looked like she wanted nothing but her own way.

They didn't know that she bit her nails to a nub or that she was terrified of new places she hadn't seen before. And she was lovable, almost more than any kid I had ever taught.

Finally, things reached a peak. It was a Thursday morning and we were all weary from the constant noise, screaming and tantrums.

"Lulululululululululu - dubdubdubdubdubdubdub," Simone's chanting and singing had reached an all time high. With no direction she yelled on and on.

"Matzaballs-a-," she was delighted with herself, "do-a-ya-like-a-matzaballs-a?" She would squeeze her own face and anybody who happened to be near her.

"Wannnnnna drink-a-milka?" she giggled hysterically, "Wanna ravioli-oli-oli-oli-oli-oli?" She ran over to me and put her hands on my neck, attempting to squeeze and embrace me all at once.

"Sit down," I said to her and looked directly into her eyes. She knew I was angry and quieted down immediately. I had all of them go to sit at their desks. The student teacher ran into my office sobbing and burst into tears.

Roxanne was screaming underneath a desk. I walked over to her and looked at her under her desk. No words were necessary. Her screaming, like Simones, stopped immediately.

The kids were absolutely silent. The only sound we could hear was the student teacher crying in my office. They knew they had taken advantage of the situation and that I was less than pleased. I let them listen to her cry for a minute longer.

"You will go to the library," I told them, "and you will pick out a book. When you come back, you will sit at your desk and look at it." I had Rose take them to the library. The only sounds I heard were Roxanne quietly murmuring, "sorry, sorry, sorry," and Simone softly humming her, "lulululu".

I went back into the office. My student teacher was still crying and I held out some Kleenex for her.

"I can't seem to control them," she sobbed, "they don't listen to me." I listened to her talk and gradually the tears stopped.

"I'm afraid of them," she whispered the words and then looked at me for my reaction.

"I know," I told her, "so are most people." We sat in silence until the kids came back.

I was none too sure that I was the ideal choice for an unseasoned student teacher. I told her that I often felt that I was not in control of the situation, too. But, she was better after that morning and I watched her confidence grow. She seemed to take more chances with them after that. Of course, she fell flat on her face more, but it didn't seem to matter quite as much. She was learning the art of flying by the seat of her pants and I tried to encourage her to experiment and remain calm in the face of the unknown. Watching her, I remembered my own early days of teaching and the uncertainty that I felt. I was glad that this young teacher had been assigned to my class. I know the kids she taught in that room helped her on her way.

June 1977

A whole year had passed by us again. I had received some great news that made all the moving from one class to another fade away. Cherry Park was still in the process of being renovated and we would not be moving back in the fall. I was elated, although many of the other teachers currently housed in the Campus School with me were not. To them it meant another year of inconvenience, to me it meant another year of the Campus School and I looked forward to it.

The best news of all, however, came from Dr. Gramm. Another class for children with both emotional and developmental problems would be added during the following school year. At last, I would have another teacher to share my experience with. The kids could be placed according to their ages. I would take the kids under the age of ten. The new teacher would take the tens and over. It would be hard to say goodbye to the kids who would go, but they needed to try their wings and I knew that the time was long overdue.

We celebrated the end of the school year with a trip to one of the nearby state parks. It had been a hot, humid spring and the cool water in the lake revived all the kids.

After a barbecue of hamburgers and hotdogs they ran off to pick wild flowers. I watched them tease and play with each other. Max and Alfie had reached the ripe old age of ten and Robert was now eleven. Could it be that we had been together four years already? Time seemed to have no meaning to me anymore. Only the trust and understanding that had built between us really seemed to matter.

Even little A.J. was growing. He was nine and still talked to anyone he could get to listen. His mouth seemed to grow as fast as his body and I was amazed at his growing independence.

Carlos and Patty, always together, sat making sand pies and sharing secrets. They had learned as much from each other as I could ever teach them. I would see if I could find another class for them, a class where they could make more friends. Perhaps, a class for kids with learning disabilities.

Roxanne was leading Simone around by the hand. They made a comical pair. Roxie so small and chunky leading our beloved 'Fish' around and enjoying playing the leader. They would both be in special classes for a long time to come.

I hoped that I could get them some psychiatric help next year. Roxie's parents had given up on the psychiatrist that I had met the summer before. A new baby in the family and the exorbitant expense of therapy had forced them to stop taking her. Simone had never been in therapy and I wondered how her parents would react to it if I suggested psychotherapy as an alternative.

She was still terrified of the water and her long hair was greasy and unkempt. She now refused to have it washed or to take a shower. Her mother told me of having to nearly drag her to the showers while her brother or father would attempt to wash her. I thought of the side excursion to the stalls that she had taken with the college students only months before. The short yellow school bus came to pick us up and I watched the kids board. A.J. still collected his treasured rocks and talked about buildings and telephone wires hurting him, but they all seemed straighter, stronger and taller to me than ever before.

On the way back to school we sang songs and joked with the bus driver. I had the driver pass by Cherry Park School on the way back to the Oswego Campus. It seemed to arouse old feelings and thoughts in the four oldest boys who had spent so much time with me there.

"Where are those darn pipes?" A.J. asked, "Are they going to hurt me on the ceiling?" He flapped his hands and cranked his head out the bus window, hoping for a better look at the school.

"Those pipes will not hurt you now, A.J.," Max was rocking back and forth, slowly mouthing the words that he had heard me say to A.J. so many times while we had been at the school. I looked at all of them and thought that nothing, no problem, was so big that it could not be overcome.

Part II - Chapter 5

September 1977

The summer had passed very quickly for me. Dan and I had spent some time camping in the Adirondacks and I felt refreshed from the vacation and anxious to get back to work. Dan had graduated from the university and located a position as an industrial arts teacher with junior high kids. I would be returning to the Campus School and looked forward to the new class that Dr. Gramm had promised us this year.

The eight children that I taught last year would be back, but due to the intensity of their problems, no more would be added to my bulging group until the new class was in effect. Already there were three children on a waiting list to be enrolled in my group.

I had seen all three of these kids over the summer months. The oldest was Miles and he was currently attending a special education class for children who were identified as educable mentally retarded. Miles was a tiny, hyperactive six-year-old who seemed to find trouble without even looking for it. His intense learning problems and mischievous behavior had nearly driven his teacher to tears. The day I visited his summer school group, he had succeeded in dumping a pint of purple paint on the carpeted floor of his class, devoured his lunch by 9:30 and peed in the garbage can, all to the displeasure of his teacher and the delight of his classmates.

His ridiculous antics were more like high jinks than emotional disturbance. He seemed like a friendly, untrained puppy. He plopped himself into my lap; his pants still soaked with pee, on the day of my visit.

"You gonna be my new teacher?" he asked, he was so hyperactive that he wriggled on my lap constantly. I felt like a wet electric fence had landed on my knees.

"I promise I won't pee out the door if you let me come," his little voice was so earnest. I must have given his teacher a green, sickly look.

"He goes whenever and wherever he feels like, even near my foot one day," she looked disgusted and Miles giggled at her.

I tried to discuss Miles impending placement in my class with Dr. Gramm. I felt he should remain in the group he was with and that a more structured, organized school day might solve his restlessness and inability to concentrate. His problems were no where near the intensity that Roxanne, A.J, Simone, Max or some of the other kids had.

Dr. Gramm had other ideas. Miles was coming and nothing I could do or say would make a difference. The two other children that were on my waiting list were girls, both five years old and had serious behavioral problems. I saw Phoebe, the previous school year, right before summer vacation had started. She was a child with a multiplicity of problems. Born with cerebral palsy, she had a form called spastic dyplegia. At an early age, she had had an operation to lengthen her heel cords. This enabled her to walk with her feet flat on the ground rather than the tiptoe fashion of many children with C.P. Her movements were slow, stiff and she had a very perceptible limp in her left leg. Daily sessions of physical therapy were recommended, although she had not been receiving any since she left the Cerebral Palsy Institute in Syracuse.

Her cerebral palsy, however, was the least of her problems. Microcephalia, severe speech and motor problems, and a diagnosis of childhood psychosis added to the list of this kids uphill struggle.

Like Miles, she was in a class for kids who were identified as educable mentally retarded. Many of these kids seemed to need intense academic remediation in reading, math, language arts and so on. Phoebe's problems were of a totally different nature.

She could not seem to connect. Her actions, what little speech I noticed and behavior were bizarre and unattached to what was happening at any given moment.

While in her class, I watched her intently. She wandered about her classroom, whispering inaudible words. Her pink tongue licked the windows, her own arms and legs and even the doorknob in the class. She walked near me, almost touching me and sniffed at my arms. Her tongue flicked out and lightly licked them.

I looked at her teacher who just shrugged her shoulders. Apparently, this was nothing new, neither was the masturbation, biting of herself and other children or screaming that would last for hours. Phoebe desperately needed a class with fewer children in it and an educational setting that was therapeutic as well as educational.

Unfortunately, she would have to remain in her current placement until the new class was in place. Rose and I were already working as hard as we could push ourselves. The pace was beginning to wear us both down.

The last child that was on my waiting list was Rudy. She was a delicate, beautiful girl with dark hair, eyes and skin like alabaster.

I'd been invited to the home of her parents during the summer months. They had given birth to Rudy late in life. Her mother was forty-five at the time of delivery and both parents were in their early fifties when I met them.

"We haven't raised Rudy like our other children," her father confided in me, "I don't know if that was right or not. But it's the way we did it." We had all been sitting at the kitchen table discussing Rudy and her entering my classroom.

"Rudy is afraid of many things," her mother added, "she's terrified of the record player, the telephone, even the windshield wipers on cars. I don't know how we're gonna get her to ride the bus, she'll be screaming all the way." Rudy obviously had other problems as well.

She had on a dainty little blue and white checkered dress with lacey frills around the collar and hem. With one swoop, she tore the dress over the top of her head and dropped it onto the floor. Standing there naked as the day she was born, her parents told me that they could not keep clothes on this little girl. She was permitted to undress at any time or place in the house.

She stood in front of her parents, myself and a psychologist who had accompanied me, rocking and swaying. Her hands held high over her head. The only sound she made was something that sounded like "EEEEEEEEEEEeeeeeeeeeeee."

Just as suddenly as she had taken off her dress, she lunged her tiny hand into her little behind, pulled it out and stood sniffing her fingers contentedly. She ran off to the bathroom where I could hear her running water in the tub.

"She takes six or seven baths a day," her mother confided in us, "just can't seem to stop her." She and her husband both laughed at this comment. I wondered if they realized how serious a problem their child had.

"What do the doctors say?" I asked her mother, "What do they think is wrong with Rudy?" Her parents exchanged looks with each other.

"Well," her father answered, "we've never taken her to the doctors... outside of when she was a little girl, that is." He looked nervous and uncomfortable. Obviously, I had hit a nerve.

"Maybe, when she's older," her mother continued, "maybe she'll outgrow it." I didn't want to squash any hopes, but I knew this child's difficulties were nothing that age would overcome. I was no diagnostician or doctor, but I knew she had serious problems.

"She doesn't eat right either," her father added, "she only seems to like junk food or chocolate. She'll eat up to six candy bars a day instead of dinner." An older daughter of theirs was walking through the kitchen. She appeared to be about ten or eleven years of age.

"Tell them what else she eats," the girl said. She was giggling nervously and bent to tie the laces on her sneakers. Rudy's mother looked at us sheepishly.

"She chews rubber bands," her mother admitted, "she likes the wide ones the best. Sometimes she'll chew them and drink coke all at the same time." The older daughter laughed at hearing this.

"What do you mean 'the best'?" I asked her mother, hoping I would not hear the answer I knew was coming.

"Oh," she said, "I buy them for her. It's one of her few pleasures, she just doesn't seem to like the things most of my other children did." I suppressed my desire to ask this mother if she knew that her child could choke to death chewing on rubber bands.

I didn't want to alienate them before she was even in my class. I would certainly have to work on some home management skills with them. They seemed extremely indulgent of their little girl's whims and moods. Without placing any restrictions on her at all, they had turned her into a small tyrant who was quietly running their household.

Rudy returned from the bathroom soaking wet. She walked over to her mother's purse and brought it near to where we were sitting. She placed it in her mother's lap and looked at her expectantly.

"She wants Kentucky Fried Chicken," the mother smiled at us, "I always know what she wants." Rudy stood naked and dripping water on the kitchen floor. She was looking at her mother and started to rock and sway again. She stopped only when her mother got up and headed for the door. In search, I guessed, of the Colonel and his chicken. The only sound in the kitchen was..."EEEEEEEEEEEEEeeeeeeeeeeeee..."

Thinking about this home visit invaded my thoughts a lot. But, Rudy was not in my class yet, nor Phoebe or Miles. I would deal with these children and their problems when they arrived. For now, I had my own group to think of.

Robert and Alfie had been having increasing problems at home. The Department of Social Services had been in close contact with me about both boys and it seemed that they were soon to be placed in foster care.

Alfie's mother had confided in me during a parent conference held last spring. She looked depressed and as overweight as she was, I could tell she was pregnant with her third child.

"I can't take that brat, no more," she raged on, "I've told him he's gonna have to go if he keeps it up. But he don't care, he just runs the neighborhood. They even threaten to call the cops on him. But he don't care. Just like his father, that kid is." I felt sick at heart, thinking of Alfie. He was usually so cheerful and happy. He returned to school this fall, angry and sullen. I hoped a good home could be found for him. His mother had already given her consent for him to be placed and it looked like a matter of time until foster placement would happen.

Robert's home had taken a definite turn for the worse over the summer. His mother's calls to my home increased and could be expected at any time of the day or night. She became hysterical, often talking of killing herself.

"I… I… I… I…," she would stutter, "I'm gonna kill myself. There's no damn reason to live anymore." She would often ramble on about her past life. She had been raped as a young girl by her father and had never resolved the conflict. If my husband answered the phone she would rant on and on to him. It didn't seem to matter who was on the phone or even if they were listening. Her calls to various county officials and administrators had really peaked. There was no running water in the trailer they all lived in and Robert began to smell terribly of urine and dried feces. He often wet the bed and frequently came to school with the soiled clothes still on his thin little body.

"What's that stink in here?" one of the relocated teachers from Cherry Park School, yelled into my classroom at the Campus School, "Open the windows!" I looked over at Robert who sat shaking and near tears at his desk. The remark had not passed by him or Carlos or Patty.

I had spoken to Robert privately about his personal hygiene, encouraging him to wash his hands and face in school. I knew he was very touchy about the subject. There was so little I could do, other than having him clean up at school. Certainly remarks like that one did little to help. Like Alfie, foster placement was imminent.

The other kids seemed to have a variety of ways to cope with the news that a new class would be added to ours. Robert, Alfie and Max had been with me now for over four years. This change would be dramatic and not without some pain involved for all of us.

Max had started to play with a particular doll this fall, clinging to it whenever he had the chance. I thought this particularly odd, since he had never shown an interest in playing with dolls before. He would bounce the doll up and down on his knees, talking to it and feeding it plastic foods. Rose brought him in some square white pieces of an old sheet from home. He would diaper and undiaper the doll constantly.

Always talking and cooing to it. His attentiveness was unbelievable. Finally one day, late in September and close to going home time, he came to me with the doll wrapped in a blanket. I was in my office.

"Can he sleep in here?" Max asked me, his voice was soft, almost hesitant.

"Sure," I answered him, "she can sleep here."

"It's a boy, Toni," he said, "not a girl. He wants to sleep here for awhile, but when he wakes up, he's going to be O.K. He's not going to be afraid anymore."

I handed Max an empty cardboard box and he put his baby in it and looked at me. I could tell this was very important to him.

"Can he sleep under your desk?" he asked me. His big blue eyes seemed dark and intense.

"Of course, he can," I told him and pulled out my chair so he could tuck the doll underneath my desk. I watched him as he tenderly put the doll to sleep.

I realized then how significant Max's sudden relationship with his doll was. It was his way of saying goodbye to me and to all that he had known with me. Not in the sense of it being a rubbing out of events or a final ending. But, a farewell of sorts.

I knew that Max and the others were growing up and away from me. But, I also knew that this separation was an inevitable and necessary fact of life. That it would be positive and good.

I watched him walk down the sidewalk that afternoon to board his bus. He walked slowly, talking quietly to himself and stopping to pick a handful of the autumn leaves that had already fallen to the ground.

I waved to him and called out goodbye, but he didn't hear me. As he turned to step up on the bus I could just manage to hear him whispering..."not afraid anymore, not afraid anymore." He was smiling and had begun to rock back and forth.

I walked back up the stairs to my office. I grabbed my keys and turned off the lights. Sleep tight I thought to the doll that lay safe and snug under my desk.

November 1977

The children were all well acquainted now with the fact that a new teacher would be coming to join us. Dr. Gramm was in the process of interviewing prospective candidates for the position. I had told Max, Robert, Alfie and Simone that they would be leaving my class sometime after Christmas. Most of them were delighted with the idea of a new teacher and I took it as a good sign. The only one I worried about was Simone.

She had been with us a little over a year and I was just beginning to feel that I was making some headway with her. But, she was twelve years old and would no longer qualify for my class of children that were ten and under.

I decided to make the most of the time left to us and set to work immediately. Simone had spent most of her earlier years in classes for children who were trainable mentally retarded. One of her teachers noticed that Simone seemed different than her other students, but the educational system did very little to support this teacher and her suspicions.

One of the saddest things that I encountered as a teacher was having a child referred to me at the age of ten, twelve or older, when the problem had been manifesting itself since early childhood or even infancy. Simone had been one of these kids.

Her mother told me that she had questioned a doctor about Simone when she was only four years old. Simone's mother had read a good deal about infantile autism and suspected that her daughter showed many of the signs of autism. The doctor had told her mother not to worry about it... that Simone would eventually "outgrow it."

Regrettably, Simone never "outgrew it" and by the age of five she had been placed in a class for severely retarded children. She stayed at the school for nearly six years until the perceptive insight of one of her teachers persuaded her parents and the COES that she needed another type of educational intervention.

Locked virtually inside herself, Simone had reverted to occupying her mind with her hands, fingers or exploring her own face, arms and neck. She seemed to have an intense need to be near and touch other people. She was aggressive and often pinched or squeezed the very people she wanted to get close to. I watched her sitting at her desk, rocking and twisting her thumbs back to her wrist. The feat seemed incredible, but she performed it with ease. Her fingers had become very flexible, almost double jointed from such constant manipulation and use. They always seemed to be twisted into a rigid, contorted position.

"Simone," I said to her, "what do you want to do today?" I always tried to occupy her time rather than leaving her sitting and rocking by herself.

"What do you want to do, Fish?" she would answer and look at me giggling. She always answered questions by asking them back to me. She generally referred to herself in the third person. If she wanted a puzzle it would be..." Fish wants a puzzle," or "She wants a puzzle."

"Fish wants the picture cards," she finally said and bit deep into her hand. It was callused, like A.J's, from years of self-abuse. I took her hand from her mouth.

Although it might seem strange, Simone often bit her hand if she was excited or happy. The picture cards certainly made her happy. They were eight inch by twelve inch pictures of food, in a variety of different colors, and designs.

I sat down next to her. I loved spending one on one time with the kids, but because there were so many of them, I seldom had a chance to do much. I wondered when we would all come to realize that many children need a teacher to themselves. It was a concept that had yet to reach its time.

"Wh... Wh...What do you want to eat, Toni?" Simone asked, it still thrilled me that she was now calling me by name. For so many months, I had been another nameless teacher to her.

"I think I'll try the pancakes this morning," I replied. She flipped through the cards, one hand around her white, ashen neck, the other fumbling through the stack of colored pictures. Finding it, she passed it over to me.

"MMmmmmmm," I said, pretending to sample them, "these pancakes are simply marvelous, did you make them yourself?" She was delighted with my response. Her hand went to her mouth again to take another bite. I shook my head 'no' and she put her hand down.

"Hold my hand, Fish," I said to her, "and squeeze it tight." She took my hand and held onto it, giggling and excited. Physical contact always made Simone giddy with excitement.

"One, two, three, squeeze!" she said and squeezed my hand. Her hand and fingers were wet and dripping with spit from her own mouth, but she seemed so alert and thrilled to be near me, it really wasn't that important.

I had been trying some different techniques with Simone for the past three months. I'd done some reading on autism and childhood schizophrenia and found that there were a variety of theories and approaches. It seemed that no one was quite sure why or how this happened to children. The more I read the more confused I seemed to get. Even the authorities in the field admitted ambiguity and bewilderment more often than not. It seemed that everyone had a different opinion or a sure-fire cure.

My idea was that Simone wanted physical closeness. But her social skills with other people left a lot to be desired. She would rush up to anyone and begin squeezing their arms, neck or waist. Naturally, most people were either frightened or leery of this child if she approached them in this manner.

I wanted to show Simone that being near to people was good, but to handle it less aggressively. We spent a good deal of time squeezing each other's hands, or touching each other's faces. I was trying to teach her not to touch so hard and to ask permission before she grabbed anyone.

"C ... C..C..CCan, can, can I touch your face, Toni?" she asked, while we were busy sorting the foods into piles for breakfast, lunch, and dinner. I knew how much she loved to do this. She picked up her two index fingers, still wet and stiff with contortion and slid them across my cheeks. She shuddered a little because she was so excited.

"Use your whole hand, Fish," I would tell her but she continued with her two fingers.

"Rose, Rose," she'd yell out, "I'm touching Toni's face!" Rose looked over and gave her a lot of encouragement and smiles. She would want to go on with this for hours, but I never seemed to have enough time to give to her.

It made my heart break to leave her. As soon as I did, the rocking, biting and strange sounds she made would start all over again. She seemed lost to me. My mind wandered back to the week when we had really lost her. It was over a year ago. The buses had just come in and I was going to the front door to greet her, she hadn't learned the way to our classroom as yet. By the time I got to the door, the buses had left and she was nowhere in sight.

I called out to Mark, who rode the school bus with her and always seemed so fond of her. "Mark," I yelled, "did Simone come today?" He looked at me, nodded 'yes' and walked away.

I ran back to the classroom. Maybe she had slipped by me and come to the room alone. But there was no Simone in sight. I began to panic, where could she be? She wasn't the type of child to hide.

Rose and I searched the bathrooms, library, classes, everywhere we could think to look. Finally, after fifteen minutes of desperate hunting, I notified the school office that Simone was missing. Somehow, she had slipped away, I hoped she was not too scared or confused.

The Oswego Campus Security Police picked her up within ten minutes. Apparently, she had gotten off her bus and walked in the school. When I wasn't there at the door waiting for her, she had followed some other children out the back door of the school. Outside in the cool, fresh air she had just wandered away.

The Campus Security had picked her up near Penfield Library; she had been heading toward Lake Ontario. I breathe a deep sigh of relief when I saw her. She looked terrified and still had on her blue raincoat and plastic white hat. I wondered what her walk with thousands of college students had been like.

"Take off your raincoat, Simone," she said to me. She always seemed to know exactly what I was going to say to her before I actually did.

"Take it off, Simone," I replied, with great relief. I was so glad she was back and unharmed. She looked down at her raincoat and popped every button on the front of it, trying to take it off. Remembering the incident brought back chills to me, as I watched her flip through pictures of Jell-O, pudding and pies. For some reason, the pictures always seemed to calm her down; she never tired of looking at them.

Maybe she felt food was one of the few things in her life she could always depend on to be there. She had so little left to her. Her fine motor skills were so poor, that at twelve, she could not write her name. Or button, zip, or snap her clothing.

I watched her again and again attempt to make an S. She would grab her right wrist with her left hand, to steady it. But it was no use; the letters would not come out right. It frustrated her and I knew it. I tried a million different ways, but it just wound up upsetting her. Then the sounds, rocking and hand biting would start.

"Lulululululululululullulululululululu," she would sing out... "I wanna choco ... lulululu... late ice-a-creama!" Unchecked, she would carry on like this for hours. Her mother told me of nights of laying awake listening to Simone's babbling aloud about food. She frequently kept her entire family from getting any sleep for days at a time.

When she was not talking about food, she was silent. In a world where it seemed she was unreachable. So, we talked about food, sang about it and even prepared it. Her favorite was making popcorn for us every Friday. She would pour a box of salt on it and I sat eating my three kernels with my cheeks sucked in like I was toothless.

"Does Toni like Fish's popcorn?" she would ask, looking at me hopefully. It was her big moment of the week.

"I'm crazy for it," I would lie and she would plop a fistful of the salty snack on my lap. Giggling and pleased with herself. I would have eaten the whole damn bowl if I thought it would help.

"Let's go lick a river," I would whisper to Rose. My whole class seemed to spend the last twenty minutes of school on Friday at the water fountain. We would suck it dry.

I hoped to get beyond the endless food inventory that Simone wanted to go through daily. She was beginning to show some interest in other things. Best of all, she was starting to trust me. And I knew that was the most important step of all.

Perhaps, I could make some arrangements with her new teacher, to spend extra time with her. It seemed both sad and ridiculous to put so much effort into working on a relationship and then have it disappear when it was beginning to have an effect. These problems would eventually work themselves out. I just needed to have some patience.

I watched the leaves fall from the trees that late November and thought about Cherry Park School. I 'd heard that it was renovated and that we would all be moving back. I'd been hoping that we could complete the rest of the school year at the Campus School. It seemed absurd to move the kids again during the middle of the year. I wondered what all this moving, constant changing and uncertainty was doing to them. They already had enough emotional problems to deal with. Adding more seemed to be courting disaster.

The icy rains that fell on us late that autumn seemed to match the mood that I found myself in. I waited for the phone call from Dr. Gramm that I knew would decide our destiny. But none came.

December 1977

"We're moving back to Cherry Park!" It was one of the special education teachers from Cherry Park School. She was jumping around and nearly fell into the green and red cupcakes that I had made for our Christmas party.

The kids were filled up with the goodies that many of their parents donated to the celebration. Alfie's stomach was swelled to twice its normal size and he sat close to me. He had been placed in a foster home this past week and his new brown plaid blazer had vanilla icing on the lapels.

"How do you know?" I asked and helped him wipe the gooey stuff off before it stained his jacket.

"Mike Donahue just called," she said, "I've gotta go. They sent boxes over and I'm going to have the kids help me pack this time." I heard her clomp down the hall and wondered why I hadn't received news about the move.

I had Rose watch the kids while I went to make a phone call in the school office.

"Hear you folks are moving back," Bob Morgan raised his eyebrows and looked at me. He had been the most visible, concerned principal that I had worked with.

"I'm just calling about it now," I said, "I haven't heard a word." I could hear the other teachers from Cherry Park moving in the halls of the Campus School. They were excited to be going back and I could hear their easy chatter.

"We're gonna miss you," Bob said, "especially my teachers. They really want you to stay. Everybody loves the kids." I knew he wasn't just handing me a line. I had felt the warmth and encouragement of the entire faculty from the very start. It was hard to think that nearly a year and a half had flown by already.

I dialed the number to Cherry Park School. The secretary answered and put me on hold while she buzzed Mike's office.

"Hello, Toni," Mike's voice floated through the lines, "I guess your calling about all the moving. The school is really fantastic, completely changed. You'll have to come over and see it."

"That's why I'm calling," I said, "are we coming back with the other classes?" There was a long pause on the line. I could tell Mike was trying to collect his thoughts.

"Well," he continued, "we really need your room. As you know, the Elm Park School is being renovated and some of the teachers from that school will be here. I've already promised your class to one of the other teachers from there."

I really didn't know what to say. I had an odd mixture of feelings. I was glad that the kids would not have to be moved again in the middle of the year and that they would be staying at the Campus School. They seemed to be more accepted, understood here. On the other hand I felt a sense of loss, a sense that this group of kids really belonged nowhere. The Campus School considered us more as invited guests rather than an integral part of the faculty.

"I see," I replied, "I guess we'll be staying on here then." Mike seemed relieved that I had chosen not to argue. He quickly said his good-byes and wished the kids and me a pleasant holiday season.

I hung up the phone and sat down. Bob and his secretary looked at each other and then back at me.

"Well," Bob blurted out, "what happened? Are you going or not?"

"Looks like we're all yours," I said to him and he rushed over and gave me a hug.

"I couldn't be happier," he continued, "you and the kids really add some flare to our school. We'll have to see what we can do to involve you more with our other programs."

"That would be great," I added, "I'm sure the kids would love it." I walked back to my classroom thinking how much like transient wanderers we were. Maybe now with Cherry Park putting us on a back burner we could become a real part of a school.

I walked in the class and looked at Rose and the kids.

"We're not going back to Cherry Park School," I told them, "we're going to stay in the Campus School." It was very hard to read the reactions on some of their faces. Only A.J., Max, Robert and Alfie had ever been in the school. The other children didn't know the first thing about Cherry Park.

"But, I want to see the pipes!" A.J. said, "Aren't we going to go back and smash those darn pipes?"

"The pipes are gone," I replied, "their gone." I tried to make light of the situation with the kids, hoping that they would not feel left out. But, I could tell they did, especially when the other teachers and children from Cherry Park were so elated. The cardboard boxes grew higher and higher the next two days and the spirits of the boys seemed to drop to an all time low. I hadn't realized how much going back to the school meant to them.

"Anyway," I said to them, "your going to get a new teacher soon. That will be a lot of fun for you." They just stared at me.

"Me too?" A.J. said, "Am I gonna get a new teacher?" His hands still flapping away in front of his eyes.

"Next year," I answered, "you'll be old enough then."

"And pretty soon we'll be old enough for junior high," Max added. They waited for my reaction, but I couldn't give one. If a public elementary school didn't want us why would a junior high? I spent Christmas vacation wondering why we had not been asked to return. I found out through the underground teacher grapevine that my class was the only group that had not been invited back. It seemed like no one had any information about it. I had a million questions, but no one, not even Dr. Gramm seemed able to answer them.

"Be happy about the room at Campus School," Dr. Gramm said, "you're an excellent teacher and they want you to stay. Your class is pretty... uh, unusual you know." As much as I loved the Campus School, I knew it was a private facility and that it only went up to the sixth grade. What would happen to the kids when they reached the age of thirteen, fourteen or older? Without the backing of the public schools, would it mean developmental centers or even worse, institutionalization? I pushed the thought out of my mind. The very word 'institution' made me think of Sophie and all the terrible changes that had happened to her there. Besides, I thought, P.L.94-142 guaranteed an education for all handicapped children. They couldn't dismiss them anymore. But, then why weren't we returning to Cherry Park with the others?

These and other questions filled my head those Christmas holidays. I wondered about the future of my students and if the public laws that were made to serve them really would.

February 1978

Our tiny three-room class was packed to the brim with people. Eleven children and three adults occupied it. By the end of the first week in February, we were all edgy. The rooms were small and we were virtually tripping over each other.

Pam had been hired as the new teacher for the upper level class. She had recently graduated from college, only weeks before. Dr. Gramm had promised her a class, but he was having a hard time locating one in the Campus School. It seemed that all the rooms were occupied. I didn't mind sharing the one I had with her, but when my own three new kids arrived unexpectedly, the situation became cramped, and tempers started flaring. Miles, Rudy and Phoebe arrived within days of each other. Miles, although hyperactive, had no big adjustment problems. Rudy and Phoebe were quite another story. Phoebe spent most of the day screaming and biting her arms, legs and hands. Rudy was equally as hysterical. The only word she knew was..."Mommy" and she cried and screamed it over and over.

"Mommy, mommmmmmmmy, mommmmmmmy, mommy, mommmmy, mommy mommy, mommmmmmmmmmy... mommy, mommy, mommy!" Over and over and over. For the first time since I had been in the Campus School, one of the other teachers came to my class and complained about the noise and hysterics, it seemed that no one in her room could get any work accomplished with all the noise that was coming from my class. I knew she was right and I called Dr. Gramm.

"Just what the hell do you think you're doing?" I demanded. I knew it was the wrong approach, but I was furious with the way the kids, me, Rose and the new teacher were being totally dismissed.

"Your backing me into a corner," he insisted, "there's no rooms available in the Campus School."

"What's the idea of sending in three new children?" I pressed him, "I thought they were going to be placed on a waiting list until the new class was established."

"The districts the kids come from were starting to crawl all over me," he stated, "I had no choice."

"Well, what are we going to do?" I said. I was getting tired of carrying on long distance phone calls with a supervisor who was never around.

"Pam will have to work out of an observation room at the Campus School," he finally said, "that's the best we can do for the time being." I hung up the phone utterly disgusted. The observation rooms were the narrow, confined quarters where psychologists or teachers observed children at work or play. Although, they were bigger than most observation rooms I'd seen, they still weren't meant to be classrooms.

I walked back to my class and told Pam the news. She seemed relieved that at least an empty room had been found for her. Even if it was just an observation area.

Pam and the four oldest kids left within a matter of days. I was sorry that Max, Robert, Alfie and Simone had to leave with such an incredible flurry of hysterics going on around them. They seemed confused and upset. Rudy and Phoebe both had serious problems and needed time, attention and a good deal of one to one teaching. Their screaming, flinging around of toys and the like had disrupted a transition that I wanted to be as smooth as possible. Especially for Robert. Like Alfie, he too was now in a foster home. He had come to school with a number of short red welts on the side of his forehead. His brother Billy had decided to play a game of darts with knives and had apparently missed his target. It amazed me to hear him recount the incident.

"Goddamn Billy," he cried, "he was playin' darts and his knives hit me." I learned that his mother had attempted suicide and been placed under the care of the local mental health clinic. All her children had been deemed 'wards of the state of N.Y.' and placed in foster care. I hoped the new foster home could deal with him. Alfie's foster home had not been able to handle his hyperactivity, occasional swearing, stealing and stubbornness. They called me up one afternoon at school to tell me that they had told the Social Service Department to come and pick him up. His biological family still didn't want him so he was placed in a new foster home.

The normally bubbling Alfie had become nearly withdrawn, all within a matter of weeks. How long did the kids have to be bounced from home to home, school to school? I wondered where it would all end for them.

Slowly, our lives returned to normal. Pam's small class was only yards away from us and I saw the kids frequently during the day. With half of my class gone, I too would have some new adjustments to make.

I had hand lettered some 'diplomas' for my four departing students. I thought they should have some memento of our years together. After all, the boys had been with me nearly five years and Simone almost two.

I handed them their diplomas and some black and white photographs that I thought they would like to keep. I remembered the frightened kids who had showed up at the Cherry Park School nearly five years before. The black and white shots showed them at various ages and in various moods.

Group shots and individual ones. One showed Max on the floor of the Cherry Park School near the yellow igloo. Another had Robert at his desk surrounded by radiators and the overhead pipes. I gave them all one of D.C. standing protectively behind A.J. In the photo I could just barely make out the year 1976 that was on a paper he was proudly holding.

It seemed that I was quietly keeping a black and white photo history of them over the years. I was happy that we could all look back on our time together. It amazed me how much they had grown up.

Despite the changes that were coming at us, from all directions, I felt that everything would work out for them. Over the years they had come to mean a great deal to me. They'd become·part of me and I cared for them and their well being. I was not only their teacher, but at times their surrogate parent, psychiatrist, social worker and friend. They may have been forgotten children to some, but I knew that nothing, not time or place or miles between us could ever erase them from my mind.

These kids had changed me and I slowly accepted the fact that they had transformed me. That was their gift to me and I loved them for it.

May 1978

Spring had returned again to the frozen, upstate N.Y community that I had come to love as 'home.' The geese were starting their long trek back from the southern states and I knew that summer was not far behind.

The kids had been practicing and preparing for weeks. The Oswego County 'Special Olympics' was soon to be held and we were going to participate in it, as we had done annually for years. It was one of the highlights of the school year. A chance for them to shine and be recognized for what they could achieve athletically.

Fund raising for the event had not been without its problems in the past, but this year, Pam and I decided to try something new. Boxes of popcorn were the traditional way we raised money to supply the kids with the T-shirts, ribbons and other things they needed for the big day.

The special education teachers throughout the county sold most of the popcorn. The money was then pooled and shared equally by all for the benefit of the kids. It was a long, tiresome chore, but we all helped out, knowing how much pleasure it was to see the looks on the faces of the kids the day of the event.

This year, we decided that the kids should help in the fund raising. Pam and I both thought that the college community would be the perfect setting for the kids to hawk the popcorn to. From my own experience, I knew that college students were generally poor, but I also knew they tended to support many worthy causes.

We weren't wrong. Although long hair, headbands and protest marches of my own college days were nowhere in sight, the students came through for us in style. I found myself growing fonder of designer jeans everyday.

I laughingly recalled how much fun they had in front of the Campus School every afternoon selling the popcorn. They had painted huge, colorful signs telling of the coming Special Olympics. The popcorn sold for $1.25 a box.

Simone and little Rudy stood near each other by the front door, swaying and rocking in unison with their boxes of popcorn clutched tightly in their hands. We decided to place older kids with younger ones. Hoping the older ones would help out. We stood back a distance from them, wanting to give them as much independence as we possibly could.

"How much is the popcorn?" I heard one student ask Simone. He had already begun to dig deep in his pockets for spare change.

"It, it, its, its, its," she stuttered and looked over at Pam and me who were standing behind her, "it's $25.00."

"That's a little out of my price range," he said and walked away. Pam and I nearly fell over laughing.

"Simone," she said, "it's $1.25 not $25.OO." Simone giggled and grabbed Rudy's hand. They stood swaying and moving back and forth. They were so much like each other; it was hard to believe. Rudy, unlike Simone, had no language at all. In the four months that she had been with me, the only word I had heard her speak or cry was..." Mommy." Still, I felt she was listening, taking in things around her. My tuned sixth sense kept telling me to keep talking. I knew that ignoring this silent child would be an error in judgement.

Carlos, Patty and some of the older kids became almost professional in their sales pitch to the college students. It was hilarious watching them jive with the sophisticated, worldly, undergraduates. I watched a lot of pretension drop away from their faces as my kids haggled with them over the 'bargain basement' prices of the popcorn.

"Give us a break," I heard Patty tell one student who had pulled his pockets inside out, "we're only little kids." She looked like she was training for a career in used cars. She just wouldn't give up. I was overwhelmed with the generosity of the entire student body. All together the kids collected over $150.00, not to mention increased social skills and some much needed practice in making change.

I knew the kids needed more exposure to the world outside of school. We could both see how much good it was doing them to meet people and talk with them. The confidence and pride that grew in them was much more than the money they collected. They were teaching themselves to be self-sufficient and take responsibility for their own welfare. Although the Special Olympics included many different events, like swimming, gymnastics and relay races, I'd signed the kids up for three basic events.

The softball throw, the standing long jump and the fifty-yard dash were the three standard events for children under the age of ten. A.J., Miles, Roxanne and Rudy were signed up to come, but I could not convince the parents of Patty, Carlos or Phoebe, to allow the kids to participate.

Both Carlos and Patty's parents did not want them seen in anything that would identify them as disabled or handicapped. They were both disappointed, but there was little I could do if their parents would not give them permission to participate. I promised I would take slides to show them of the Olympics, but I knew it was little consolation.

Phoebe's parents were not responsive to the whole event. They never responded to notes or permission slips that would allow her to participate in the Special Olympics.

The day of the games was sunny and streams of kids, chaperones, parents and well wishers roamed the athletic field of the local high school, where the Special Olympics was being held.

The organization of the games seemed to improve with each passing year. But it was totally dependent on volunteers and the generosity of people who wanted to help. I had been on many committees to help organize the Olympics in the past. The most gruesome was the 'food committee.' I remembered sitting up, several years ago, with several hundred bologna sandwiches, apples, candy bars and milk. Dan, a few other die hards, and I sat up until the wee hours of the morning packing food in brown bags. But, it was worth the effort the next day, to see the kids pigging out on their lunches.

This year I volunteered to chaperone Rudy to different events that I had signed her up for. She was much better now, than she had been a few months ago. Her hysterics had slowly faded away and she was beginning to let me get close to her. I had done a lot of homework on emotionally disturbed children, both in my classroom and my reading. Rudy seemed to have a textbook case of autism. I gradually convinced her parents to have her seen by a neurologist and a psychiatrist.

The neurologist had confirmed my suspicions of autism, but he asked to see her again; he wanted to perform a brain scan on her. Her parents refused, the hospital would have to medicate her and they did not want to see their daughter hurt anymore than she'd already been.

There was a huge parade before the Special Olympics began and Rudy and I stood at the sidelines watching it. There were mobs of people pressing in around us, but Rudy seemed oblivious to them. She stood, rocking back and forth with her little hands directly in front of her face. Like Simone, she would twist her fingers until they turned white from the pressure. She was playing what I had come to call the 'doubles game.' It was a name that I made up to describe what she did with her fingers. She would take one tiny hand and put up several fingers, then do the exact same with the fingers of her other hand.

I watched her do this same thing many times before while she was in school. One day, I sat down near her and began to play the 'doubles game' with her. I would make shapes with my fingers or throw out several on each hand. I felt like I was in a craps game with her, but I kept on anyway. Later, I told one of the school psychologists about my discovery.

"You really shouldn't do that," he said, "your only reinforcing inappropriate behavior."

"But, I got her attention," I refuted, "she smiled at me. We were on each other's wave length. She even took my fingers and put them in different positions!" He looked at me and checked his watch and briefcase.

"Still," he continued, "you shouldn't even permit her to do it with her fingers. If she likes to use her hands, show her how to draw or... write the alphabet."

But, I continued on, despite the warnings not to. If Rudy would not come to my world, then I would enter hers. The psychologists could go study the Wide Range Achievement Test, or whatever it is that they all seemed to do so much of.

Now she was standing in front of me, with the parade almost directly in her line of vision; her hands were still in front of her face. I saw her eyes cross and she put her arms high over her head. She moved them quickly, back and forth in a rapid motion; it looked like she was pushing against the wind. I felt her arms when she did this once, they were rigid.

I knelt down close to her and began talking. She never at any time acknowledged me with words, but she often responded to my directions or things I said to her.

"Look at the parade," I said, "can you hear the music?" She put down her arms and looked in the direction I was pointing. The local high schools had volunteered their marching bands and the flutes, drums and other instruments were blaring away. The noise was incredible.

"See all these people," I went on, "we're all watching the parade." No response. But, she continued watching the long stream of young, high school musicians with fascination. Maybe she liked music, I would have to bring my guitar to school and find out.

"Isn't this a nice parade," I persisted, "do you like parades?" Still no answer. I looked at her deep brown eyes and wondered what silent, secret mystery lay behind them. I finally stood up and continued watching the parade in silence. No use pushing too hard, we had plenty of time. She stood with her eyes glued on the events, watching everything. Taking everything in. It always seemed like she was either completely absorbed in herself or something that was happening outside herself. Usually, it was herself.

I remember hearing her say in the tiniest, little voice...

"Look at the parade." I stood for a few seconds hardly believing my ears. Then I dropped to my knees, next to her.

"What did you say?" I asked, you said, "Look at the parade." She turned away from my voice. I knew she heard me.

"I heard what you said, Rudy," I pushed on, you said, "Look at the parade." Still no response. I put my hands on her shoulders and turned her around, so that she was facing me.

"Get off my back," she said, not looking at me. I just stared at her. I really didn't know what else to do. I was in absolute shock. Rudy had spoken her first words. Not just words, but a complete sentence.

I stood up, still awed by hearing her speak. There were mobs of people surrounding us and I didn't know any of them. I turned to the man next to me.

"Did you hear her?" I asked, "She told me to get off her back." I looked at the man for some sign of confirmation, but he pretended not to hear me. Probably thinking I was some kind of nut. He looked a little uncomfortable.

I turned to the man on the other side of me; he'd been listening to my conversation with the first man.

"She told me," I said again, "to get off her back." He looked at me; a wet, smelly cigar was stuck between his thick lips.

"Then get off the kid's back, lady," he said, "I think she knows best." I was laughing now and grabbed Rudy's hand. She had started to play the 'doubles game' and rock back and forth.

"EEEEEEEEEeeeeeeeeeeeeeeeeeeeee," she yelled, I think she was as happy as I was. The first words, the most important, were out. They had been said. I had heard them.

I ran off with her and looked back at my two male friends, who stood staring at us. The one with the cigar was shaking his head. He looked at the other man.

"Want to know why kids are so weird," he said, "take a look at the parents!" They watched us run off until we were out of sight. I was beside myself; I had to tell somebody the good news.

I managed to get Rudy through the softball throw and the standing long jump, without many problems. She liked playing ball, although it was hard to get her to return the catch. She usually just stood with it in her hand, rocking and staring at it. I had to really coax her, to get her to throw it.

At the fifty-yard dash, Roxanne spotted us and came thundering over. She threw her arms around me and then Rudy.

"ROOOddeeee, ROOOdddddeeee!" she yelled, happy as a puppy to see her, "Wan run race?" Roxanne, as usual, was overflowing with life and happiness. Her red pigtails flopping around in the wind. I noticed that Rudy played with Roxie's pigtails, if she happened to be sitting near her. Strange to some, perhaps, but I took it as a sign of affection.

"Wan run race?" she said again and grabbed Rudy's hand. They raced, or rather; Roxanne half-dragged Rudy over to the group of kids who stood near the starting line of the fifty-yard dash.

I noticed that Rose was standing on the sidelines of the race, waiting for it to begin. Even though it was Saturday, she volunteered her time to help out at the Special Olympics.

"Rose," I ran over to her, screaming, "Rudy told me to get off her back!" I smelled cigar smoke and looked over to see my friend, of earlier that morning, standing and staring at the two of us embracing each other.

"Jesus," I heard him say, "not this crap again." I waved at him, but he continued to smoke his cigar and shake his head.

"She talked to you?" Rose said, "She actually said something?"

"Yes," I told her, "she said...'Look at the parade' and then she said, 'Get off my back.' Rose and I looked at each other and threw our arms around each other again. She felt as deeply about the kids as I did.

"Now there's two of them," I heard the man with the cigar say to the woman standing with him, "this world is going to the dogs. Take my word for it. Full of loonies."

He walked over to us, still puffing and blowing out billows of blue smoke. He chewed at the end of the cigar and spit out a piece of it.

"You know, ladies," he said, "I've heard that professional help can really do wonders for people like you." He walked away with his cigar still stuck between his lips. "Or have we just been self medicating again?"

"Who was that?" Rose asked, "What did he mean?" I fell out laughing. Although the clouds in the sky, were beginning to threaten rain, the Oswego County 'Special Olympics' had turned out to be the best one I ever attended.

June 1978

It was late evening and I was sitting up with a glass of red wine trying to recover from the parent conferences I had been through earlier that day.

Normally, conferences were held in November and again in April. But, I had received notification from Dr. Gramm that I had to complete an I.E.P. on Rudy, Phoebe and Miles by the time school was over.

"What's an I.E.P.?" Dan interrupted my deep thoughts.

"A new regulation from Albany," I explained, "it stands for Individualized Educational Program. All the kids have to have them."

"You special ed. people have more acronyms and abbreviations than anybody I know." He was flipping through my mounting pile of documentation, progress reports and anecdotal records.

"Tell me about it," I said, "we just don't teach kids. We have E.D.kids, L.D. kids, E.M.R.kids, T.M.R. kids, S.M.H. kids, D.E. kids, N.I. kids. God, the list is endless."

"What's your class labeled?" he asked.

"Hold onto your hat," I warned, "it's E.D.-F.M.R."

"What's that?"

"Emotionally disturbed," I explained, "functionally mentally retarded." He looked at me as if I'd gone mad.

"I wonder what kind of a class they'd put me in," he asked "if I was in school now as a kid? Probably the A.M.P. class." We both laughed at his comparison, but it was true, the labels really helped stigmatize our kids. I hated them, but the list seemed to grow longer every year. Only cans of corn should be labeled, I thought.

"I'm going to bed," he said, "and leave you with your I...E...P" he walked off to our back bedroom.

My mind drifted back to the conferences I had that day. I was exhausted and to a certain extent disgusted. How could I hope to accomplish anything with the kids if their parents were doing one thing and I was doing another? Sometimes I felt like all we were trying to do in school was being destroyed at home.

I had met with Rudy's mother at their home. Rudy was sitting on the sofa, while her mother and I talked; she was watching Sesame Street and sniffing her soiled underpants that she had removed from herself. It was shocking for me to watch this child who had so much potential, being allowed to behave with no restrictions placed on her at all. She pulled off her dress and sat naked, still sniffing at her underpants. Finally I could take no more.

"Why do you let her do that?" I asked her mother. I was starting to wonder if her mother had mental health problems.

"Well, I don't like the fact that she does it," her mother said defensively, "but, what can I do?" She had snatched the underpants from her and put them back on her.

"Just what your doing now," I answered, "lay down some rules for her. She can take her clothes off in her bedroom, not anywhere she feels like. What do you do when company comes over?"

"We send her to her room," she said, "and by the way, we can manage just fine without your fancy advice."

I hadn't meant to put her on the defense, but I knew Rudy could keep her clothes on. She had attempted to remove them many times in school, but I just put them back on her. As soon as she realized, I wasn't going to let her sit around naked, she stopped taking them off. No big deals, no long drawn out solutions, I had just let her know where I was coming from. In my class, she had to keep her clothes on.

Rudy's family was not poor. They were a middle income family who lived in a modest, but comfortable house. Her father was in state politics and both her parents were involved in the community. Rather than buying 100% cotton clothing, which many autistic children preferred, they allowed her to undress when and wherever she chose.

Miles family was quite another story. They were very poor and I had to help his mother fill out forms that would put Miles on the free lunch program at school.

"He never has any lunch to eat at school," I said to his mother, "his driver tells me he eats it on the bus."

"I know," she said, her voice was tired. She had probably heard complaints about him from everybody connected with him. I had seen him digging for scraps in the garbage cans at school and decided to try and do something about it.

"Why didn't you fill out the free lunch forms before?" I asked. She lowered her head and I realized how insensitive and stupid the remark had been.

"Can't read 'em," she mumbled, "don't know how." I put my hand on her thin shoulders. Life had not been easy for this young mother. At age twenty-eight she was already toothless and had been an alcoholic for years. Miles had the facial features of many children who were born with the fetal alcohol syndrome.

"The kids drive me crazy," she said. Big tears had started to fall from her clear blue eyes. They were the only part of her that didn't look old.

"I try not to drink," she continued, "but, it's the only way I can handle things. Sometimes I feel like puttin' all the kids back in foster care again." Miles and his two younger sisters had been placed in foster care years ago. Child abuse was stated as the reason in his cumulative folder, I knew if things got much worse at home, they would be placed in custody again.

"How's he been at home?" I asked. He and his sisters were running wild in the house, while his mother and I talked. They were dragging a dog and two kittens with them. We both stared at them.

"Already found one of the kittens mauled to death this week," his mother said, "I don't know if it was Miles or the girls. They probably all had a hand in it." I felt sick, thinking about the dead kitten, my own cat was a fat Russian Blue. Dan and I laughed frequently, about how she permitted us to live with her.

136

Miles younger sister, Annie, was watching me from the stairs. I had noticed that she had a black eye and walked on her tiptoes.

Annie was enrolled in the pre-school class at the Campus School for disabled children. I had seen her before, and talked with Annie's teacher. She was very concerned about the bruises that Annie constantly came to school with. At the age of five, she had developed no language skills at all.

The upstate medical center, in Syracuse, told her teacher that Annie's lack of language was due to emotional problems rather than a hearing loss. I knew they were thinking about placing Annie in my group, but I was so depressed over the things that her mother told me, I didn't even bother to bring it up.

I excused myself from the conference, explaining that I had another conference back at the Campus School. I nearly broke my neck, tripping down the rickety front steps.

Miles, who had dashed outside, was playing in front of his house. He laughed when he saw me stumble and yelled out, "You better watch it, teacher," green snot was dripping off his nose, "you gonna break your face." He and his sisters laughed hysterically at this remark.

Back at the Campus School, I had received a message to call Phoebe's mother. She called several times while I was out and the school secretary told me she sounded desperate.

"I just wanted to tell you that I can't make it," her mother said, "so I'm sending my husband instead." I was glad, I had never met Phoebe's father and this would be the perfect opportunity.

"How are things otherwise?" I asked.

"Well," she said, "we've been trying some new things. I have a friend who's a psychic and he's done a few readings with Phoebe."

"A psychic?" I said. My mind silently roamed to the background information that I'd read on Phoebe. It had stated that her parents were interested in the occult and had delved into astrology to try and help them explain or learn more about their child.

"Yes," she continued, "he says he picks up some evil vibrations around Phoebe. I don't know if it's a case of reincarnation or what. Phoebe seems to have some knowledge of things that happened before she was born."

"Reincarnation?" I said. The school secretary looked over in my direction. I wished I could have private conversations with parents. I ended the conversation quickly and promised to get back to her. Her mother had a right to some privacy; I knew this was neither the time nor the place for this conversation.

Phoebe's father was waiting for me in my classroom. He was sitting in the dark and I turned on the lights as I walked in.

"I'm sorry," I said, "I hope I didn't keep you waiting long. I was just talking with your wife on the phone."

"Don't worry about it," he answered, "I'm glad somebody can talk to her. I sure can't." He was a big man, slightly overweight and in his mid thirties.

"Listen," he continued, "let me tell you a few things about my wife. First of all, she's a manic-depressive. I never know how she's going to act. One day she'll be baking pies and the next day she'll be hysterical, throwing things and carrying on like a crazy woman." I had met him only moments before and he was launching into a tirade about his wife.

"You really don't have to explain," I offered, but he ran on.

"I just want you to know," he said, "in case she seems... odd to you. She is not a well woman." He was very nervous and was talking very fast.

He leaned closer to me and put his hand on my arm, "I come home from work and she's plastered...flat out drunk, at 3:00 in the afternoon." He paused for a second.

"We haven't been... Uh, man and wife, you know...for a long time now. I even threatened to take the kids and leave. That's when things finally straightened out a little."

He left as abruptly as he had come in. "You'll have to come out to our house," he said, "we have a boat. We'd love to have you." And he vanished out the door. I was amazed; he hadn't stayed more than a few minutes. Although I had read in Phoebe's folder that her parents had quite a bit of money, I would never have guessed it. Her clothes were old and ragged. Almost every pair of pants she owned had holes in the crotch. She masturbated so much that she had ripped most of them apart.

One day she came to school screaming and biting herself more than she usually did. Her hands were in her pants all day and I knew something was desperately wrong. We sent her home, but the next day she was back in school.

A note from her mother explained that Phoebe had been to the doctor and that she'd developed a vaginal infection. A tube of medicated cream accompanied her. It was a prescription drug and had the label from the pharmacy typed on it. Her mother wanted the school nurse to apply the cream three times a day to her.

Phoebe was screaming so loud that Bob Morgan had come to my door, wondering what all the commotion was about. I handed him the note.

"This is ridiculous," he said, "she has to go home. Her parents should be handling this, not us. Our responsibility has certain limitations to it." There were deep, red bite marks on Phoebe's arms; she was obviously being tormented by the infection.

We sent her home and I received a phone call from her mother later that morning. I could tell she was very irritated with me.

"I'm surprised at you, Toni," her mother said, "I thought you cared more than this."

"I do care," I answered, "that's why I sent her home."

"Well, my husband sleeps during the day," she said, "and I work. There's no one here to watch her."

As I sat in my living room and thought about the three conferences that I had gone through, I wondered if all this effort I put into teaching was really worth it. At times it seemed like it wasn't. What good was it to ask Rudy to keep her clothes on in school, if she could rip them off anytime she wanted at home?

I pushed these thoughts out of my mind. I generally tried not to think along these lines, but talking with the parent's of the kids had brought home a stark reality to me.

I needed the help and cooperation of the parents. Without it, all the effort and determination in the world was useless. Somehow, I had to reach them, as surely as I had reached out and touched their kids. I didn't know how I would do it, but I knew I would have to try.

Part II - Chapter 6

September 1978

A new school year, once again, had started. Over the summer, I had attended the local Committee on the Handicapped, that every school district was now required to have. I wanted to see if I could convince them to recode both Carlos and Patty. As it turned out, I had few, if any, problems.

The Oswego Committee on the Handicapped was a big group. More than most I'd seen in the past. Nearly twenty people sat around a huge, round table in the education center. I was surprised to learn that only a few other people and myself actually knew who Carlos or Patty were. Both sets of the kids parents had been invited to the meeting, but neither showed. I felt a tremendous responsibility to them. I knew I was the only advocate they had and I also knew that if Carlos and Patty were to leave my group, it would be my word that would get them out.

Carlos had been tested by the school psychologist and his full scale I.Q. was in the range of the educable mentally retarded. He'd spent two full school years with me, and although I could see some minimal emotional problems, they were not nearly as devastating as some of the other kids. I had very little problem in persuading the Committee to have Carlos placed in an EMR class. I'd hoped for a class of children with learning disabilities, but there were none that existed.

Patty just barely scored within the average range of intelligence on her achievement tests and although I could tell the Committee was loathe to do it, they had to place her in a regular first grade class. I was thrilled beyond words, she was the first child I had ever taught to make it back to a class that was not restricted to only the disabled. I knew that Carlos and Patty's parents would be very excited over the good news, I just wished they'd attended the meeting. They begged off at the last minute. I talked with Carlos's mother on the phone, the day before the meeting was to be held.

"I'm not comin', Toni," she told me, "I don't know what to say to them education people. They always make me feel lousy. Like some Mexican trash. Don't you let them treat my Carlos that way."

"Why don't you come and help me out?" I asked her, "I need you there, Carlos does too. We have to stick up for him."

"You can do it better than me."

"No, I can't," I said, "I'm his teacher, not his mother. Tell them what it's like. They'll listen to you."

"They ain't gonna listen to no Mexican," she said, "and my husband can't come either, he don't speak English at all." I'd talked to Carlos's father a few times in the past. My college Spanish had come in handy and we barely managed to communicate.

"Me Carlitos es un bueno muchacho," he told me, "me desgracia es la falta de dinero." I looked at this small man who reminded me so much of his little Carlos.

"Dinero es no importante," I said to him, "Carlos quiere un padre." We looked at each other for awhile.

"Si," he answered, "pero, hablas como todos los ricos." And so, I went to the Committee alone. A part of what Carlos's father considered the wealthy and influential members of society. I did not press his parents to come, although part of me said I should. I could empathize with the alienation that they felt and I was as angry as his father that Carlos and his family were cut off from the educational system through lack of language, money and schooling.

Carlos's father had been right in one respect. The Committee members were all bastions of the educational system. Trying to talk to the well-heeled, fashionably dressed members of the group was intimidating for me, but I placed my fears aside and in the end, both kids were placed in new classes.

I would miss them, but I knew they were better off going to a class that was less restrictive. Other special education teachers had an easier time 'mainstreaming' their kids than I did. One scream from Phoebe or Rudy was enough to scare some teachers off for a whole school year. They probably thought if one child screamed and bit their arm, they all did.

My own little class included Roxanne, Phoebe, Rudy, Miles and Jane. Jane had come from a private school for emotionally disturbed children and like Miles, was small and blond. Miles little sister, Annie would be coming to my class in the afternoons. It was hard to believe, but I now had nearly all girls in my group. It would be a change from teaching boys and I looked forward to it.

We were still in our tiny three-room class at the Campus School and Pam and her group were right down the hall from us. A.J. turned ten and was overjoyed to be going with the 'big kids.' His progress had been remarkable and after four years, he was more than ready for a new situation. Although he still screamed, bit his arm and talked continuously, he had been able to control these things more as the years went by. His hand flapping was less frequent and he seemed not as fearful of things. His obsessions with objects and feelings had begun to fade away. I hoped that Pam would not come to know the hysterical fits he used to have over the pipes at Cherry Park. He rarely even mentioned them anymore.

My class size had decreased and things seemed to be going very smoothly. No longer did I have kids from age five or six to age thirteen or fourteen. With the addition of Pam's class, I would never have a child over the age of ten. It would be a strange experience teaching kids who were all the same size.

I was not an individual teacher anymore, but a part of a program for kids. A program that looked as if it would expand even further. Dr. Gramm mentioned a third class starting for kids with these problems. Perhaps, to be placed in the local junior high school.

In my wildest dreams, I couldn't imagine this happening. I had been told many times before that my class would not make it. That it was easy to forget about children who sat and rocked all day. Who only talked when necessary. Now it seemed as if we had caught the attention of many people from the school districts all across the county.

The children in my class and in Pam's came from half a dozen different districts in the county. At last, they were listening and like A.J., I had little intention of remaining quiet.

October 1978

It was a bright October morning. The leaves on the trees had turned a delicious orange and were still clinging tenaciously to the dark branches that held them. Fall was one of my favorite seasons and the only sadness it brought me was in knowing the brutality of the following wintry weather that I knew would come.

I had been preparing Rudy all week for the inevitable shock that I knew would be hers today. Her mother and father told me of her intense fears. One of them was the stereo or record player. They didn't know where she had picked up this strange fear. Perhaps, the loud rock music that her older siblings played had frightened her as a young child. She had broken the arms off a number of different stereos they had in their home. Finally, they just didn't play them anymore. At least, not when she was at home. The cost of replacing the arms was big and they were not interested in placing restrictions of any kind on their daughter.

I had promised them that I wouldn't force the record player on her immediately, but I had no intention of letting it lay silent for years. She had been so hysterical last winter during her introduction to our school, that I'd put it out of my mind completely. There were too many other problems to deal with. Getting her to keep her clothes on, eating food without spitting it and just getting adjusted to life without her mother was a major hurdle.

She had developed some speech since our last trip to the Oswego County Special Olympics, but no language at all. She would not talk to me, Rose or any one else in our class. However, if I held up a picture card of an object, she would repeat the word after I said it for her. Just hearing her say the words of the pictures was enough to keep me going. The kids and Rose were equally as thrilled.

"Rooodeeee talk!" Roxie would exclaim, and pound her emphatically on the back. Both Roxie and Rudy were placed on the 'severely speech impaired' list. They received speech and language lessons daily from a certified speech pathologist. Miles and Phoebe were also involved in speech therapy. My noisy, talkative class had suddenly become oddly quiet. I had become accustomed to years of unending questions from A.J., Max and the others. Most of the children I had now, at best, could barely make their most basic needs known. I knew I would have to work hard with them. Children without speech or language were cut off from the rest of the world in a very isolated way. I had to learn to break the barrier. Fortunately, Jane and even Miles, had some speech and language skills. I would draw upon their ability to help me teach the younger kids.

Whenever Rudy said any words, she had the undivided attention of everyone in my group. Even little Phoebe, who had very little language development, would look up. She loved Rudy and would try to get as close to her as possible, even though her efforts were rarely rewarded. Rudy just never seemed to notice her, or anybody else for that matter.

Earlier in the week, I'd brought in my guitar. We sang some old familiar songs and Phoebe and Rudy were delighted with it. Phoebe bounced up and down, clapping and singing at the top of her lungs. None of the words were right, but nobody cared or even noticed.

"Oh Mish babble hab a yarm," she sang, "E-i-e-I-o!" We all laughed and sang along. I had never seen Phoebe so animated, clearly music was the way to entering her world.

Even Rudy rocked back and forth, humming along and smiling more than I had ever seen. They all loved the guitar and the rhythm band instruments that I brought out for them to play. I was astounded that Rudy could play along on the kazoo any song that I mentioned. She couldn't sing the words, but she could hum out the melody. I just knew there was more to this kid than met the eye.

Roxanne was the sociable conductor of our singing group. She picked up a wooden stick and led them in song, looking like a red haired version of the New York Philharmonic's, Zeuben Mehta. Because she could now control her behavior more, I let her assume the role that she loved best, that of the conductor. Just watching her would make my eyes tear up. She was a natural comedian.

The next day, I decided to show the kids a record. I passed the warped black object around and the kids touched it with a great deal of curiosity. It was easy to hold their attention with simple things. I had to keep reminding myself to go slow. Only Rudy was upset.

The next day, she was more cautious. After our singing, I brought out the old, worn record player that I kept in my office. I knew it was time and I would have to help her overcome her fear. Hiding the record player or denying its existence would only help her to believe there really was something to be afraid of. The day after, I turned the record player on. I held my breath as I waited for the reaction that I knew would come. Although, I had only turned on the switch that started the turntable moving, Rudy had begun to scream and pull at her clothing and her hair. I moved by her side and put my arms around her.

"It's O.K.," I reassured her, "I'm here. Nothing is going to hurt you." She pushed me away and ran screaming to the closed doors.

"Mommy, mommy, mommy, mommy, mommy," she screamed the word over and over, "mommmmmmmmmy... mommmmmmmmmy, mommmmmy." Unable to unlock the closed door, she stood pounding on it. I felt like an ogre, but I knew that if I gave in and turned it off, it really would give her the subconscious idea that there was something to be afraid of in this square box we all called 'the record player.' The other children watched, more in confusion than fear, as Rudy screamed on.

"Rudy afraid," Roxanne remarked, and began to bite her already short nails. Watching other children in scary situations brought out her own anxiety. It was too close to home to be comfortable. This was not going to be easy for any of us.

"Don't be scared, Rudy," Miles yelled over her screaming, "why don't you boogie wid me." He jumped up and started a crazy gyration that would have put Elvis Presley to shame. But nothing helped. She continued screaming until I had one of the kids turn the record player off.

Now today was the day of reckoning. I would have some low, mellow music playing on the record player, when the kids came in every morning, so she knew when to expect it. I wanted it to be predictable and not arouse her anxieties anymore than I had to.

Rudy was the first one in the door that morning. She stood at the entrance to the classroom and stared in, shocked at the music coming from the record player. She ran over to it and attempted to rip the arm off the player as I had been pre-warned that she would. I gently but firmly, pushed her back.

"No, Rudy," I said, "the record player stays on. It's only music. It won't hurt you." Her face had turned white and I prepared for the battle that I knew was coming. She punched and shoved at me trying to get to it, screaming hysterically.

"Mommmmmmmmmmmmmmmmmmmmmy, mommmmmmmmmmry mommmmmmmy," her screams broke my heart, "Mommmmrmmy, mommmmmmmy, mommmmmmmmmmy,... turn it off, turn it off... turn it off!" I couldn't believe my ears. I had heard her speak another sentence. And even though she was hysterical with fear, I made a mental note of it.

I calmly grabbed hold of her, although inside I was shaking as much as she was. "I'm not going to turn it off, Rudy," I said, "it's going to stay on in the morning. It won't hurt you, I promise." She raged on and on. Screaming, punching and kicking at me. Trying to get next to the record player.

Finally, she stepped back and flung open her lunch pail. She threw the contents of it against the window and her jelly sandwich stuck to the windowpane. I watched the purple, sticky mess slide down the glass while she continued screaming. The song came to an end and the brown arm of the record player slowly moved across and clicked to 'off.' Rudy ran over to me again and I picked her up in my arms. She was still screaming and beating against my chest and arms. My blue vest had been torn.

Suddenly, she jumped out of my arms and threw her whole body against the concrete wall. When she turned around she was bleeding from her nose. Still screaming, and now bleeding, she ran from the room and raced down the hall.

"Mommmmmmmy, Mommmmmmy, Mommmmmmy," she screamed, "turn it off... turn it off, turn it off!" Her screams echoed in the halls of the Campus School. Children were pouring in as they got off their buses; they stopped to stare at us as I ran down the hall after her. I passed Rose and just dashed by her, no time to talk. I had to catch her or there was no telling what would happen. Finally, I grabbed her in the basement.

Exhausted, we both sat on the gray cement floors near the custodian's room. I was completely out of breath from chasing her and she was still crying. Her beautiful little face smeared with tears. I wiped them off and sat rocking her until she calmed down.

"It's O.K. Rudy," I said to her, "nothing's going to hurt you. The record players not going to hurt you." We sat and rocked for a long time. Gradually, her heart stopped racing and both our breathing and heartbeats returned to normal.

With her face cleaned and washed, we walked the now quiet halls back to our room. I could hear Rose talking to the kids, as we neared closer and closer.

At the door to the room, Rudy stopped and looked in at the now silent record player. It sat where it had been earlier that morning. The record was still on the turntable and I noticed that Rudy's crusty sandwich was still stuck to the bottom part of the windowpane.

"Good morning, everybody," I greeted them, as we came in. They eyed the two of us curiously.

"Where you been, Toni Baloney," Miles demanded, "why you chasing Rudy down the hall?" He stuck out his lower lip. Probably thinking how much he would enjoy being chased.

Rudy watched the record player closely the rest of the day. Although the following weeks were difficult, nothing would compare to that morning. There were still tears, screaming and hysteria, but she knew the record player would be on every morning.

She eventually came to tolerate it, but slowly... ever so slowly, she would make her peace with it and I would watch her tackle other problems that fell in her path. Gradually, she learned to touch the record player. After many years she even turned it on and off every morning.

November 1978

We had just come in from the playground and the faces on our kids were red with sweat and the cold, crisp air that had started flowing in from Lake Ontario. Miles had lost his green pullover cap and Jane's new sketchpad had blown away in the spirited wind.

Pam's kids were with us and Max had on a paper Batman cape that he made. It was long, white and dragged on the ground as he walked. He had taken to making several of them everyday during his free time. Pam had informed me that drowning people and intense black clouds he usually drew were now replaced by these Batman capes. If you listened closely, you could hear him whispering.

"I'm not going to die, I'm not going to die...I'm not going to die." Always when he had on these capes. Apparently, they gave him an unrivaled feeling of immortality. I'd seen his mother recently, she told me that Max had taken all her towels and cut half-moons in the bottom of them. Furious with him, she had admitted that the two of them actually got into a fistfight over it. I knew Max and many of our other kids needed psychotherapy, but when I questioned my direct supervisors about it I usually received a very haughty answer.

"Sure," one of them told me, "they can get therapy. I'll just put it on my master charge card." This was the typical, arrogant response we had learned to expect. Gradually, over the years, I had stopped asking. But Pam was new to the game and she persisted in futile attempts that only wound up frustrating her. I knew there was no use asking for help because none would be given. I had learned to cope by providing my own answers and solutions. I was grateful that Pam's class had finally been added.

"I'm sick of the whole thing," she said, "we're still stuck in the observation room and now Dr. Gramm says he's going to send me another kid. That will make seven. We'll have to crawl over each other." After nearly a year of teaching her attitude had changed from complacency to anger.

"Alfie's been in and out of foster care two times since I've met him," she added, "and most of the other kids need psychiatric help." I knew how she felt, I had been there myself many times in the past.

"How do you do it?" she asked, "How do you keep from going crazy, sometimes I feel like everybody wants a piece of me." Her short, dark hair bobbed up and down as she talked.

"Just take it easy," I advised, "these kids were here long before we got on the scene. You're only one person. You can only do so much." I looked at her and thought I recognized the classic symptoms of burn out, teacher overload and fatigue. I had seen it before and had guarded against it myself. It was a very easy thing for an involved teacher to find himself or herself in the midst of.

"You need a cup of tea," I suggested, "go get one and I'll take your kids back to class." She wandered into the teacher's room to grab a cup and I thought about how tense and out of sorts Pam had seemed lately. Even Bob Morgan had remarked on it to me.

"Whatever her problem is," he said, "tell her to clean it up. I can't have her kids screaming in the halls." Bob had usually been very responsive and accepting of the kids. But Pam didn't seem to be able to handle their outbursts very well. One of her kids frequently had screaming sessions in the hallway. This past week, she had come to my room, upset and in tears. She had slapped one of the kids and was feeling guilty about it.

"He bit me," she exclaimed, "he actually bit me." She was talking about a boy that was brand new to our program.

"What happened?" I asked.

"I don't know," she continued, "all of a sudden, he ran up to me and bit my finger. I slapped his face." I looked at her finger, it had a small, red welt on it and was swelling a little.

"Maybe he was testing you," I tried to suggest gently, "maybe he just wanted to see if he could rattle your cage. Or if you would let him do anything he wanted." I was certainly no paragon of virtue and the kids often tested my patience. The most aggressive I'd ever gotten was with Roxanne. I sometimes had to physically move her. But I never hit her and I did not look upon it as a healthy alternative.

I knew if I ever hit a kid, they would never again trust me. That's not to say that the thought never occurred to me. Occasionally, I had to step out of the room for a quick breath of air or a cup of coffee. It was not easy teaching children, and I was well aware of it. Teaching was more an art than a science. I was totally empathetic with her.

"Maybe you could have found a better way," I tentatively said, "to let him know that you don't like being bitten."

"Well, I'd do it again," she replied and walked out of my room. I knew some teachers did use force with kids. It was an easy solution, but one that left devastating effects.

I dropped Pam's kids off by their class and left them with her teacher aide. Rose and I walked our own group back to our room in silence. We had both waited so long for this additional class and now things didn't seem to be going the way they should.

"Maybe everything will work itself out," Rose's voice sounded encouraging, "remember how confused I was in the beginning?" We both laughed; thinking of the weeks that Rose had sat behind Roxanne, riding shotgun.

"I was scared to death," she added, "Roxanne was like a wild, uncontrolled, bolt of lightning." She looked thoughtful and I could see memories slipping past her eyes, it had been over two years since we had met each other. Her assistance had become invaluable to me; I didn't know what I would do without her.

"But, I came around," she sighed, "you and the kids helped me out more than anything. Pam just needs more time."

Just as she said that, we could both hear Simone yelling at the top of her lungs.

"Roast-dubba-roast-dubba-beefa!" The sounds poured out of Pam's room and they sounded like they were going to last the rest of the day. I knew something would have to be done and quick.

January 1979

I had seen many kids from the Campus School racing up and down the stairs to the industrial arts room, located in the basement, near the custodian's office. They always looked exhilarated and their arms were usually loaded with the wooden projects they made. No one, not even the little four and five year olds were excluded from this fascinating place.

The man who ran the shop was a tiny, middle aged college professor, who decided he wanted to be a schoolteacher again. His handlebar moustache was about as big as he was. One day I saw all the six-year-olds in Campus School walking back from shop class. Their hands and arms were raised over their heads and they were laughing hysterically.

"Guess what we are?" one of them yelled out to us, as we were walking by. My kids looked at them like they were all crazy.

"We're Dr. Steven's moustache!" Obviously, he had put them up to that I thought. I strongly suspected him of actually liking kids.

"When we gonna come to your room?" Miles asked him one day, "I wanna use your saw blades!" The kids usually swamped the man with attention.

"How about right now," he answered, "that is, if it's allright with Toni." Five pairs of eyes looked at me, pleading their case.

"O.K." I said, "but, don't touch anything." Nobody stayed around long enough to hear the last part. They were charging down the hall with Murphy Stevens leading them like a divine nymph.

"Oh my God," I said to Rose, "they'll kill themselves." Roxanne looked like she was chomping at the bit. All those tools in her hot little paws, I could just imagine her examining every one.

The room was vast, packed with every kind of tool and equipment imaginable. The place was incredible. It must have had thousands of dollars worth of machinery. I knew that the university specialized in industrial arts, but to sink this kind of money into an elementary shop program was very unusual.

"Look at these funny glasses," Miles came charging over to me. His little face was covered with a pair of goggles that were way too big. He looked absurdly funny.

"Those are to protect your eyes," Murphy said, "so they don't get hurt if you're using a machine."

"Turn one of those things on." Jane pointed to a huge table saw that was over at the far end of the room. Her blue eyes were sparkling with excitement. How she had ever wound up in a private school for emotionally disturbed kids was beyond me. I didn't even think her problems were severe enough to place her in my group.

"Let's see," Murphy answered, "how about if we turn on this band saw instead." The kids were scattered all over the room, but when he turned the machine on it really scared them. They all came running over to Rose and me.

"GODDAMN, SHIT ... GODDAMN! SHIT,COCKYSHIT!" Phoebe's screams must have carried out way down the hall, because a passing college student stuck his head in the door, to see what all the commotion was about.

"See," I said to Rose, "Phoebe can really speak up, if she feels like it." Murphy looked at her and then me.

"I know how she feels," he said, "I always say that when one of the machines breaks down. Maintenance is not my thing." Well, at least the man had a sense of humor.

Rudy was busy hiding her head in one of the green lockers that were jammed up against the back walls. "Mommmmmy,... Mommmmmy, Mommmmmmmy... Mommmmmmmy!" She was screaming like a pin was stuck in her little rear end.

"You certainly know how to keep a captive audience," I yelled over the noise of the machine and the screams of the kids, to Murphy.

"Well," he answered, "we try to please. Maybe that was too much for the first visit, huh?" He looked at me, slightly surprised by the reactions of the kids.

"Nah," I said, "they greet me like this every morning." I wasn't exactly telling a lie, Rudy and Phoebe had lungs on them that could challenge the metropolitan opera singers.

"We'll have to talk to Bob Morgan about having you folks come and visit us again," Murphy said, "how would you like that?" Jane and Miles were all over the man, they loved him.

"I wanna make a pool table," Miles said, pulling at his gray shop coat.

Murphy's shop coat was filthy, covered with unidentifiable goo. But, somehow, he always managed to look tidy.

"A pool table," he said, "you like to play pool, do you?" Miles was jumping up and down. He looked like he had been electrified. "Yeah," he answered, "my daddy teach me to shoot pool and Toni and I shoot pool in school." I grinned sheepishly. It was true, Miles and I did shoot pool in school. Of course, it wasn't a regulation table, but then neither one of us cared particularly.

Miles would take the colored beads that Carlos made spaghetti and meatballs out of. I showed him how to rack them up to form a triangle.

Then, both of us would lay out on the floor and shoot the small, colored beads with the wooden pointer that I kept near the chalkboard. It was great fun and good for fine motor coordination, which he needed plenty of practice in.

One day, Dr. Gramm and the Superintendent from the City School District, showed up in my class just as Miles and I were involved in a hot game of pool. We were both sprawled on the floor, and I was furious because I had just missed an easy shot.

"Having fun?" Dr. Gramm asked from a corner of the room. I almost died when I heard his voice. Why did he have to show up at the most incongruous times?

"We're shootin' pool," Miles yelled, "and Toni Baloney's losin' the game." He took a shot at one of the colored balls and they scattered all over the floor, some coming to rest right near the superintendent's feet.

The Superintendent had caught me years before in the yellow, plastic igloo making 'potato soup' with Alfie and Sophie. I was sure he thought I was right out of Looney Tunes.

"Very educational," he said, handing me some of the colored beads, "is this what they call 'play therapy'?" I prayed for the floor to swallow me up, but none of us vanished.

"Well," Murphy said, returning me to the present, "we'll have to see if we can find some scrap wood to help you make a pool table. How will that be?" Miles was beside himself by now. I looked down near his feet and a small yellow stream of urine was starting to flow out from his pants.

"Time to go," I said, looking down at the puddle, "right now!"

"Looks like my friend already did," Murphy replied, looking down at the growing puddle. We both burst out laughing.

The weeks flew by and one cold winter morning, Murphy showed up at our door, complete with his gray shop coat and some good news.

"It's all set," he told us, "the kids can come every Wednesday morning. I have a college student to work with each one." I was so happy. This would be better than any psychotherapy session. Working with tools would teach them independence and some practical life skills.

"Thanks," I answered, "you don't know how much this means to me. It's really going to help the kids."

"Don't mention it. It'll be good for the college students, too. A lot of them have requested to work with special children."

"Goodbye, Professor Sawdust!" Jane yelled, "Go take care of your machines." From that minute on, he was known as Professor Sawdust to my kids. The ones who could talk that is.

"SHIT, GODDAMN, COCKYSHIT!" little Phoebe screamed at him as he left. She probably associated him with the noise of the machines. The memory of their last encounter had stuck in her mind.

"And goodbye to you too, Phoebe!" he responded. I knew we were lucky to have him on our side. And best of all, the kids behavior didn't seem to faze him in the least.

The college students were quite another story. I had been teaching emotionally disturbed children a long time. Their ways had become second nature to me; nothing they did surprised me anymore. I had a tendency to forget that most other people viewed them in quite a different light. The student that was working with Rudy acted like he had been teaching gifted students how to draw up plans for construction of the World Trade Center.

"Take your rule," he said to her, "and measure out the length of these boards. Make sure you come to the nearest quarter inch."

She stood near him, oblivious to his words, and rocked back and forth. Her little hands playing the doubles game in front of her eyes.

"Measure out the length of these boards," he repeated himself, and then threw a fast glance in her direction and mine.

"Rudy," I said to her, it was first important to make eye contact with her. She stopped rocking and looked in my face.

"Ruler," I said the word to her. I held up the object.

"Ruler," she repeated back to me and started rocking again. The student looked like he was going to pass out. He was accustomed to giving directions quickly and having them complied with. I wasn't sure Rudy even knew the name for 'ruler', never mind measuring boards to the quarter inch.

The student who was working with Phoebe was in a similar state. He picked up a hammer and showed her how to pound nails into a piece of plywood. Her motor coordination was very poor, but she picked up the hammer anyway. Fascination covering her appealing little face. She whacked away at the board, missing the nails completely, and the plywood went sailing across the room.

"SHIT, GODDAMN IT! COCKYSHIT," she yelled, "COCKYSHIT!"

She bit into her arms and hands and I tried to soothe her crumpled feelings. Her lack of motor ability always frustrated her to tears.

"You shouldn't swear, Phoebe," the student said, "it's not nice for little girls to swear." She looked at him and a huge grin covered her face. I really wished he hadn't said that, it was like telling her to swear all the more.

"YOU SHIT," she yelled out again, "COCKYSHIT! GODDAMN IT!" She was smiling a toothless grin and attempting to bite her arm all at once. The college student looked horrified. Phoebe had learned very few words, but her parents told me she picked up quite a few swear words from their older teenage children. I had been waiting for other language skills to follow, but in almost a year since she'd started school, all she did was swear.

Roxanne was in a corner of the shop tussling with a young, slender college co-ed. Roxie was, hands down, definitely getting the best of the struggle. At nearly eight years of age she weighed over 110 pounds. The co-ed was not more than that herself. The

A. R. Magaletta McClure

two of them looked like they were in training for a mud-wrestling match. They were yanking a Phillips Head screwdriver between themselves. I knew Roxie would not give in and when the college kid let go Roxanne landed firmly on the dusty, wooden floor, the screwdriver held triumphantly in her pudgy hands.

"I got it, I got it," she yelled, "I got scoodiver!" She was busy congratulating herself, when she caught hold of my disapproving look from across the room.

"Sorry, sorry," I could hear her mumbling.

"Give it back," I mouth the words to her, still standing near Phoebe and Rudy. Roxanne and I knew each other very well by now, she knew I would follow through if I gave her a direction, so she handed back the screwdriver and burst into tears.

"IT'S MY SCOODIVER!" she cried, big tears dripping off her face, "MY SCOODIVER!" She lay down on the wooden worktable, her fat hands pounding its surface. I hadn't seen her have such a temper tantrum in a long time. The college student was standing by her, looking helpless and spellbound by the scene.

Jane and Miles were the only ones who were quietly working alongside Murphy Stevens. Murphy was helping them cut plywood into pieces for a wooden structure that was to be a play store. It would stand about six feet in height and have four shelves. Perfect for putting empty boxes of food on. Miles's hyperactivity seemed to vanish in thin air when he was working with Murphy. I thought that perhaps, the real cure for hyperactive children was not medication and suppression, but increased mobility. Maybe the doctors and psychiatrists who were always recommending medication should come visit the kids in the industrial arts workshop. They might learn a few things.

"What do you think?" Murphy asked me, "Was it too much at once?"

"Not at all," I smiled at him, I was still keeping my eye on Roxanne and her now cautious college friend, "it's just a new

158

experience to them. New things are always exciting to my kids. They need it though, it's good for them."

"Good for the college kids, too," Murphy added, "they think they want to teach 'special children' but, this may show them what it's all about."

How true it was. I had many college students come to my class, anxious to volunteer their time and energy. Many left with frustrated visions backfiring on their brains. Teaching was not easy to begin with; teaching oppositional children was extremely difficult.

"Well," Murphy continued, "then we'll see you all again next Wednesday." He walked back into his office while Rose and I helped the kids clean up and put away the tools they'd used.

"How do you do it?" one of the college students asked me, while we were sweeping up the floors. He looked about nineteen or twenty years old. His blue college windbreaker was wrinkled from having Phoebe pull on it during the past hour.

"I drink," I said to him and he stared at me, the joke passing him by like a train whizzing through a tunnel.

"Actually," I went on, "it's very simple. I do what I can and leave the rest for the next day."

He looked over at Phoebe who sat staring in his direction. She smiled when she saw him looking at her and quietly giggled... "cocky-shit," at him once again. Even at her developmental level she was clever enough to figure out what made him angry, and had succeeded in throwing it in his face. He unconsciously touched the delicate gold cross that hung around his neck and turned away from her. She smiled up at me and I could feel victory showing in her blue eyes. How strange that a child with so few skills could manage to manipulate a grown, educated young man. I had seen it happen many times before, even with the kid's parents. I called the kids over to the door, it was time to leave. Phoebe ran over to a corner of the room and stood giggling and swearing. Roxanne stood near the worktable trying to figure out a way to smuggle her prized 'scoodiver' back to our class, without me noticing it. Rudy stood, rocking and swaying.

Only Miles and Jane had come over to the door. I looked over at Rose, we both knew it would take most of the morning to get the other three back to normal. But, I felt this new, exciting adventure was well worth the problems it would surely cause.

"Goodbye," I said to the college students as we were leaving, "we'll see you next week." They tossed knowing looks at each other and I wondered who would show up again the following week.

The industrial arts program proved to be everything I hoped for and more. That winter our grocery store was completed and painted a royal blue. It stood proudly in our classroom. Mounds of empty, cardboard food containers lined its shelves. All donated by parents. I had to stop the kids from bringing in too many boxes. The grocery store was fast turning into a food distributing conglomerate.

The college students also helped the kids build a wooden car. It was complimented with two green car seats that Dan and I donated from our own Dodge Van. A steering wheel and a busted radio were locked in place on the dashboard. Even the principal of the Campus School had generously contributed a rear view mirror. Needless to say, the car was the envy of every kid that passed by our class. We had many visitors to our room after that, all looking for the special privilege of 'riding' in our fuel efficient car. A beautiful contraption, complete with orange racing stripes.

Even Miles, had his long sought after dream come true. He and Murphy began the complicated task of constructing his 'pool table.' Even though some eyebrows were probably raised, I was personally relieved. I was getting sick and tired of going home with filthy flannel shirts everyday. The dirt from the floor, that I had to lay on while we played pool, made me look like I worked in a gas station rather than a school. After it was finished, Miles and I could play on the table. It was close to being completed, but little did I know that we would never have it in our possession.

Unknown to all of us, events were about to unfurl themselves right before our very eyes.

March 1979

Spring was coming closer everyday. The kids were getting restless and Pam and I decided that it was time for something new. Although I knew that she was still dissatisfied with her position teaching, I hoped things would iron themselves out for her.

We frequently combined our two classes for lessons, plays, parties and lots of other activities. It gave me a chance to keep up with Simone and the boys. The feelings of nostalgia that the kids and I had for each other, renewed itself each time we met. Watching them grow into their adolescence was a rare and unexplainable experience. One that I knew few teachers ever had. And one that was almost too big for words. We had spent so much time, so much of our lives together.

One late winter afternoon, we were all walking by the student union, where the college kids hung out. We decided to take our kids in the center before we got them ready to board the buses for home.

The union was crowded with hordes of laughing, joking college kids. Rock music was blaring out of a jukebox. The sounds of the Rolling Stones came blasting past us, as we sat at our table in the union. Our kids were fascinated watching the college kids dancing, talking and eating junk food. We had taken them in the union many times before. The fantastic opportunity of being on a college campus was one that I made sure we took total advantage of.

The kids were perpetual visitors to the campus art exhibits, displays, and cultural happenings. It had enriched their lives, and mine, incredibly, over the past three years. It was hard to believe that we had not always been in the Campus School.

"We should take the kids out on some field trips," I yelled over to Pam, the music was ear shattering.

"Yeah," she agreed, "Centro bus goes right by the college administration building." I nodded my head, thinking of all the local stores we could visit.

"Turn that goddamn music down," I heard Robert mumble under his breath. I couldn't have agreed more. It was enough to shatter glass.

"MOOSIC! MOOSIC! MOOSIC!" Phoebe yelled, she was hopping up and down like a rabbit. Hopping about so fast that her speed amazed me, normally she dragged herself around. Lately, I had heard her whispering words, but when I came close to her, she turned me off. It was one extreme or the other with her. Either she screamed or she whispered, nothing in the middle. There was certainly nothing dull about the kids at all.

I brought her back to the table and continued talking with Pam.

"Why don't we start Friday?" I was getting excited. I loved going on trips as much as the kids did.

"Where to?" Pam cupped her hands around her mouth, so I could hear her better. I had to think about that for a minute.

"The maple syrup farm?" I hollered back, "Then to McDonald's for lunch." I waited for her reaction. She gave me the O.K. sign with her thumb and fingers.

Friday came quickly. Instead of Centro bus, I wrangled a bus from the transportation people out at the COES. They sent us a rickety, yellow heap and a driver that thought she was trying out for the Indy 500. I held my breath all the way.

"Damn bus breaks down constantly," she yelled to me. I was sitting in the back with the kids; "battery went dead on it twice this week already."

"Dead?" Max jumped to his feet, his ears perking up at the mention of the word. Pam looked at him, exasperated.

"DEAD," he repeated, "this bus is definitely gonna die!" His voice had become very self-righteous. I could hear his imaginative mind clicking away explanations to himself.

"Ever been to this farm before?" the driver asked.

"No," Pam answered.

"Well, watch out for the farmer's wife. She's crazier than hell." Rose and I exchanged glances. Oh God, I thought, what have I gotten us into now.

The farmer's wife turned out to be a fat, white haired, friendly, old lady. She had on red rubber boots, the kind everybody wore as a kid and she smelled distinctly of manure. I liked her instantly. Her hair was wild and stuck out under the straw hat that she wore on her head. A beautiful, brown and white, longhaired cat was hanging off her shoulder. It looked like a scene right out of Lil' Abner.

"You kids glad to be out of school?" she asked. The kids yelled back their appreciation. She turned to the side and hissed out a long, yellow, stream of spit. About three of them tried the same thing. Simone's spit hanging in a gooey, glob near her mouth. She giggled with pleasure.

"Not like that, Honey," the old woman said, "like this." She spit again, showing Simone how to direct the spit more accurately. She had the attention of Phoebe and Rudy, I watched her talk to them, and knew a genius was at work.

"Want to see the maple syrup first?" she asked the kids. They were so excited to be on a real farm. Their eyes were filling up with all the new sights. It was still winter and a little snow covered the cold, frozen ground. We sloshed our way through it, over to the maple trees, with the worn buckets nailed into them. Syrup dripped out in slow, laborious drops.

"Can't rush these things," she told them, "everything in due time." We all had on our winter coats, but all she wore were a pair of farmer jeans and a flannel shirt. I think it was the first time I'd ever seen a pair of farmer jeans on a real farmer.

"Come on over to the shed," she continued, "we'll show you how we boil the syrup up." The shed was across the road and looked like it had been there for a century.

She opened the door to the shed. A ton of smoke from the boiling syrup poured out and covered us. Two or three cats screeched and ran out from under some wooden barrels when she opened the door. Phoebe's nails dug into my arm and Rudy started screaming.

"Mommmmmmmmmy, MMMoooommmy!" I couldn't say I blamed her, the shed looked like a good prop for a Halloween play.

"Don't worry, sweetie," the old woman consoled Rudy, "your mother wouldn't be caught dead in this dump."

I could hear Max whispering the words... "Dead, dead," as she walked us through the dark insides of the little lean-to.

The syrup was being slowly boiled in huge, cauldron like pots. She gave us a taste of the sweet, sticky stuff. It was the best syrup I'd ever had and before we left I bought a quart of it from her. I thought we'd make pancakes next week in school and pour some on them.

"How about seein' the animals now?" she asked the kids. They had grown used to the darkness of the shed and were beginning to trust the old woman's words.

"Do they bite?" Jane asked. Her big eyes, full of suspense.

"Only each other," she answered, "and only on occasion."

The barn, where the animals were housed, was near the white farmhouse that the woman and her husband lived in. He waved to us as we walked by. His thin, wiry body had seen many days of hard farm labor.

"Enjoy yourself!" he hollered out to us as we went into the barn. If this was what the bus driver thought was crazy, then bring on the crazies. These people were beautiful, natural and had an innate understanding of kids.

The barn was filled with several dozen mooing cows. The place smelled terrible and I could see why.

"Hold your noses," she warned us, "the girls have been really crapping up a storm in here!" The 'girls' were cows lined up in stalls. Their rear ends pointing toward us. Huge, globs of brown manure came plopping out of them from all directions.

A.J. was flapping his hands and started laughing so hard he could barely talk. I knew he had experienced some difficulty in

164

being toilet trained. I guess watching the cows poop brought back old memories. When he was very young, about six or seven years old, he would take playdough and make short rolled pieces of it and lay it around his desk. "Poopie" he would yell out, "poopie ... pooopie!" But gradually, he stopped. This whole scene brought it all back home to him again.

"COCKYSHIT! COCKYSHIT!" Phoebe giggled, practically bent over with laughter. It was all affecting her the same way as A.J.

"That's right, Honey" the woman said, "and there ain't nothin' wrong with that either. Just plain old cow shit!"

The kids ran up and down the aisles, some daring to touch the cows or watch them chew the grassy food that was put out for them. I had rarely seen them so fascinated. Miles was jumping around so much that he fell in the sewer where the manure was being collected. I quickly fished him out.

"Time to go." I called out to Pam and Rose. They were watching the woman feed a newborn calf with an over sized nursing bottle. I really wasn't in the mood to dig anymore kids out of the manure pile. Although I'm sure they could have happily stayed the rest of the day. The kids seemed to have some kind of instant rapport with the animals. Unspoken but felt. It was as strong as the smell of manure that hung in the air.

The clean, fresh breeze outside almost knocked me over. My nostrils had filled with the stench of animal excrement in the barn. The kids waved goodbye to the old farm couple as we drove away. Even Phoebe and Rudy stood at the window, excited and laughing.

The lunch at the Golden Arches was equally as enjoyable. I was very happy to see that they now had a menu in Braille for those who couldn't see. Fortunately, none of us had to use it.

With the exception of Roxanne, who insisted on digging in the garbage, in search of a 'Big Mac', we all had a peaceful lunch. The child was constantly in pursuit of food. Only when I held up her chocolate milkshake, pretending to drink it, did she come bolting back to our table.

A. R. Magaletta McClure

We visited the sheep farm, the zoo and the goat fields after that. Every Friday was devoted to exploring the charming countryside that was a big part of the heritage of upstate New York. The friendly, bigheartedness of many of the farmers, artists and craftspeople in the area never failed to amaze me. They gave of themselves and their time with no thought of anything in return.

April 1979

Easter was late in coming, but the kids wanted to dye eggs and make our traditional holiday baskets anyway. We were all in the room next to the school office, where the stove, refrigerator and cooking utensils were kept.

Roxanne and Phoebe were dunking their eggs in blue and purple dye. It was staining their fingers and they were spilling more of it on the table than on the eggs. Jane, Rudy and Miles were stuffing grass into Easter baskets. I was busy eating all the black jellybeans I could find.

The school secretary walked in. Her arms were loaded with a stack of cumulative folders and she looked bone weary.

"Toni," she sighed, "it's Dr. Gramm on the phone. He says it's an emergency, can you take it?"

"Be right there," I told her and gave my bag of jellybeans to Rose. Hoping some black ones would be left when I got back. I wondered what the big emergency was, it was too late in the year for a student teacher, probably a new kid was coming.

I picked up the phone, puzzling over the dozens of phone calls we had traded since I had started to work for the COES.

"Toni," he said, "I have news, and none of it's good."

"What is it?" I held my breath. This was not a new student and I knew it.

"You're leaving," he rushed on, "Cherry Park wants you back."

"What are you talking about," I was in shock, "it's the end of the school year. There's only six or seven weeks left until schools over."

"I know, I know," he replied, impatiently, "but, you're still leaving, now." I couldn't believe it, I hadn't heard from Mike Donahue or anybody from the school in over a year.

"They say they want you back," he paused long enough to collect his thoughts. I could hear his mind clicking away.

"I don't get it," I said, "what's this sudden concern with me and the kids?"

"Look," he answered," just between you and me, I've heard they need to fill up some extra classrooms or the boys from downtown are going to grab them. You know how they feel about administrative offices being in the school. They want your class back so they can fill the place up."

"And you let them do it?" I was furious, "It's your class, not theirs." I couldn't believe it. Just who did they think they were, yanking kids around like so much cargo.

"I'm sorry," he said, "I really have no choice." Yes, you do, I thought. You can fight back. But, I knew he wouldn't.

"It's been three years," I said slowly, "we haven't been there in three years. We like the Campus School. I want to stay, the kids want to stay."

"I know," he replied, "I really thought they were just going to leave you there, but, like I say, if your old class isn't occupied, Donahue says the Superintendent or some of the other administrative personnel people are going to move in."

"Well, what happened to the teacher who's been in my class for the past year and a half?"

"Elm Park Schools been renovated," he answered, "she's moving back. That leaves your room empty."

"Oh great," I said, "they want us if we're of use to them. If not, we could have stayed here for the next thirty years."

"How do you think I feel," he was growing stubborn, "I don't like it anymore than you. They could have at least waited until next year."

"We never finished the pool table," my voice beginning to wane. I was thinking of how to explain all this to the kids. How to uproot them in a matter of days, tear them away from all that was familiar.

"What?" he said, interrupting my thoughts, "What pool table?"

"Never mind, you wouldn't understand."

"By the way," he interjected, "tell Pam. She's going too."

"Why?" I asked, "She's never even been in the school." I could tell from the impatient grunts and sighs I was hearing that Dr. Gramm was growing tired of explaining the whole mess to me. Why couldn't I be a nice, quiet teacher and mind my own business?

"I've already told you," he was getting testy, "they need classes in the school filled up. I'm sending over some boxes for you and Pam."

I could tell our conversation was almost over. Three years of hard work in Campus School over in one five minute chat. Who were the schools for anyway, I thought, the kids or the administrators that ran them? The answer to my question had been lying in my head for years.

"Have a Happy Easter," I said and hung up the phone. I walked back into the room where the kids were still dying eggs and making Easter projects. But, everything was changed. I would have to take their peaceful world and shake it up. On my way to our classroom, I stopped off and told Pam the news. She gave me a look of resignation and pointed to the brown, cardboard boxes that the COES had sent over. A ton of them were neatly stacked in the corner. They could sure move fast on things, if they wanted to.

"Am I gonna get to smash those pipes now?" A.J. asked. He had overheard our conversation. His hands started flapping away.

"What pipes?" Pam asked.

"Don't ask," I said, "you'll find out soon enough." I looked at A.J., Robert, Alfie and Max. Could these be the same kids that I had met so many years ago in that grimy, pipe filled room? It seemed like a dream. One that we were glad to escape.

Rose and I packed our class into boxes, once again, within two days. Rudy, Phoebe and Roxanne growing more alarmed as we crammed and filled the boxes up.

By the last day of school before Easter break, mounds of boxes were heaped all over the room. The kids had their Easter party sitting virtually on top of them. Children from the Campus School came by all day, to say goodbye and wish us good luck. They were as sad to see us go as we were to leave.

Pieces of chocolate rabbits lay mashed on the floor, along with boxes, and all our equipment. Our last day of school, before Easter break, was filled with good-byes and some tears.

I was sitting in our forlorn looking classroom, after the kids had all gone home, feeling depressed. I wondered if any school really wanted the kids. Not just to fill a quota or satisfy a state law, but really wanted them.

I heard a soft tap at my door and turned around to see the teacher from next door. She was standing at the chalkboard. Her usually prim, neatly tailored suit unwrinkled and fashionably cut. Two delicate hairpins held her auburn hair in a tight bun. She looked absurdly out of place among the heap of boxes.

"Can I talk to you?" her soft voice, drifted over the mound. Her brown eyes looked troubled and concerned.

"Sure," I said, "come on in and grab a seat." I dusted off a spot on the box that I was perched on and patted the area for her to sit down. I knew she rarely came in my room, the kids seemed to disturb her reserved manner. But, she was always very nice to us and I liked her very much.

"I just wanted you to know," she said, "you and the children have helped me so much."

"Helped you?" I was confused. How had we helped this seemingly flawless model of the perfect educator?

"You see," she continued, "I use to be afraid of the kinds of children you teach. That is, before I met them."

"I didn't know you were afraid," I answered. I had always thought it was her cool attitude that kept her so far away from knowing us.

"I hide my feelings well," she added, "but, I just wanted you to know, before you left, knowing your kids and watching you teach them has been inspiring as well as educational for me."

Her thin lips twitched, I could tell this had not been an easy confession for her to make. I felt guilty and ashamed. All these years I had assumed her aloof manner was due to coldness not fear.

"Thank you," I said. It was all I could think of. On impulse, I gave her a hug and added, "I needed to hear that."

I left the building, after our talk. Although I never returned to the Campus School, I knew I would always keep good memories of it.

May 1979

To say that Cherry Park had changed would be the understatement of the year. Transformed would be a better word. Unlike many of the other teachers, I had never come back while the renovation was taking place. After it was completed, and we were not asked back and I saw no reason to return.

Now, being in the school was surreal, to say the least. I was put back in my little pipe room, but there was a big difference. The pipes were gone; they vanished into nowhere. I looked up at the ceiling, amazed that they weren't there. The ones near the floor, where Sophie had thrown me against, were also gone. But that wasn't all, wall to wall carpeting, chalkboards with floodlights, tinted windows and a brand new sink lay placidly where there once had been concrete, wood and cracked frames.

A new, orange phone that connected me with the office and any other class in the school was ringing. The noise startled me out of my reverie.

"Toni," the voice said, "this is Cookie." One of your buses has just pulled in. They're having trouble with one of the children. Can you take care of it?"

I'd met the new secretary over my Easter vacation. I'd come to unpack the boxes and straighten the room up. I tuned her out instantly when she began talking about 'those children' and how much patience I must have.

"Right away," I answered and strode up to the door near the side entrance. It seemed fugue like to be back in the school again. Seeing once familiar faces, that had somehow lost their names and meaning to me.

From the door, I could see Phoebe and her bus drivers struggling with her. She was biting herself and attempting to throw some poorly directed punches at them. I could hear her swearing and crying, while the bus aides looked on. It had been a long time since Cherry Park had seen anything like this.

I walked down the path to where Phoebe stood crying. She had ugly, red welts on her hands and arms from the biting. Her drivers looked irritated.

"We'll have to get a harness for her," one of the drivers told me, "if she keeps this up." She was rubbing her chest and pulled me off to the side. She wanted to speak with me in private.

"She gets up on the bus," she continued, "punching and biting the other kids. Today she bit me on the breast." Her fat hands massaged the spot.

"I know she's hard to handle," I said, "but, she'll get use to the new ride. Changes are hard for her."

"Well," she added, "it better be quick. I'm not going to put up with this. A seat harness would keep her from getting up."

"How long is the ride?" I asked.

"Over an hour."

"That's unbelievable," I said, "over an hour just to come to school." It would drive almost any kid to the edge.

"Plus," the driver went on, "over an hour to go home. She's the first one on the bus and the last one off." The rides that some of the kids had, just to come to school, were absurd. They had been like this for years, but with more and more kids coming from farther points in Oswego county, the rides became longer and longer. How sad it was, that Phoebe's local school district, could not provide an appropriate classroom for her. Instead she was bused hours everyday to attend my class, one that the COES operated. Now, she would have to get accustomed to a new school as well.

"I guess we're all going to have some adjustments to make," I said, "just give her a little time to get use to the whole thing. Then we'll think about a harness."

I walked her back to our new class. She was still whimpering, probably wondering what had happened to the Campus School and the old familiarity that she was acclimated to. Shifting gears would not be easy for any of the kids, particularly so close to the end of the school year. I wished they had waited for the following school year to start, before they moved us. But no one waits for children, least of all the educational bureaucracy that serves them.

It was peculiar to watch the kids working, playing, laughing, just being... in Cherry Park School, once again. It floored me to realize that none of them had been here when the original group started all those years ago. Rudy, Phoebe and Roxanne were disturbed by the change.

By the end of the first week, Roxie had scribbled in black magic marker on the new green rugs. Rudy reverted back to tearing at her clothing, screaming and pounding on the door, if it was closed. Her fears of being locked in, behind the door, were too much to handle. Phoebe's incessant crying and screams brought a few phone calls to my class.

"Who is that screaming?" it was Cookie, calling on the intercom, "Is everything O.K.?"

Her voice full of curiosity as well as concern. The screams were audible from the second floor office.

"Everything's fine," I reassured her, "it's Phoebe. She's just getting use to the classroom. She'll adjust."

"FUCK FACE," Phoebe screamed in my direction. I prayed the secretary hadn't heard it.

"What was that?" she asked. "What did she say?"

"Duck legs," I answered, "we're studying ducks. I just showed Phoebe some duck legs. And she knows the answer."

Please God, I thought, let this woman go back to her typing.

"Duck legs," she said, "isn't that cute. I'll have to come down sometime and visit the children."

"Do that," I replied, "we'd love to have you. I'm sure the kids would love to show you what else they've learned."

Well, if Cherry Park was in such a hurry to have us back, they would have to put up with the adjustment period. Screaming, swearing, tantrums and all.

Pam's class was placed behind the gymnasium. They couldn't have isolated them more if they tried. But, the kids were excited to be back in Cherry Park again. Watching them come to visit me in my own class was like experiencing dejavu.

Could this newly remodeled classroom really be the place where we had first met each other? So many springs, summers, falls and winters ago? The boys had all equaled me in height. It was hard to believe they had once been so tiny. Now Robert was at thirteen, a young man, and the others were not far behind.

We toured the building, fascinated with the changes that had taken place. The renovation had made the school completely unrecognizable from the way it was. It was so odd to think that we were in the same place, the same school.

Walls had been knocked down, opening up classrooms. Wall to wall carpeting extended into the hallways, library and even the cafeteria. I shuddered thinking of all those mashed peas lying on the rug. Whoever had dreamed up that idea did not have young children in mind.

The library was now known as the 'media center.' It had been expanded and its location had been moved. The reading section for the primary grades had several elongated steps leading down to it. I wondered how a child in a wheelchair could possibly get to the books? Perhaps they thought Mary Martin was coming in to give flying lessons to kids who used wheelchairs.

The librarian and I exchanged greetings when we saw each other. She was awed seeing us again. Maybe she remembered pulling Sophie off me all those years ago. She carefully scrutinized my young students.

The bathrooms had been totally revamped. Gone were the steel containers that held brown paper towels to wipe your hands. Instead, hand blow dryers, adorned all the washrooms. I'd observed many of the Kindergarten and first graders twisting the blow dryers to blast hot air on their hair, arms and other body parts. They looked hilarious; blow drying their wet hair, and dunking their little arms in the sinks, trying to get them drenched. As far as they were concerned, the blow dryers were the best part of the school.

The list of new additions went on. But teachers complained about many of them. They had not been consulted and many of the changes were not to their satisfaction.

Andy Spano, told me they insisted on laying carpeting in the art room, only when he tried to logically debate the wisdom of such an impractical idea, did the planners relent. Purple paint on a green rug, would not be the most harmonious color scheme I could think of.

The school was grand, all the way from the centralized heating and cooling system to the chic potted palms that graced the new 'media center.' Like it or not, we were all members of the ultramodern, streamlined school of the twentieth century.

When I became melancholy during the month of May, I would wander to the boiler room. It remained untouched and the still, grotesque furnace and oversized, hulking pipes reminded me of the timeworn, seasoned veteran that this school had once been. No amount of modernizing or facades could ever change that. Even the pipes, that I had once detested, came to hold a special meaning for me. In my heart, I would always retain memories of the 'old' school, my pipe room and even the Campus School, but for the sake of the kids, I knew the future would have to be welcomed.

June 1979
I received a telephone call from the Department of Social Services. It was the child protective worker for Miles and Annie.

174

She wanted to speak with me and I knew it was serious from the sound of her voice.

Annie had been attending my class in the afternoon for most of the school year. She'd come to school with numerous bruises and even several black eyes. She still walked on her tiptoes and had acquired no language at all. Social contact with other children was nil. Annie preferred to play under the table, usually with the same toy. I was very worried about her and recommended that she be placed in my class full time next year.

It was hard for me to believe Miles and Annie were brother and sister. He was so outgoing, energetic and curious. Constantly getting into things, he had been labeled 'immature' by a number of school psychologists. I, however, did not feel this was criteria enough for placement in a class for emotionally disturbed children. I recommended another group for him, the same class that D.C., and Carlos had been placed in. The other kids he would meet in this new class would be more talkative and I felt he could communicate with them. Annie, was the complete antithesis of Miles. Withdrawn into her own world, she spoke to no one. Fearful, if I should make a sudden move near her, she always covered her face with her hands. I knew something was desperately wrong, but exact circumstances were cloudy.

I read from the cumulative folders of both Miles and Annie that both their parents had a history of alcoholism, child abuse and neglect. Apparently, their mother had called the Social Service Department and told them to come get all three of her children. Life had become too difficult, her drinking unmanageable and things were quickly getting out of hand.

"We're going to pull Miles and Annie out of their home," the worker told me, "they're both in your class aren't they?"

"Yes," I said, thinking not only of Miles and Annie, but Robert, Alfie, and Sophie. It was no coincidence that all these kids were targets for foster care placement.

"The mother's requested it," the worker added, "so it's strictly a voluntary placement. Probably for the best anyway, I think the drinking is getting out of hand."

175

"Yeah," I admitted, "she told me."

"We're trying to guide her toward A.A. or one of the other agencies that can help her and her husband deal with the problem." The child protective worker sounded tired, resigned. I wondered how many kids she had placed in custody during her years as a caseworker. As a teacher, I'd seen more than my share.

"So many kids seem to go this route," I said, "it makes me wonder why?"

"No need to wonder why," she replied, matter of factly, "kids with problems wind up getting abused or neglected a lot." A straight, up front answer. But, I wanted more.

"Why do you think that is?" I pressed on, searching for something.

"I don't know," she said, "maybe their slow or hyperactive or have emotional problems. Whatever it is, it's harder to deal with them. Tempers fly and you already know what the end result is."

"How about the youngest child," I asked, "is she being placed in foster care too?" I'd seen Miles and Annie's youngest sister. She seemed alert, more vigilant than her siblings.

"Her too," the worker said, "and all in different foster homes. We had to split them up. Couldn't find a family that wanted all three." My stomach bottomed as I thought of the kids being separated.

I hung the phone up feeling sad. I would be going home soon to my husband. I thought of the kids I'd taught, of Miles and Annie, who would be going home to poverty, illiteracy and abuse.

I'd talked to so many parents over the years. And with most, the strong desire to be a good parent was foremost in their minds. Perhaps, as with Miles and Annie's parents, giving them up was the only way they could accomplish this. I held that dream into the long, hot months that lay out before me.

Part III - Chapter 7

September 1979

Things changed drastically during the summer months and I returned to school thinking that this was certainly not a profession for those who were inflexible. Pam resigned from her position as teacher of the intermediate level class. I did not try to persuade her to stay on for another year, knowing that her discontent was growing daily. This was not an easy job, it was uphill work dealing with kids who not only didn't respond, but also seemed to look right through you. As if you were not even there.

A man who was her complete opposite replaced her. He was a strict behaviorist, in every sense of the word. I wasn't sure that he would meet with any more success than Pam had, but I also realized, that there were many ways to reach kids. Maybe, he had a new one.

Like Dr. Gramm promised, a third class was added to the two that already existed. I was so happy; the small class that I started years ago was becoming a program. Not just an isolated class, but an ongoing program that would educate children with emotional and developmental problems from ages five to age fifteen. Maybe now, we could work on procedures for entry. I knew there were many kids in special classes for the developmentally disabled that also had emotional problems. I also knew that many kids who were autistic were in these same classes.

Somehow, we had to find a way to figure it all out. This was not as easy as it sounded. For every child I'd ever taught, at least three or four different diagnoses were recorded. Even the professionals could not seem to reach an agreement. I'm sure it was confusing to parents. I know it created confusion in my brain. Labels like autistic, schizophrenic, mentally retarded, neurologically impaired, behaviorally disordered and so on could all be different evaluations on just one child.

Since all the kids were multiply handicapped, both emotionally and developmentally, it was not easy finding exactly the right classroom for them. Now with this program, an alternative had been developed. And one that was in public school, not a separate, segregated class in a school for only the disabled. I hoped, that in the future more kids like Phoebe or Rudy, would be identified.

With the third, junior level class added, our age spans among the kids would be even closer than before. I would teach kids who were under the age of eight. Josh, the teacher who replaced Pam, would teach the nine to eleven year olds and Mindy, who had been hired to teach the third level would have the twelve to fifteen year olds.

Josh and I would be staying on in Cherry Park School. I would still be in the newly renovated pipe room and Josh would take over Pam's old class, in back of the gymnasium. Because the third class was added over the summer, we would have far fewer children. Josh had four children, one of whom included Roxanne. And I had three, Rudy, Phoebe and Annie. The entire situation seemed nearly perfect, one that I had been striving for over the years.

Strangely enough, Cherry Park refused to let the third level of the program remain in the school. It made me sad to see Simone, Robert, Max and Alfie have to pack up once again and move all their belongings. They had only been back in Cherry Park a few weeks and now it was moving time again.

The most ironic circumstance of all was that they were moving back to the Campus School! I wondered what mental chaos they were going through. Being moved about like a pawn in a chess game. More than anything, I wished power for them, power to determine their own destiny.

It saddened me to see them manipulated like so much mush. I knew that we were all at the mercy of the educational bureaucracy.

For the first time in six years, I would not be seeing them every day. I knew eventually, we would all go our individual ways. The only thing that made it easier was knowing they had all grown up.

They were no longer in need of constant supervision. We would not see each other nearly as much, but my forever friends would always be close to me.

Getting accustomed to Cherry Park School proved to be more difficult than I had anticipated. The almost constant activity of life on Campus was a sharp contrast to being in the singular world of public school once again.

It seemed so odd to see kids sitting in rows, marching down halls in lines and sneaking whispered secrets. I had grown familiar with the unconventional, almost rowdy behavior of the Campus School kids. I suppressed longings that I had to be back there again, freed from the restraints of learning by rote memorization. There would be no classes in the halls here, and the sooner I learned that fact of life, the faster my girls would adjust.

The combination of having Phoebe, Rudy and Annie together in one room proved a fascinating one. At last, without noise or interference from other children, I could attend to these soundless little girls.

It would be very unusual for me. I had always taught kids with at least some language. Now, there were no other children to rely on. Either I would break through their barrier and establish communication or I wouldn't. It was as simple as that. But the thought scared me and I knew I would be facing a year that was unparalleled in challenge.

To lean on language, books or words would mean to court disaster. I would have to find another way into their silent world. This trial by fire would test not only my patience but my endurance as well.

October 1979

We sat on the rectangular, fuzzy rugs that I managed to secure from a local carpet business. Remnants and scrap pieces of rug or fabric were always handy in a classroom.

Rudy seemed oblivious to the alphabet bingo game that we were all attempting to play. She sat rocking. Her thin little body, arms and hands held high over her head, her small chest arched out like an eagle. Her eyes crossed and transfixed themselves on the tip of her nose. The only sound she made was the one that I had heard her make for over a year and a half.

"EEEEEEeeeeeeeeeeee..." she laughed and mumbled a few other incoherent sounds.

"What did you say?" I whispered quietly to her. She ignored my attempts at communication.

Phoebe was sitting next to her. An odd blend of curiosity and amusement cover her wide eyes. Her blue eyes have thin flecks of silver in them and they seem to dance while she watches Rudy moving back and forth.

"Do you like Rudy?" I asked Phoebe.

She smiled in my direction, and then looked back again at Rudy, who still continued her never-ending motion. Phoebe's full, curved mouth was open and drool was beginning to dribble down the sides of her chin.

"Rrruuu - dddeee--," she managed to say and I smiled my approval in her direction.

"Very good, Phoebe," I said, "Rudy likes you too." I put my hand gently on Rudy's arms and she stops rocking.

"Rudy," I said, trying to focus her attention, "can you say 'Good Morning' to Phoebe?" She shrugs off my touch and moves back to her rocking. But my insistence on entering her world is just as strong as hers to keep me out.

I touch her face again and her deep brown eyes meet mine with impatience. She will do anything to get me to leave her alone.

"Can you say 'Hi' to Phoebe?" I asked again. Rudy looks at me restlessly. In an impetuous moment and without so much as a glance in Phoebe's direction she vehemently says...

"Hi to Phoebe," and picks up where she left off with her rocking. Phoebe, nonetheless is thrilled, and attempts to bite her hand. Drool now covers her hand as well as her chin.

Annie, still terrified of most everything, sits beside me. She seems safe and secure here on the rug, next to the ground. Green globs of gummy nasal mucus are running from her nose. She leans near me, pressing up close to my side, and I gently, but firmly give her a warm hug. She needs so much attention and praise. The complex needs of these three little girls hits me squarely. I feel like a new teacher, learning things I thought I had long since discovered, all over again.

"Can you get me the box of tissues?" I asked Annie. She looks up at me and follows my pointing arm over to the desk where the tissues lay in their orange, cardboard box.

Quietly, she gets up and tiptoes over to the box of tissues. She looks at them and then back at me.

I nod my head vigorously, "That's right, bring them here, to me." Annie tiptoes back to where we are all sitting. Although there is no medical reason why she walks on her toes, she does it almost constantly. Like a suspicious feline, wary of any impending danger.

I slowly take the tissues from her, careful not to make any fast or unnecessary movements. I know by now that any rushed or quick motions will send her off into the corner, hiding and cowering. Her small hands covering up most of her face.

I gave her a tissue to blow her nose while I set to work on Phoebe's dribbly chin. Only Rudy's rocking and bird like noises break the stillness in the room. Suddenly she stops and the four of us stare at each other. We smile soundless feelings and unspoken words, floating in, between and around us. I find myself wondering if I have ever really taught children before. Ever really been with them, without words getting in our way.

I can hear the sounds of 'learning' going on in other classrooms down the hall from ours. Children reciting what they have learned or what their teachers think they have learned. Regurgitating ideas, thoughts, and information. Is this really what school, what education was all about?

I go back to our forgotten alphabet game. Phoebe has taken the cardboard sheets and begun to shred them. Rudy is now sitting on hers while she rocks and Annie has made a crude version of a play hat with hers. It has grown more than obvious to me over the past two months that the girls are not ready for any cognitive work. I have already banished the desks that I used in previous years to the school storage room. Hoping that another teacher would not lift them.

"What would you like to do now?" I ask the girls.

No response. Phoebe looks at me, or rather through me while Rudy has busied herself with playing the doubles game with her fingers. Only Annie seems alert and somehow connected to what I am saying.

I look over to our long wooden table where my lacy, white tablecloth from home lies peacefully. I had intended to use it as a tablecloth where stuffed dolls, animals and trucks could be placed. Instead, a better idea suddenly came to me.

"How would you like to paint?" I asked.

Phoebe jumps to her feet, excited with just the mention of the word 'paint' and begins to hop around the classroom in quick, short jumps. Her agility amazes me, usually she moves very slowly, almost painfully, her legs stiff and unyielding.

Annie looks at me expectantly. "Pai?" she said, "Me pai?"

"That's right." I put my arms around her. I had never heard her say any words before. Not to a person anyway. Only to her toys.

"We're all going to paint," I said and moved over to the cupboard where I kept smocks, paint and our other art supplies.

The raggedy shirts I used for painting were years old. Ripped and splattered with paint and clay from kids who had used them many years ago. It was fun for me to pass them on from one kid to another.

I helped the girls into their painting shirts. I buttoned up Phoebe's shirt while Annie attempted to button Rudy's. Annie's fine motor ability was far greater than her language skills.

"Thank you, Annie," I told her, "your really a big help." She looked up at me and smiled. Green mucus was again dripping from her nose. It was incredible, like Mount Vesuvius. Just when

I thought we had dried up the volcano, it would erupt all over again.

With one hand, I gave Annie a tissue and with the other I finished buttoning Phoebe's painting smock. I pulled out all the tempera paint I had and some over sized brushes. Then I proceeded to cut my tablecloth into three large squares. One for each of the girls. Even Rudy had stopped rocking by now. She was watching me cut and I noticed her middle and index fingers opening and closing as I continued cutting.

"That's it," I said to her, "I'm cutting!" I opened and closed my own fingers to show them.

"Cutting," I repeated again and moved each of their little fingers. They were perfect mimes. I knew then that kids learned by doing, seeing and experiencing. Words, talking, language would come. But for now, being and doing, was not only enough, but all that there was.

I spread a large plastic sheet on the floor. I used it when we were doing projects I knew would be messy. I didn't want to create anymore clean up than necessary or make the school custodian mad as we had done so long ago.

"Hey, I've got an idea," I said to them, "why don't we paint with our feet?" They looked at me, still unspeaking. My words were getting in the way again.

"Look," I said, "watch me." I began taking off my sandals and knee socks, then rolled my jeans up. Rudy and Annie needed no further encouragement; they delighted in the sensuousness of their own bare feet. Phoebe struggled with her orthopedic shoes, until she finally yanked them off her feet. One went sailing across the room and landed incredibly in the garbage can.

"SHIT!" Phoebe screamed, "COCKY SHIT!" I knew she must feel frustrated. To want to do something as basic and simple as taking off your own shoes, and not be able to, would push the patience of even a saint.

Annie ran over to the garbage can to retrieve her shoe while I helped Phoebe with her socks. Scars that were reminders of her operation for heel cord lengthening were still visible on her ankles just over the soles of her feet. Although many of the reports in her folder stated that she was minimally involved in her cerebral palsy, she still needed daily sessions of physical therapy.

When we all had taken off our socks and shoes, we sat looking at our feet. I touched my feet to Rudy's feet. She giggled hysterically and Phoebe and Annie did the same with each other. It was so much fun watching them interact. But what a struggle it was to keep their attention. It seemed only seconds long and wandered as often as not.

I poured red, green, orange, purple and white paint into round, plastic dishes. Slowly I dunked my own foot into the squishy red paint. Then the other foot into the orange paint. I walked on one of the pieces of tablecloth I'd cut up. It left a perfect footprint.

"See that," I said proudly, "that's my footprint." The girls were mesmerized. Drunk on colors and bare feet.

"Want to try?" I said to no one in particular. Without any hesitation at all, Phoebe jumped up and plopped her two feet in the red paint. It splattered up her legs. I was glad we'd rolled up our pants, maybe we should have worn bathing suits.

She laughed gleefully and Annie and Rudy were testing the paint out within seconds. They tramped up and down the once white tablecloth and I watched both fascinated and satisfied.

Rudy was not rocking and Phoebe seemed totally absorbed while Annie was having the time of her life. We would have to make a mess more often. They seemed to revel in the whole experience.

After they had worn themselves out, I set about the chore of clean up and washing their feet. Rudy and Annie were washed and still sockless while I was busy helping Phoebe wash her feet. Suddenly, the alarm for a fire drill sounded. Phoebe bit her arm and ran screaming from the room. The noise had frightened her and she reacted in fear.

"GODDAMN," she yelled at the top of her lungs, she was racing up the steps to the outside door as fast as her wobbly little legs would carry her. I was right behind her and managed to grab hold of her just as a flood of second and third graders came pouring into the hall.

"GOD..." she started to say, but I put my mouth close to her ear and began whispering into it. It always seemed to calm her.

"Shhhh..," I said, "its O.K. Phoebe, only a fire drill, just a fire drill." Rudy and Annie had followed me out of the room and stood huddled near us.

"Fire drill," I could hear Phoebe softly murmuring to herself, "fire drill, fire drill." Usually Mike Donahue told me before he sounded the alarm for a fire drill, but for some reason he didn't do it today. It had taken me, as well as the kids, by surprise.

We were all standing out on the steps by now. We were still sock and shoeless. Rudy was swaying, rocking and sighing. Phoebe was calm now and staring out into space. Annie stood close to me whimpering. How quickly things could change for my small group of kids. One minute they were cavorting happily and the next screaming, confused and crying.

I looked out over the rows of silent, statue like children and teachers. The October leaves seemed to be falling all around them, alive with their autumn colors. Still, they all stood quietly and obediently. There was no talking during fire drills. It was a rule that was understood.

The only things that seemed alive to me that brisk fall morning were the falling leaves and the little rocking girls I stood with.

December 1979

Christmas loomed quieter than ever. The girls seemed to move about the classroom with more ease, more freedom than I'd noticed before. But the stillness, the solitary feeling of isolation and quiet always hung in the air.

The contrast of the whole situation to the other years I spent teaching were nothing short of remarkable. Noise, confusion and at times aggressive behavior, had marked my time as a teacher in the past. Now, I moved slowly, with deliberation. Like a cautious stranger on unfamiliar ground. Watching, always watching their small faces closely for signs of recognition or understanding.

Rudy was standing in front of me, sweating and breathing hard. She had taken a short break from the game I was playing with her. It was the same game I stumbled on only weeks before. I had, quite by accident, discovered that Rudy loved being chased. Perhaps, adored is a better word. She could never get enough; it appeared as if I had unearthed a direct line of communication to her. She actually enjoyed being with me when I chased her.

Rose, who was now in my classroom only part of the day, had taken Phoebe and Annie to the library. I stayed alone with Rudy, to complete her reading assignment and for our little game, that she knew would come afterwards.

It was amazing, but I had managed to teach her to read and write over fifty words since the start of the school year. Her reading was very robotic; it sounded like it was on automatic pilot. Her writing was huge. The letters engulfed the blackboard, scrawled and shaky. But letters they were and I was delighted that she had allowed me to introduce her to the world of books. Even her parents were astonished at her ability. But, I felt she had more, much more to show us, if I could only find that mysterious key that would unlock her. But for now, this was more than enough.

She looked up at me, her breath returning to normal. Her eyes were dancing with delight. She was laughing outloud!

"What do you want?" I asked her, knowing perfectly well what she wanted. Maybe, if I was lucky, I would get a response.

She looked at me; I could see her defenses crumbling.

"Chase me!" she whispered and like a dutiful servant, I responded in kind. Around and around the classroom we went. Me always in pursuit, Rudy always running. I had yet to teach her to chase me although she seemed to prefer it the other way around.

She laughed hysterically, I loved the simple, pure beauty of her voice. Those moments meant more to me, than all the time in the world with lesson plans, curriculum or IEP's. She seemed so in touch at those moments. Perfect eye contact and direct feelings.

Rudy ran out of our class into the hall. She slipped behind the large steel and glass doors that led to the stairwell.

"Rudy," I said, walking calmly out into the hall, "where did you go? Are you hiding?" I knew exactly where she was, but this was not a game for the unimaginative.

"EEEEeeeeeeee..." I heard from behind the door. She was laughing and had hidden her head with her hands.

"If I find you," I continued, "I'm gonna tickle you."'

More laughing, but she wouldn't budge. After a great deal of pretend looking and searching, I would suddenly 'find' my little friend behind the door.

"I see you now," I would laugh with her, "you can't hide on me!" I would grab her and tickle her until she was bent over with tears of laughter. Then the whole game would start all over again. Around and around. I'm sure she could have gone on for hours, and I'm not so sure that it wouldn't have been the best therapy for her in the world. But other children needed my attention too and I was happy when Rose returned with Annie and Phoebe.

"Tell Toni about the big Christmas tree we saw in the library," Rose encouraged the girls. Annie's eyes lit up and Phoebe began hopping up and down.

"Chrish ... must tree," Phoebe yelled, "Chrish... must tree." She was excited and her callused hand went to her mouth for another bite. Rose gently removed it and held her sticky fist in her own warm hand.

"Big tee, Toni," Annie whispered, "big kiszzzzzmast tee!" Her speech had really bloomed recently. I never interrupted or corrected her when she spoke. The sound of her voice was enough to keep me going for days. I wasn't altogether sure we would ever hear it.

"Good girl!" Rose assured her, "Your talking so nicely!" Little Annie smiled back her pleasure, green mucus pouring out of her nose. It flowed continuously, and I suspected the cause to be the tubes that were placed in her ears recently rather than a head cold. No cold could possibly go on for months at a time.

Rudy returned to the small wooden table where she, Phoebe and Annie had their lessons. She was rocking back and forth, still smiling and playing the 'doubles game' with her fingers. I caught her eye and for a second she thought we would return to our chasing game.

"Oh no you don't," I told her, "I am tired and that's a fact."

"And that's a fact," she repeated in a loud voice, much louder than her own usually mumbled words. Rose and I both burst out laughing. We had both noticed that Rudy had started to repeat words, even complicated phrases and sayings.

"And now the DOW JONES average iissssss..." she said in an equally loud voice. Rose looked over at me in shock. Rudy had always watched a phenomenal amount of television at home, but commercials and public announcements were somehow creeping into her vocabulary. Her parents told me that she would sing and repeat ads for household products over and over. Now, apparently, Wall Street had made its debut too!

"Silver is up $1.70 and gold is down!" she ranted on. Her words in a rush and slurred together. Even Phoebe and Annie were fascinated. Lately, we never knew when she would come out with these incredible pronouncements.

"How's IBM doing?" I asked and she turned her body away from me. I had barged in on her world and she didn't like it. She went back to filtering light through her fingers again. Still reminding me of Simone in so many ways.

"What if we eat the cookies you baked this morning?" Rose asked, breaking the familiar silence.

"Cookie!" Phoebe screamed, "Give her a cookie!" She often referred to herself in the third person.

"Give the Princess a cookie!" she yelled on, referring to the nickname that we all frequently called her. Food always excited Phoebe, and as thin as she was, the child could eat grown men under the table. Never had I seen an appetite as voracious as hers. She could hold her own, even more than D.C. or Roxanne was able to.

We sat down at our wobbly little table eating Christmas cookies shaped like candy canes and milk in waxy looking drinking cups. Phoebe and I shoveled in cookies, while Annie and Rose took delicate bites of theirs. Only Rudy sniffed at hers in a disapproving manner. She was still very picky about food, but I was surprised to see her turn down a cookie.

That's not the only surprise I had that afternoon. We all sat munching and sipping, the lights blinking on and off our little artificial Christmas tree. Since the renovation of the school was completed, no real trees were allowed in the classrooms. Only our 'media center' held one. The rest of us would have to content ourselves with artificial trees or none at all.

I looked up from my cookie feast and saw Gwen Casher standing at the door, knocking. She'd taught Kindergarten in this very school for over thirty years.

"Hi," she said, "can I come in?"

"Of course," I responded, "come in Mrs. Casher."

"Mrs. Basher!" Phoebe screamed, "Mrs. Basher!" Phoebe jumped up from her milk and cookies and hopped over to Mrs. Casher. Although Phoebe was not an overly affectionate child, she threw her arms about her waist and wouldn't let go.

"Hello, Phoebe!" Gwen responded to her, "Are you having some Christmas cookies?" Phoebe looked up at her and smiled, but offered no comment to her question.

"Just wanted to wish you all a Merry Christmas," Gwen went on, "maybe sometime, you and the girls could come to visit Kindergarten?"

I looked up at her, my mouth hanging open. Here was a woman who not only knew the names of each of my kids, but also frequently greeted them in the hall. Regardless of the fact that they never answered her, she kept on.

"Did you hear me?" she asked again. I was so stunned to be given an invitation to another teacher's class, I was speechless.

"Visit," I asked, "as in mainstreamed?" I was referring to the popular term used by many special educators. Basically it pertained to educating the disabled and the non-disabled together.

"I think that's what they call it," Gwen continued, "used to be called 'integration', now they call it..."

"Mainstreaming," I quickly answered, finishing the incompleted sentence for her. My mind was far away, already making plans.

"Of course," she added, "we'll have to have it O.K.'d by Mike Donahue. But he won't be any problem."

I had brought up the idea of mainstreaming my kids in with the Kindergarten to one of the school counselors. He had spoken with Mrs. Casher and evidently, she liked the idea.

"We'll discuss it after the holidays," Gwen said, and walked out of the class without another word, leaving Rose and I staring at each other bewildered.

"Is this the Mrs. Casher," I said to Rose, "that so many teachers in the school don't like?" I had heard many jokes and snide remarks being passed about her teaching competency and her bad breath. Someone had even gone so far as to leave bottles of Listerine on her desk. I thought the whole thing was sad and clearly remembered the days when my kids and I had been target practice.

Rose shrugged her shoulders and resumed gobbling her cookies.

"We're going to Kindergarten," I said to the girls, "we're really going to Kindergarten."

"KIMBERGARSHEM!" Phoebe shrieked, "Princess goes KIMBERGARSHEM!"

After nearly seven years of teaching we were all finally being promoted. I still couldn't believe it. Although many other kids in special classes within Cherry Park had been mainstreamed, my own unique group of kids, had remained peerless for all these years. They befriended each other or no one at all. My mind reeled with excitement that Christmas vacation and I found myself wishing for school to begin.

February 1980

The chairs in the Kindergarten were ridiculously tiny and I felt like a giant perched on top of one. I looked out the windows and saw the never-ending snow coming down in sheets. The cold bit right through me, but the five and six year-old children who were in the room with me seemed oblivious to it.

It was play time and they were totally engrossed in their world. One corner of the rectangular room was set up with housekeeping toys. Stoves, a refrigerator, cooking utensils and plastic fruits and vegetables lay strewn over tables and floor. Some of the kids were concocting a make believe mess of peas, prunes and a rotting plastic object that looked like it had once been a carrot.

Several of the large 'riding' toys were out in the middle of the floor. The kids were racing around the room on them looking like the first place winners of the Grand Prix. One of the boys, a blond, chubby kid with red cheeks, rammed his riding truck into a table and sent a tray of brushes, paints and crayons tumbling to the floor.

"Alright," I heard Mrs. Casher say in a loud voice, "that's enough. We'll just have to sit down if you can't play properly." The children quieted down quickly and returned to their low tables to sit with their hands folded.

Mrs. Casher was flicking the lights on and off, probably this was a warning to go back to your seat. I had noticed she frequently did this if the kids were really noisy or loud.

"Now," she continued, "you'll just have to put your heads down on your tables. You've gotten yourself too worked up."

I watched my own kids sitting with the other Kindergartners. We had been coming to the Kindergarten every morning now for about two months. All of us, including me. I laughingly thought that I was probably one of the first special education teachers ever to be mainstreamed along with the kids.

Mrs. Casher liked the idea of me coming with the girls. She didn't have any assistance or student teachers and I suppose she thought I could be a help to her.

"Some of them just can't handle all the activity," Gwen whispered to me after the kids had settled into their chairs, "they remind me of their parents."

"Do you know their parents well?"

"Know them," she responded quickly, "I taught most of their parents when they were children themselves." She left me to contemplate this incredible statement while she busied herself with another child. Imagine having taught the parents of the children who were in your class. The thought amused me.

"Gina Passalacqua!" I heard Mrs. Casher's voice booming, "Will you puleezzze stop pinching John." I looked over to the child I knew was Gina. I had seen her skipping down the hall earlier that morning.

"Gina," I said to her, when she interrupted her skipping to tie an unlaced shoe, "how are you today?" Her long, dark hair was in baloney curls and snow was sticking to her eyelashes. The kid was absolutely beautiful.

'Well," she answered, "today I'm Shirley Temple, but yesterday I was Jonathan Winters... you know how it is." Without another word she finished skipping her steps down the hall to the Kindergarten.

"That one's gonna be the death of me," Gwen said, her upper lip twitching from nerves.

"She's got quite an imagination," I said, "a real inventive thinker."

"Imagination," Gwen answered, a bit irritated, "can you imagine that she went home and told her mother we had been cooking lobsters, shrimp and clams in school?"

I buried the strong urge to laugh outloud. Gina Passalacqua was certainly one of the more colorful children I had met in this room and apparently, she had an I.Q. to match.

"I administered an achievement test to her recently," Gwen added, "I showed her pictures of different breakfast foods. Poached eggs, shredded wheat, cereal and pancakes and coffee."

Gwen looked back at little Gina who had busied herself picking off some old, red nail polish from her nails.

"Guess which one Gina thought was the most nutritious?" Gwen asked me, shaking her head.

"Pancakes and coffee?" I ventured, thinking that no five-year-old in her right mind would pick a poached egg over pancakes dripping in syrup.

"You got it," Gwen said, "how that child's mind works is a sheer wonder to me."

I looked back over at Gina who was still attending to her nails. Phoebe sat in the chair next to her. I could tell she was beginning to get impatient. She was scanning the room, probably wanting to get up and move around.

I saw her hand ball itself up into a fist and come crashing down on the table. Lately she would pound on the table in order to get my attention.

"Cocky Shit," I heard her say in a low feeble voice. I looked over at Mrs. Casher, praying she hadn't heard. She didn't and I casually walked over to Phoebe, hoping she would keep her thoughts to herself.

"Toni," Gina whispered, "did you hear what Phoebe said? If I say a bad word at home, I really get it from my mother."

"Yeah," John added, "and that's not all she says." The other children around the table nodded in quiet agreement.

"She says," Gina bravely volunteered, "the F word."

"Oh no," I played up to them, "not the F word. Did she really say the F word?"

"Yes, she does!" Gina continued, "Phoebe always says the F word."

"You mean," I continued, taking a deep breath, "she actually said the word... FROG?" The children all look around at each other and suddenly realize that I am putting them on. The table bursts out laughing and Mrs. Casher is by our side within seconds.

"What's going on here," Mrs. Casher insists, "are you children annoying Phoebe?"

"No, no," I interjected, "they just wanted something explained." The kids are still tittering and Phoebe has put her head down on the table, giving into exhaustion and sleep.

"At any rate," Gwen continued, "it's time to finish up our Valentine's Day present for Mommy and Daddy."

The children slowly come back to life as Mrs. Casher pulls out old, worn pattern cards for the kids to trace their Valentines on.

"We used to do a lot of these things years ago," Gwen says and her voice drifts off into a soft whisper. I found myself wondering about the kind of teacher she used to be. Many of the other teachers in the school ask me how I like working with her. I usually shrug off their questions. I really enjoy coming to the Kindergarten with the girls. It is only for an hour every morning and it's a fantastic opportunity for my girls to be with other children. Something no other teacher has ever offered.

Annie has grown unbelievably since we started coming. She adores the attention that Mrs. Casher gives her and I am pleased that another adult has given some time to Annie. She has actually begun to misbehave! No longer the shy, frightened child on tiptoes, she now struts around like a rooster. Talking, joking and laughing with the other kids. Rudy and Phoebe, however, remain the same. They stay apart from the other children and unless I engage them in play with another child, they are content to sit, rock or stare. But still, I can't help feeling the exposure to other non-disabled peers is helping them in ways that I do not yet understand.

Rudy is cutting snips out of her red valentine and the other boys at her table are watching her rock. Her hands arched in the now familiar lines over her head.

"Why does she do that, Toni?" John asked, "She does it all the time." The other Kindergartners watch her, fascinated and confused. Rudy is small like them, but her ways are as complex and confusing to them as they often are to me.

"EEEEeeeeee... she says, "Hey, buddy can ya' spare a dime?" Her eyes cross and she rambles on in disconnected sentences that are daily becoming a working part of her vocabulary.

"Rudy," I told them, "is very into herself. Kind of like how you might feel if you didn't want anyone to bother you."

They continue looking at her and listening to her ramblings. I am not at all sure I have said the right thing. Theories on autism, probable causes and remediation techniques seem absurdly incongruous right now. Explaining to a six year old why their eight-year-old friend and classmate rocks and speaks in seemingly nonsensical phrases is not as easy as it seems.

"But," I continue on, "it's very important to keep talking to her. She really knows what you're saying."

I interrupt Rudy's quiet self-absorption.

"Who's that?" I ask her, pointing to one of the kids.

"John," she whispers, much to his delight. She names the other six kids who are sitting at the table with her. And has proven my point to them and to me once again. The child who is with us, but who rarely chooses to be among us. She hears, but will not speak. And only I know how much she has taught me. I hope we have all done the same for her.

She picks up her silver blunt edged scissors and cuts right through the red heart that another child cut out for her.

"Mrs. Cashers gonna kill you," Gina says and proceeds to cut her out a new one. I walk away from them. They are best left to themselves, to grow and learn without too much 'help' from their teachers.

It is time to go back to our own small classroom down the hall. Annie is reluctant to leave her friends and has stuck out her lower lip into a pout. I marvel at her changing moods, she seems so alert, in charge, and I find myself wondering if I will keep her with Rudy and Phoebe next year.

We slowly make our way down the hall, dragging bits of ripped valentines, glue and tape along with us. The halls are dead silent despite the 'open classroom' areas that the renovation has produced.

The only sound to be heard is Phoebe chanting over and over.

"G'Bye, Mrs. Casher, G'Bye Mrs. Casher...G'Bye!"

April 1980

I sat in my class waiting for the Kindergarten kids to arrive with Mrs. Casher. Jelly beans, colored eggs and worn black socks that have been made into Easter rabbits await each of the kids.

Dan has donated his old socks to be used for the occasion. Annie, Phoebe, Rudy and I have been making the sock rabbits as a special surprise for Mrs. Casher's kids. The socks are loaded with tons of Elmer's glue and the rabbit ears are grubby and gray from being handled so much, but they are some of the first presents my girls have ever made for other kids and I am very proud of them. It is good for them to give things to other people and not always be on the receiving end of the situation. To break down the mythology that surrounds kids with disabilities is part of the reason I was so anxious to have the girls involved with Mrs. Casher's morning Kindergarten.

Every Thursday her class comes over to my small room down the hall. Never have I had so many children from mainstream classes in my room at once. It is just as new and thrilling to me as it is for the kids. I have prepared several lessons, one on animals and the different parts of their body and another on matching things that go together -- like hammer and nail, toothbrush and toothpaste and knife and fork.

Suddenly they are all at my door, Mrs. Casher in the lead and the tiny Kindergartners lined up faithfully behind her. They pile in my class and a few of the bolder children break away from convention and hug Phoebe, Rudy, Annie and myself. We

196

have all become fast friends during the past months and I have grown to care about these younger, smaller kindergartners as I do for my own kids.

"Toni," Benjamin said, "I want you to meet my friend Ziggy." Little Benjamin is holding up a raggedy hand puppet with a huge hole where it's mouth used to be.

"He wets the bed," Benjamin continued, "what do you think we should do to him?" He looks at me with his deep, soulful eyes and I think how much alike, how much in common all kids have. How ridiculous labels, classifications and separations are. All it ever teaches kids is that there are some kids who are 'different' from them and that they must be placed in a special class, a special room, apart from the others. There will be plenty of time for separations later, but not today.

"Why don't we," I told him, "try to find out why he wets the bed. Maybe we can help him out?"

Benjamin digests this information carefully and walks away with his friend Ziggy. No need for additional words. I have as few solutions for problems as the kids do. It seems like all of us, young and old alike are searching for answers.

"Benjjjeee," Phoebe screams as soon as she spots him, "Benjjee, Benjjjee," Phoebe loves Benjamin. She too, has developed a special relationship with a small doll that is in my class. It is the same doll that Max, so many years ago, rocked, loved, nursed and nurtured. The same doll that he once placed under my desk, for love and protection.

Phoebe has this doll with her. She calls it Baby Nancy. Through the years Baby Nancy has not only lost her diapers, but all of her clothes. Regardless, Phoebe loves her just the same.

"Hi, Baby Nancy!" Benjamin says to Phoebe's doll, "Has Phoebe been a good girl this week?" Phoebe is delighted with the attention being showered on her and in the excitement of the moment, she puts her hand to her mouth ready to bite it.

"No, Phoebe," Benjamin says, "don't bite your hand. It'll really hurt you." Since he is one of the more bold children in the Kindergarten, he takes her hand from her mouth. I am touched watching these small kids care for each other. We give them all so little credit for being loving human beings. Phoebe stares at Benjamin and obediently takes her hand from her mouth. So many times I've noticed that the kids seem to understand each other so much better than we do.

The kids have been divided into several different groups so that each of the two lessons can be going on simultaneously. Rose has just come in the door from Josh's class, behind the gymnasium. Her time has been divided this year between my class and the class that Roxanne and A.J. are in.

"It's like going from one extreme to another," Rose said, "I just can't seem to make the adjustment." I know she is unhappy with her situation, but I've learned I have no control on what goes on in other teacher's classes. I'd tried earlier in the school year, to establish communication between us. But, Josh, the kid's new teacher was appalled at the freedom my own kids enjoyed. He needed more control, both physical and psychological over his students.

Playtime in my room particularly upset him. A.J. made a mad dash over to his old, favorite toys, picking up a doll that he once enjoyed playing with years ago.

"Why don't you play with another toy?" Josh asked him, he was clearly uncomfortable with A.J. playing with dolls.

"Because I want to play with this one," A.J. answered, his hands still flapping in front of his eyes.

"Put your hands down," Josh told him, "don't do that." A.J. put aside his doll and walked away pouting.

"They play too much," Josh told me, "they need to learn that adults don't play."

"What about your football games," I said to him, thinking of all the athletic games and sports he himself was involved in, "aren't they play?" Josh looked at me, but did not respond.

Rose has had to learn to be teacher assistant, this year, to two very different teachers, with teaching styles that are the complete antithesis of each other.

Now I watch her as she settles down with the Kindergartners and my own three girls, comfortable and happy. Talking and laughing with them in her own way. She's been with us four years now and I've come to think of her as indispensable.

The kids are attentive and enjoy the lessons I've prepared. So many times, in the past, I've taken hours with plans that have fallen flat on their face. The Kindergarten seems alert and inquisitive. Annie watches them with interest while Phoebe and Rudy stare blankly out into space.

"Do lobsters shed their skins like snakes?" Gina asks me, always curious about sea life, I wonder if she will grow up to be a marine biologist or maybe run a fish market.

"Aren't they shellfish?" John asks, "Don't we call them mollusks?"

I am intrigued by their store of information and answer their questions as best I can. Even Phoebe has begun to watch them intently. If only I could read her mind, to see what she is thinking, just for a few minutes. But, I am granted no such wish and the lessons are soon over.

The kids are preparing to go to dance class and to art class. My own kids have been included with these activities. It is fascinating watching Phoebe dancing. Her stiff body becomes graceful as I watch her sliding across the floor with the other kids. Pretending she is a tree or a flower, blowing in the wind.

We have a few minutes left before these two classes start and I suggest that we all enjoy the new 'hospital' the girls and I have recently finished painting. It is the wooden structure that we built years ago at the Campus School. It had been a store for a while, stocked with empty food containers. But, the girls seemed so interested in the dolls and stuffed animals I had that I decided to help them change it into a hospital. Annie and Phoebe spent a fair amount of time in hospitals and I wanted them to get a positive view of the place. Dolls and animals lined the shelves that had once been filled with containers of yogurt, cereal and peanut butter jars.

The word 'HOSPITAL' is painted in bright red letters across the top baseboard of the wooden building. Tons of hospital face masks, bandages, surgical caps, and ace bandages lay waiting for the kids to play with.

They made a beeline for the 'hospital' when we let them go from their lessons and within minutes, the play area is a shambles. But, I do not mind, it is good to see them enjoying themselves. Engaging Rudy and Phoebe in play is not always the easiest thing in the world. Often, they sit and stare at the most magical of playthings. Their eyes, minds and hearts elsewhere.

Mrs. Casher seems to enjoy watching them cavorting about like puppies. Teasing and playing with each other. Administering shots in the fanny or 'medicine'.

Benjamin has taken Phoebe's doll, Baby Nancy, and placed a cream colored Band-Aid on her hand. It is in precisely the spot where Phoebe bites most often.

"That's so Baby Nancy won't hurt herself," I hear Benjamin telling Phoebe. She picks the doll up and wanders off to deposit it behind the classroom door, as I have seen her do so often.

"Baby Nancy bites her arm," I can hear Phoebe murmuring to herself, "she is a bad, bad, girl."

Mrs. Casher has made the last minute call for her kids to pick up their toys and get themselves ready for art and dance class. The kids begin the process of making tidy piles of toys, one on top of the another. Scattered mounds of stuffed animals that lay lifeless, not long ago, will be played with at some other time.

As the kids are filing out the door, Phoebe is still with Baby Nancy behind the door. Some of the kids are fascinated watching her act out this scene.

"Bad girl," she says over and over, "Baby Nancy is a bad girl."

Suddenly, Benjamin breaks away from the line and comes charging up to Phoebe. He stares at the doll, who Phoebe has placed face first against the wall.

"Baby Nancy's not a bad girl, Phoebe," he tells her, "why don't we try to find out why she bites her arm. Maybe we can help her?"

She smiles at him and I watch Benjamin race off down the hall.

June 1980

The classroom was stifling hot and I could see pieces of the fuzzy rug from the floor stuck on Annie's warm, sticky legs. Mike Donahue had told us, repeatedly, not to open the windows. The school had a new, centralized air conditioning system, but it rarely seemed to work. Most of the classrooms were smothering with heat in both the winter and the summer.

Finally, I could take it no more. Phoebe and Rudy were on the verge of going to sleep and Annie stared off serenely into space. The hair on the back of my neck was matted down with sweat. I took off Phoebe's sweater that came down to her wrists and put it in the coat closet. She seemed to always be dressed like she was taking a trip to Barrow, Alaska.

I opened the windows and let in the warm breeze. The smell of freshly cut grass came wafting over to the girls, along with the aromas of newly bloomed flowers. The smells of summer made me smile and the looks on the faces of the girls were like a lazy contentedness. We were all too hot to even move. I could see other kids, moving slowly and silently in the halls. It was even too hot to run.

I went back to the language lesson I was teaching to the kids. Phoebe's head had nodded off to one side, she had fallen asleep. I let her rest while I continued on with Annie and Rudy.

"What's this?" I asked Rudy, holding up a colorful picture from the Peabody Language Development Kit.

"Rake," she said, correctly.

"Tell me in a sentence," I answered her. She usually tried to escape with as few words as possible. Although, by now, I frequently heard her speaking in long, elaborate sentences. Two, three or even four syllable words. But never to other people, not even her parents. She spoke for and to herself, repeating what she heard, from t.v., radio or other individuals.

"YOU--MOW--THE--LAWN--WITH--A--RAKE,"   she repeated, in a static voice that sounded like a machine cranking out words.

"No," I told her, "You rake leaves with a rake." She looked at me and repeated the words I told her, more out of exasperation than understanding. Rudy had come a long way, but there were moments, many of them, when she did not want any part of what was going on. I had slowly learned to respect that. Here in this room, with these kids, there was no such thing as 'rote learning.' You either understood that fact or you didn't survive as their teacher. Rudy was not in the least bit interested in appeasing me.

"GO--ANSWER--THE--PHONE," she told me, although the phone was not ringing. She frequently told me to do this, if she wanted to be left alone.

"Tell me in a sentence," I repeated, the summer heat had made me stubborn, although I felt like I could barely talk.

"YOU--RAKE--LEAVES--WITH--A--RAKE," she repeated suddenly and lapsed back into rocking herself in her chair. Pulling answers out of the kids in this heat seemed futile and stupid.

I gave up trying and sat back in my own chair, staring at them. They looked beautiful to me even in this weather. We all sat for minutes, quiet and blank. Phoebe making little snoring sounds out of her mouth. I couldn't believe I had ever not been a teacher, it seemed like I had been doing this forever.

"What you doin' Toni Baloney?" It was Miles, Annie's brother standing at the door. He looked in and then sauntered over to where we were sitting.

"Nothing," I told him.

"Us too," he said. I think the whole school felt like this.

"How come my sissy is in your class and not me?" Miles asked, pointing to his sister Annie.

"Annie's going to get a new teacher soon, too," I told Miles. Annie had made remarkable improvement over the year and a half she'd been with us. The Committee on the Handicapped had already approved her new class. She would be going to a class for developmentally delayed children. It would be less restrictive, she would have more classmates and Mrs. Casher had agreed to her still coming to the Kindergarten. Unlike Rudy and Phoebe, Annie was only six.

"What school is Jane in?" Miles asked. Memories of Jane came flooding back to me. She had only been with us for a year. So quiet, almost shy, it amazed me that Jane had ever been in a school strictly for emotionally disturbed children. Usually private schools handled only the most seriously disturbed kids. I'd kept Jane for a year and then recommended a class for learning disabled children. She had learned to read, spell and compute math problems very rapidly. Rarely, if ever, was she a behavior problem.

"Elm Park School," I told Miles. And I could see him store this piece of information in his mind for future use.

"How you doin'?" I asked him. He had been in a special class that was next door to mine all year. Still hyperactive to the point of never ending motion, he had driven his teacher to the edge. But, she liked him and I could tell he was happy in this new class.

"Good," he answered. Soon Annie was on my lap, looking for my attention.

Both Annie and Miles had been placed back in their home with their mother and father. Back and forth, back and forth. This was the typical way, I learned that the kids were moved around. Miles had been in a foster care situation twice already in his life, and he was not yet nine years old.

"I--HAVE--TO--GO--MAKE--PEE--PEE," it was Rudy, her voice was soft, an almost inaudible whisper.

"Go on then," I told her and she walked toward the door, stopping to examine both the record player, her old fearful enemy and the tape recorder, who she had not yet come to grips with. She sniffed at them and then quickly hurried off to the safety of the bathroom.

"Remember when I used to pee the floor?" Miles asked me. And suddenly it seemed hysterical to both of us. Laughter filled the hot, steamy classroom.

Just as suddenly as he appeared, he bolted out of the room and into the cooler hall corridor, probably on his way to speech class.

Phoebe's snores were filling the classroom. With only three days left until the close of school, I decided to start packing away a few things for the summer months. Annie insisted on helping me and I couldn't help but notice how firmly, how sure, her little feet walked around on the floor. The days of tiptoe had long since vanished. I wished that Phoebe and Rudy could experience this same thing in their own way. But I knew it would have to be on their terms, not on mine.

"No mo' ool?" Annie grinned up at me, her nose still pouring out green gum.

"No more school," I said to her.

The past year had been a difficult one for all of us. Pulled out of the familiar environment of the Campus School, I felt the girls had made an excellent adjustment. I was just glad we didn't have to move again. For once their future seemed settled. We were back in Cherry Park School and it seemed like we would stay.

"I want my pool table!" Miles yelled into my room from the hall. He was on his way back from somewhere and I thought of our lost pool table. He never finished it and I guessed that it lay somewhere at the Campus School on some shelf, forgotten or mislaid.

I looked up, but he vanished into the room next to mine, the door slamming with a resounding bang.

The pool table would have to wait, I thought.

And so would a lot of other things. This class had found itself on a new path. From one small class it had grown into three. I'd heard, through a good deal of communication, that the junior level class at the Campus School was doing very well. Their young teacher was excellent. The kids all seemed to be happy. Simone was now not only in the pool, but on the trampoline as well!

Part III - Chapter 8

September 1980

I am sitting at my wide, gray, teacher's desk, feet propped up on the tabletop. The last section of a Florida orange I am eating is oozing over the math lessons I'm preparing. I look around for a napkin and find it on one of the kid's desks. I walk over to it, and for the hundredth time that month, marvel at the number of desks and chairs that once again are in this room.

Over the summer, Dr. Gramm has eliminated the intermediate level of the program. Instead of hiring another teacher, because Josh has resigned and returned back to college, Dr. Gramm put all the kids in his class with me. Josh's four kids plus Phoebe and Rudy would have been enough, but an additional two kids are thrown in for good measure. My class size is back up to eight again and the span in ages goes from eight year old Rudy to three of my other kids who are nearly thirteen.

I wipe my sticky fingers off and listen to the sounds of the kids coming back from lunch. They sound wild and I know that the cafeteria must have been rocking today.

Roxanne comes charging into the room, nearly knocking me over. She is now close to 140 lbs. Her weight has sky rocketed and she has put on nearly 50 lbs. since I met her almost four years ago. At the age of ten and not quite 4'7", her weight attracts more than its share of attention from many of the kids in school.

"Katie bite me," she yells in my ear, her breath smelling of the spaghetti sauce she has just eaten, "she bite me, she bite me!"

"No, I didn't." Katie smiles and slides her tight, blond braids into her seat, grinning like she has successfully held up the Brink's truck and gotten away with it.

Katie has proved herself to be quite a match for Roxanne and they seem constantly to be engaged in a battle of wills. Struggling over who will be first in line, get a favored toy, or have the last word. The power struggle seems never ending.

206

Katie has come from a class for the trainable mentally retarded, where she ruled the roost. Like many of the other children I have taught, Katie is currently in foster care and has been for years.

Despite her aggressive nature, I like her very much and find it easy to joke her out of situations rather than provoking her into an explosion.

"Human flesh for lunch?" I ask her and she smiles a look at me that goes clear over Roxanne's head and understanding.

"Keep it up," I continued on, in a more serious tone, "and you won't have your free time."

I found that the best way to deal with Katie was instantly and directly. Her smile turned into a frown that lowered her blond eyebrows to her cheeks. I refused to become involved with her screaming temper tantrums and had frequently left her yelling and writhing on the floor of our classroom. She was use to wrestling with her past teachers. Something I refused to do. The tears, explosions and screaming of the past few weeks were nearly gone and I learned how difficult it was for kids to have a temper tantrum without an audience.

Only the biting was left and I felt like I could help her deal with that. In spite of everything, she was only a nine-year-old girl, without the care of her biological parents and probably confused and scared a lot of the time.

Roxanne sat rubbing her bruised arm, while I contemplated sending her to the school nurse. More kids were pouring into the room. A.J. who had grown as tall as I was myself, and as talkative as ever, went directly to his desk to pick at his newly sprouted adolescent acne.

He rolled his head around and grimaced. His hands still fluttered in front of his face, although he was more cautious about hiding it now. He had become a closet flutterer. Perhaps embarrassed by the stares or questions of others, he had subdued this part of his personality. He now flapped his hands only when really pressed or under extreme pressure. The cafeteria must have really been frenzied today.

"Are you Wonder Woman?" he asked me, staring at me with unabashed curiosity. Where his questions came from, I'll never know.

"Only to the City School District," I told him and he went back to picking at his face.

"Toni's not Wonder Woman," Nolan said, "she's Daisy." I know he is talking about a character he's seen on the popular t.v. show, "The Dukes of Hazzard." He showed me a picture of 'Daisy' only days before, taking a worn, creased, t.v. guide cover photograph out of his wallet. He had shoved it in front of my face.

"She looks like you," he said and shyly blushed. The photograph was of a lanky, voluptuous, blonde starlet. I had all I could do to keep from busting out laughing. The only resemblance between us was that we were both human and women.

Like Katie, Nolan was new to our class. He'd come from a class for educable mentally retarded children. Although he seemed bright enough, he had not yet learned to read and had compensated by escaping into a world of fantasy. At the age of ten, he was preoccupied with a world he created. And where I suspected he lived much of the time.

His mother told me how unhappy he was in his last school. She reported that his teacher made him stand in the garbage can with a 'DUNCE' cap on his head. No wonder his world was made up of illusion.

Both he and Phoebe ride the same school bus, for more than two hours a day, depending on the weather. The Committee on the Handicapped, in their school district, has recommended they both be placed in this class. Two more different kids could not be found. And in spite of that fact, they are both here. How I can possibly meet both their unique needs bewilders me. I wish that the various Committees on the Handicapped in the county would take the time to visit classrooms before placing kids in them. It staggers the imagination to picture a group of 'learned educators' sitting around tables, discussing the fates of kids they don't know and then placing them in classrooms they've never seen. And yet, I'd seen this happen time after time.

"RRRRoooodddeeee" I hear Roxie yell from her seat, while she stretches out her arms. Rose is walking through the door with Rudy and NaDean holding onto her hands. Rudy is rocking back and forth, her lean body nearly touching the floor.

"It was wild today," Rose says, "I think they throw more food than they eat!" I know she is talking about the daily insanity that goes on in the cafeteria. Lunchtime has become a battle ground for the kids of Cherry Park. A noise level that reaches pandemonium, food throwing, fights and hysterics are an everyday occurrence. The digestion of food is out of the question and it is not uncommon to see kids dumping their lunch in the garbage half eaten.

I am not thrilled with the prospect of having my own kids watching this spectacle daily. But, the only other choice is having them eat lunch in our room, which I feel would further isolate them from their peers. I choose the insanity and usually have to pay for it after lunch when the kids are keyed up from watching other kids out of control.

Rudy walks past Roxanne's flopping arms and backs into her own seat. She has messed her hair up with her hands and it is sticking out in small clumps all over her head. A disheveled reminder of the cafeteria scene she has just watched.

"AH-.-AH--AH--AH--AH--AH," I hear NaDean's breath coming in distorted sounds. Her irregular breathing occurs when she is tense, like Rudy she is rocking and her eyes look wild.

She runs over to my desk and picks up a pair of large shears, opens them up and then places them on her throat.

"What will I do now?" she screams at me. I have seen her act out this episode many times before. And though it no longer panics me, it is not an enjoyable situation to watch.

"Put the scissors down," I say to her calmly, "and take a seat."

She grumbles, balls her hand up into a fist and then punches herself, hard, in the chest. I point to her chair and she placidly, without another word, goes quietly to her seat.

NaDean has come from the now dissolved intermediate level class. For years, she'd been in classes for the trainably mentally retarded. And then, on a recommendation from one of her teachers, she was placed in the intermediate level of this program. Her behavior was bizarre and erratic.

"Do you love me," she asked, "yes or no?"

"Yes," I told her and meant it.

"Then why does Mommy call me an asshole?" she turned her face from me and continued chanting, "Asshole, asshole, asshole." "That's enough, NaDean," I said to her or I knew she would go on for some time like this. Her ideas and thoughts jumped around so outlandishly, that I never knew what would come out of her mouth next. She smiled up at me, a glazed look and I knew what was coming. A grand mal seizure engulfed her and she slumped over and dropped to the floor.

"Get the nurse," I said calmly to Rose, "she's having another one." Rose picked her long body up from a chair she had flopped in and walked over to the phone while I tended to NaDean. These seizures happened several times a week. They had been increasing and I was becoming very concerned about it.

NaDean's eyes looked glassy and she smiled up a weak grin at me.

"Fruckin bish," she tried to swear, but the seizure had made her words slur and run together, "a fruckin bish asshole."

Just then the school nurse came in the room. NaDean took one look at her and then her head nodded off to the side in blissful sleep. I wanted to move her, but the nurse stopped me.

"Let her sleep," she said, "we have to have this looked into, she's been having way too many of these. Maybe her medication needs to be changed."

We both looked at each other and stared. The problems seemed overwhelming. NaDean had been in foster care, but was now living at home with her biological parents. She'd been removed from her home after repeated neglect and abuse charges had been reported to the Social Service Department.

NaDean's past teacher notified them when she showed up for school one day with her body covered with magic marker pictures and words.

'Daddy loves NaDean' was scrawled on her. When I read these and other documentations in her cumulative folder, I felt as sick and discouraged as I have ever been.

The nurse and I looked at NaDean as she slept. I hoped her dreams were peaceful because I knew her real life wasn't. NaDean's hair was filthy and her body was so black with dirt it looked like she had been rolled in soot.

"Maybe I better check her hair again," the nurse said and I knew she meant for head lice. NaDean had several outbreaks of head lice last year while she'd been in Josh's group.

"I better call Child Protective Services," I said, "maybe they need to pay another visit to her home again." My mind and heart were torn. On one hand, I didn't want to start the merry-go-round that I knew foster care placement could mean. I had seen it happen too often. On the other hand, something had to be done about her physical problems and personal hygiene. Perhaps, we could work with her parents.

I sat on the floor near NaDean, watching her lips trying to move and form words she was unable to make.

"I'M SICK." I heard from the doorway, "I'M, REALLY SICK!" I knew it was Drew. He too, had come from the intermediate level class. Small, stocky and stubborn, Drew's mother had confided in me that she felt he was really a miniature version of an adult.

I watched Drew go through this ritual several times a day for the past month. My patience, only five minutes past lunch, was wearing thin. Drew, although only twelve years old had been in nearly half a dozen elementary schools. His mother reported that he had succeeded in intimidating even the most experienced teachers.

"I'm not comin' in," he informed me, "start without me." With that last remark he plunged his teeth into his arm and began to gnaw at it.

Not really biting as Phoebe or occasionally A.J. still did, but actually chewing up his arm. I could see blood starting to trickle out of his open wound.

"Come here, Drew," I said to him.

He looked up at me, his arm still in his mouth, and shook his head 'no.' My impatience turned to empathy for this little boy who knew no other way to resolve problems other than hurting himself.

"Where's the Princess?" I said to Rose, and quickly scanned the room looking for Phoebe.

"She's in the cafeteria," Drew said and took his arm out of his mouth. He was pointing back around the corner where Phoebe was.

"Oh my God," Rose said, "I must have left her there."

"Don't worry about it," I told her, "it's impossible to keep an eye on everyone all at once." I headed off in the direction of the cafeteria with Drew strutting by my side.

"I knew where the Princess was," Drew said, "didn't I, Toni?"

"You sure did," I answered and thought that maybe responsibility was the way to reach him. He had built up a wall of steel around him that I knew would be difficult to penetrate. His short stubby fingers were moving rapidly while he talked. He held them, one fist on top of the other, by the right side of his face. His squat fingers moved so easily, they looked like he was typing or maybe sewing.

"What are you doing?" I asked. I knew this was what the psychologists called 'self stimulation.' I had seen many of my kids do some unusual hand or body movements many times before.

"I'm playin' the flute," he told me and laughed hysterically while his fingers played a soundless song. I wondered what the intern school psychologist would say to that?

212

We found Phoebe standing in the middle of the cafeteria, holding her green lunch tray and chewing on a piece of waxy milk carton. She seemed frozen, mesmerized by a group of 6th graders who were busy crumbling brownies and dumping them on the cafeteria rug. The lunch assistants, who were hired to supervise the noon time fiasco, stood at the far end of the room looking vacant and exhausted. The noise, screaming and insanity was deafening. We walked back to the room and I closed the door.

October 1980

It was nearly Halloween until I'd completely overcome the shock of our new school circumstances. The year I had just completed with Rudy, Phoebe and Annie had been an intense one. I'd been forced to grasp and then interpret the singular, silent worlds that each of these three girls lived in.

Now, with little explanation, other than a lack of funding, the intermediate level class had been dropped. My exhaustion and energy were nearly depleted, but for the sake of the kids and for the concept behind this school program, I kept on going.

Dr. Gramm asked me on occasion to consider a change in teaching positions. A variety of different classrooms for emotionally disturbed children were springing up all over the county. But I'd watched the kids grow from early childhood into adolescence. For many of them, particularly the kids who had been in foster care, I knew I was the only constancy in their young lives.

It was with this attitude that I moved on that last year. At least, the junior level class was still in operation at the Campus School. I took great pride and comfort in knowing that Robert, Max, Simone, Alfie and the others were still hanging in there. Their teacher, Mindy, had stayed on for another year and she appeared to really be enjoying them.

My own tribe of kids were active, noisy and always on the verge of some catastrophe or another. I had gone from the still world of Rudy to the wild one of NaDean. After experiencing so many changes over the years, this one did not seem much different. But never had I had a group of kids with such a wide variety of problems. Rose and I seemed to be caught in a never-ending state of perpetual motion.

In spite of all this, I kept the kids busy with a schedule that put many of them to sleep on their return trip home from school. I felt confident most of the time. But I was grateful that I had been spared this group of temperamental, moody kids until I was a well seasoned veteran. They would have eaten me alive my first year as a teacher and I knew it.

Hilarious is the closest way I can describe the Halloween play my kids put on for Cherry Park School that year. The week before the play had been filled with fits of screaming, swearing and general hysterics. But then, the producers of Broadway never seemed too calm to me anyway, so I figured we were par for the course. The kids, all naturals at comedy, could have put Uncle Miltie on the floor laughing.

It was a classroom play and we were to put on three performances. I sent out invitations that the kids colored and wrote, to every grade level in the school. Rudy and Phoebe delivered them, with Rose's help, to the different rooms. They rocked, swayed and occasionally screamed, but deliver them they did.

The day of the play dawned dark and I let myself into school with the custodians. I was as excited as the kids. I'd written, directed and was acting in this play along with all the kids. It was an original and I was as anxious and nervous as any new playwright.

The classroom looked appropriately strange and eerie. Dark brown tree branches hung overhead from the ceiling. They were scattered across the length of the room. Little orange and yellow ghosts, made out of an old sheet hung from the branches. They cast a friendly look on an otherwise mysterious scene. They hung low and gave the appearance of a concealed forest.

Another orange and yellow sheet lay spread across the length of the floor, where we were to act out our impromptu play. The props, mostly broken down pieces of discarded junk, lay quietly in wait for the kids.

One by one, from six different buses, they arrived. Some kids irritable, some tired, some just plain excited.

"Mommy says the plays an asshole!" NaDean screamed and started rocking, breathing hard and mumbling irrational, disconnected words. Her face had deep, scabbed scratch marks on it. These were reminders of the times she had tried to hurt herself. It seemed like I was forever stopping her from injuring herself. A child protective worker from the social service department had been to the run down trailer that she, her parents and her brother lived in. He told me that it was the worst, the filthiest situation he had ever seen. The family was without running water and was forced daily to lug buckets of it from a generous neighbor. It was no wonder NaDean was always so black with soot, she would literally roll in the ashes from the wood burning stove her family operated. Refusing to wash, the grime and dirt built up over weeks. Attempting to clean her was like trying to bathe a twenty pound tomcat. Her parents had been told to either clean up the situation, move to a new home or NaDean would be taken from them again, due to negligence.

"I love you!" she yelled in my direction, "I love you! I love you!" I walked by her and she grabbed my hand, kissing it and muttering words all at once. Much of her behavior was not only shocking, but unpredictable as well. I never knew what to expect from her.

"Settle down now, NaDean," I said to her in a soothing voice. She balled up her fist, ready for a fast punch to her chest. Instead, she dropped her hand and dashed over to the rubber food that we were using as props for the play. She began chewing on them.

"I'll take care of her," Rose said and walked over to NaDean, to retrieve the rubber food from her mouth. I was afraid she would choke on it. I hoped her behavior was not an omen for the way the play would go that morning.

215

A.J., Katie and Nolan arrived with cupcakes, juice and apples for the party afterwards. None of them looked like they had slept all night. They were all so excited. "Are we gonna have the play?" A.J. asked, he had barely taken two steps inside the classroom door.

"Is a bear Catholic?" Nolan asked him, "Does the Pope shit in the woods?" He and Katie broke up over this while I tended to Phoebe who was crying and screaming at the top of her lungs. The play and all the rehearsals were frightening to her. Rather than exclude her from it, I had decided to let her lead our 'audience' in the pledge of allegiance, something she loved doing.

"Shhhh,"... I said to her, "everything's O.K. Princess, we're going to have a play this morning." Even after all these years whispering in Phoebe's ear still calmed her down.

"Gonna have a play," she whispered back, "gonna have a play." Her eyes glazed over and she immediately turned quiet. Learning to soothe Phoebe had been a skill that I had perfected over a lot of time. Getting worked up over her screaming or swearing only enraged her more, and magnified her excitability.

Only Rudy stood rocking back and forth. She was laughing while she swayed to and fro. Her hands still in front of her eyes, moving endlessly in their small spider like way. Perhaps her life was not as still as I thought. It was just her own, where she lived. Like it or not, I would have to learn to accept that fact of life.

She caught my eye and for a split second she thought I was going to chase her around the room, our old familiar game.

"Oh, no!" I said to her, "Not now you don't." I was so busy with last minute details that I hardly noticed Drew and Roxanne hanging out by the door.

Roxanne was crying and mopping up her tears with her red pigtails while Drew was trying to shove her in the door. He was pounding on her back with the homemade cookies his mother had sent in.

"She's tryin' to eat my cookies!" Drew yelled and sent his bag of cookies, or rather... crumbs, flying to the floor. NaDean, who never had enough to eat, was over to them within seconds. Face down on the floor, she was attempting to gorge herself on cookie crumbs.

"Alright!" I shrieked, because that was the only way anybody could hear me, "Sit down and cool it. Everybody, right now!"

Fortunately, most of the kids and I knew each other well enough to know when we were at our limit. They all either walked or were gently steered to their seats. Within minutes, calm replaced the crying and swearing. The changeable, uneven moods of this particular group of kids was puzzling even to me.

I tried to relax them with several of the Yoga breathing exercises they knew. But feelings ran high on Broadway that morning and my young actor friends were very anxious.

We shoved our desks, chairs and all the furniture we could out into the hall, making room for our guests. I had invited everyone from the Superintendent to the night custodians.

The shades were drawn tight, lights dimmed to a soft, yellow glow. The television video recorder sat in the far corner of the room. It would catch the entire play so the kids could watch themselves on t.v. afterwards.

Rose and I had taken our two large, orange cabinets and placed them strategically, so that the kids would be out of sight to the audience, except when they were actually on stage. I was behind the cabinets with them now, jumpy as a cat and filled with last minute advice.

"O.K.," I told them, "you've all practiced hard and you know what you're doing. Just go out there and break a leg!"

"YOUR GODDAMN LEG!" Phoebe yelled back at me. Nolan put his hand on her shoulders. He had seen her like this many times on their school bus, going to and from school.

"Shhhh..." he said, "you don't want them all to think we're weird, do ya'?" He looked over at her with his earnest, blue eyes and I found myself praying. Please God, I thought, if I have any coupons at all to cash in with you, I want to do it now.

How my tiny classroom could hold all those kids and adults I'll never know, but for each of the three performances we put on that morning, forty to fifty people stuffed themselves in an area that never even seemed big enough for my own kids to work in.

I walked Phoebe out to the front of our audience, when they had all quieted down, the tension in the air was as tight as a jeweler's saw that was about ready to pop.

Phoebe walked along with me, the picture of tranquility, her beautiful mouth open. She stared at all the people in our classroom. She'd never been in a play before and I wondered what was going on in her mind. Only when she heard the pledge of allegiance being recited did she snap out of her reverie.

"AND TO THE REPUBLISH FOR WISH IT STAMS..." she chanted on, while everyone suddenly grew quiet, "ONE NASHUM UNDER GOB, WIV LIBERTY AND GUSHUS FOR ALL!"

Although I'd never seen it done, everyone broke into spontaneous applause at the end of the pledge. I choked back tears as I watched the Princess hop off our 'stage' completely delighted with herself. Rose had Baby Nancy waiting in the wings for Phoebe and I could just manage to hear her talk to the doll.

"A good girl, Baby Nancy...a very good girl!" She grabbed the doll from Rose and sat with it, content for the rest of the play. I continued my silent commune with God, during the rest of the show, hoping the creator answered the prayers of a tenured teacher.

We ad-libbed our way through all three performances, but the audience seemed to thoroughly enjoy our improvised, off-handed comedy. The kids were hysterical and every time they played a scene, it came out different. Katie and Nolan played the part of two mummies. I had wrapped them to the teeth in ace bandages and they were the hit of the show. But by the end of the performances, Katie was tired and her muscles were growing cramped from being jammed inside the bandages.

While the last audience, clapped, laughed, and enjoyed themselves, I could see the kids growing restless behind the orange partitions. Katie's eyes narrowed to thin, blue slits and I could tell she was preparing herself for a mouthful of someone else's arm. Good luck or chance was with us and the play mercifully ended.

"You've really got guts, Toni," one of the other special education teachers in the school whispered to me, as people charged their way out of my room. So much could have gone wrong, but miraculously, nothing did. Cherry Park School had witnessed a curious blend of psychodrama and humor that I knew they would not soon forget.

December 1980

I wandered around my classroom picking up bits of wrapping paper, tinsel and broken pieces of candy canes. The Christmas party was over and most of the kids had gone home for the weeklong Christmas vacation. Only NaDean was left, fretful over her late bus. She industriously busied herself with her huge bag of toys, games and food.

I had over-indulged the kids in the Christmas glut of presents and gift-giving that I usually hated. Normally, I preferred a quieter celebration. But for some reason, unknown to me, I had quietly managed to secure a load of donated presents, stockings and food. NaDean, who normally had so little of her own, had actually hugged the gifts and food close to her own body.

Putting her thin, pale arms around them, she had smiled and whispered out into space...

"These are mine, all for me! Not you, not you!" Her eyes were still glassy from the unexpected deluge of Christmas presents.

I watched her rocking, talking to herself and coloring with precise, meticulous strokes in her new coloring book. Her fine motor and fairly fluent language skills were markedly superior to her still confusing behavior. She made facial grimaces that would scare the pants off a confirmed atheist. And her seizures

219

were happening with increasing frequency. The child protective worker had talked to NaDean's mother about this. The seizures were more frequent at home too and a doctor's appointment had been made for early in January.

NaDean's small, claw-like hands were red and chapped. The winter weather, as usual, had been brutal. She had no gloves or boots and I looked at her reedy legs with new eyes.

"I'll be right back," I said to Rose and left her with NaDean while I went in search of the office.

"I can come too!" I heard her yell as I walked out the door.

"Stay here," I heard myself calling back to her as I ran up the flight of steps that led to the school and principals office.

"I wanna go with Toni!" I heard NaDean yelling from our classroom. Impetuous and headstrong NaDean. I smiled to myself when I heard her calling out after me.

The school office was empty, even the secretary wasn't at her desk typing. I looked around the office again, checking to make sure no one was around. The light in the room was growing dim even though it was only 3:15 or so. I walked over to the Lost and Found box and started rummaging through it. Feeling a little like a five-year-old hunting around for cookies in the middle of the night.

The box was gigantic and I was bending over it, the top half of my body practically in it. Lost mittens, gloves, scarves, broken lunch pails, gym socks and sneakers lay in a rumpled mess. I was looking for a pair of mittens or boots for NaDean. Nothing seemed to match and the harder I looked, the deeper I dug into the box.

"What the hell are you doing?" It was Andy Spano, still covered with paint and clay from the day's work with the kids. He startled me so much that I fell headlong into the box, only my feet stuck up over the edge.

We were both hysterical laughing while I tried to pull myself from the smelly contents of the box. There's really nothing like the odor of mildew on damp mittens.

"I've seen everything," Andy said, "but this really fits the bill. What are you doing in there?"

"Sssshhh"... I answered, "I'm looking for boots and mittens for NaDean." I was still hunting around while I talked. Andy offered to help and the two of us must have looked like dogs scrounging around for bones.

"How 'bout these?" he said triumphantly, holding up a pair of red mittens with furry little white fuzz balls all over them.

"Perfect," I whispered, "and they match!" I grabbed them and heaved myself over the top of the box; I thought for sure that someone would hear him laughing and come to see what all the commotion was about.

I ran down the steps to our class, holding the red mittens, Andy was right behind me, still laughing and holding his sides.

"Look what I've got!" I said, holding up the mittens for NaDean and Rose to see. NaDean was by my side within seconds.

"Mine?" she said, "Mine?"

I shook my head yes and she put them on her little hands. They were sizes too big for her but she loved them anyway. Rubbing the soft fabric on her face, you would have thought we gave her the world. Perhaps, to NaDean, the world was those red mittens.

A yellow station wagon that was NaDean's school bus pulled up outside the window and began laying on the horn.

We waved goodbye to her and I watched her slip and slide her way to the bus. Her ripped and torn sneakers were useless in this biting cold weather. The zipper on her thin jacket was broken and I had put three safety pins in it, trying to keep it closed.

I knew there would be no Christmas celebration in her house. I only hoped there would be wood for the stove.

"I'll bring her a pair of boots after Christmas," Andy said, "I think my daughters got an old pair around somewhere."

"Thanks," I said, "it beats stealing from the Lost and Found box." We looked at each other and smiled.

221

We watched as the yellow station wagon pulled away from the school. Snow was falling fast and the wind was picking up in short, cold blasts, sending garbage can lids sailing around the front of the school. I could see NaDean, from inside the bus, proudly showing the bus driver and the other kids her new red mittens. Still making faces and punching at the air around her.

As the bus turned the corner all I could see was NaDean's grimy, pink jacket. Rocking back and forth near the rear of the bus. Moving in the steady, slow rhythm that I had come to know as her own.

My small, artificial Christmas tree was still up and its lights blinked on and off, casting strange shadows on the walls. I decided to leave it up until we all returned back to school. Maybe some of the magic of this special holiday would work its way into the hearts of the kids.

January 1981

It was a cold, Saturday morning and I was driving toward the city of Syracuse. The sounds of the Beatles were blaring out of my tape deck. I thought of the recent death of John Lennon. I had loved his music and his untimely death had shocked me. Like most of the kids I taught, John had been a victim in the struggle between love and hate. All the rest of my generation could only hope to carry on the ideals that he sang about.

I was going to Syracuse to meet with Phoebe's psychiatrist. He had a private practice in the city and Phoebe had been seeing him most of the school year. Her parents had taken Phoebe for a five-day stay in Boston earlier in the school year. Her screaming, swearing and temper tantrums had reached a peak at home. Her mother wrote me long, painful letters describing the impossible living situation that Phoebe was creating at home.

"It's like living with a crazy person," her mother wrote, "she's destroying our family." The empathy I felt for the family was very real. I imagined how difficult life could be with a kid who seemed to understand no rational thinking. The screaming, for hours on end, could send most people to the point of desperation. I hoped that the Children's Clinic in Boston would help.

They came back with a diagnosis of childhood psychosis. I wasn't surprised but I thought it would send her parents into a deep depression. Instead, it seemed to relieve them. At least now they had a name for it. Psychotherapy was recommended and her parents found her one immediately. The cost of therapy was high--$90.00 for fifty minutes, once a week. But if it helped, it was worth it. I only wished my other kids had the benefits of such medical care. After nearly eight years of teaching, I still worked without the assistance of a trained psychiatrist.

If any of the kids received psychiatric services, it was not through the schools, even though the schools had placed them in classes for emotionally disturbed children. Only parents who could afford this luxury, had the freedom of seeking out alternatives.

I parked my van in the garage for the State Tower Building and then rode the elevator up twenty floors to the office where Phoebe's psychiatrist and mother were waiting.

The waiting room was dark and empty. I settled into reading magazines and comic books for children that were scattered around on tables. I was contemplating turning on the radio that lay under one of the tables when suddenly a door opened and a young man, about thirty two years old, appeared as if by magic.

"Coffee?" he asked as I walked into his office. Phoebe's mother had just arrived and was trying to decide what to do with her coat, hat and handbag.

"Please," I said and tried to adjust my eyes to the blinding light that was in his office. It was quite a difference from the waiting room. The morning sun was pouring through the windows and seemed to reflect off every object in the room.

"Where shall we start?" the doctor said and looked at the two of us. Phoebe's mother was clearly uncomfortable, she had built up a mystique around psychiatrists. This particular doctor was doing very little to help break her illusions.

We sat and stared at each other for what seemed like minutes. Finally, I grew weary of the game. It was Saturday, my day off, and I had driven over an hour to come and see this doctor at his request. At more than a dollar a minute, something should come of this meeting.

"What kinds of things do you do with Phoebe?" I asked. He looked at me, his eyes and face seemed frozen, unblinking.

"All kinds of things," he answered after a while in his best Dr. Freud voice. He was a man of little words and our discussion turned into a two-way conversation between Phoebe's mother and myself.

I had seen many psychologists and therapists during my years as a teacher but, this was one of the most uncommunicative. He sat like a monk, who had taken a vow of silence, staring at the two of us.

Finally a buzzer went off and signaled the end of our therapy session. I had learned little, if anything, of what Phoebe was doing with the doctor. Was it just an expensive play session? Phoebe talked so rarely it was ludicrous to imagine her and this taciturn doctor talking.

"Can you show me where you work with Phoebe?" I asked, as we were about ready to leave. I knew they didn't sit around and discuss life in the room we were just in.

He opened another door that held one of the tidiest play areas I've ever seen in my life. Even the blocks and Lego's seemed lined up. There was a small cubbyhole with dolls, and puppets tucked neatly into a corner of the room.

He saw me looking at it. "Children like Phoebe want to play in areas like this," he said, "it makes them feel secure."

I laughed. This doctor took himself much too seriously. I had learned a lot about kids; Mrs. Casher's Kindergartners as well as my own students, had seen to that.

The over heated building and our 'therapy' session had made me irritable. It seemed ridiculous that Phoebe's parents were paying so much money for such a lack of services.

"What do you think?" I asked her as the elevator glided us down to the first floor.

"'Well," she said, "he's young, and he's good looking."

"He really doesn't say very much," she added, "sometimes I think he's got a problem himself." I was having a hard time trying to imagine him understanding kids; he could barely talk to adults.

"Some things are best left to the Gods," her mother said as we got into our cars for the drive home. If she was satisfied with this doctor then I guess I had no reason to be concerned.

But on that ride home I couldn't help thinking about the fantasy that we all tended to form around doctors, particularly psychiatrists. This very doctor admitted he had no solutions, no answers to Phoebe's problems. Why do we trust so much in them and so little in ourselves? For once, I knew that 'the Gods', the therapist's of the world, were shopping for insights themselves.

March 1981

"Campus School is closing," I heard the words and turned to look at the two sixth grade teachers who were talking to each other. They were engrossed in conversation and went on from one topic to the next, but I was blown away by the words I had just heard. Campus School closing? Impossible. The school had been with the college community for nearly twenty years.

But it was true. Budget cutbacks, financial problems and other concerns had forced the school to close its doors. In a few months there would be no Campus School. It was so sad. I had loved the school and had not wanted to leave, even after the renovation of Cherry Park had been completed.

I walked back to my classroom. Rose was working on a science lab with the kids. Planting seeds that would sprout into flowers and vegetables within weeks. Spring was just around the corner. But I felt sick at heart. What would happen to the junior level class that was at the Campus School now?

I tried to push the thought out of my mind, but it kept on returning. Simone would be sixteen years old this coming fall.

What public school in this county would take her? Or the others for that matter. Still extremely involved in her autistic world, it would take a school with a humanistic philosophy to offer a class for her and the boys. The only other alternative was to have her returned to the 'special school' for trainable mentally retarded children where she had spent the first six years of her education.

I felt panicky during the next few weeks of school. If my own class had been retained on the Campus, we too would be without a school. I began looking at Cherry Park with different eyes. We had been well received on our return back and many of the teachers were beginning to understand the concept behind the philosophy of educating emotionally disturbed children within the schools. Our Halloween play had led to many other things. Every student in my class was now mainstreamed, at their appropriate age and grade levels, for art, gym and music. It had taken years to break down the walls.

The kids had all made such big improvements over the years, it hardly seemed possible. These were the very same kids that many doctors had predicted doom and disaster for. Instead, they had proven the professionals wrong. They still had intense problems but, not one of them hadn't improved. Each in their own way. Some taking big steps and others, like Rudy and Phoebe, smaller ones. But just as important, just as meaningful.

I looked at them now, as they sat quietly at their desks. The circle of desks that they sat at drew me in. Roxanne, still round and stubborn. Her language skills had improved very little over the years but, incredibly she could read and spell on a third grade level. Her tantrums had ceased and I knew she felt secure here in this room.

Her friend and foe, Katie, sat near her. Together they had come to a truce. Perhaps they had learned, each from the other, that cooperation rather than competition would get them both what they wanted. Rudy, still rocking, smiling and playing the doubles game had learned for the first time ever, to walk with her mother through the grocery store. Without screaming, running or crying. Still afraid of many things, she was learning to overcome the unknowns in her young life.

Drew, still with his steel wall around him, chewed his arm and looked at me with caution. Was I one of those to be watched or trusted? He still had not made up his mind. Nolan, the quickest, had completed an entire year's program for reading, math and language arts. He would be leaving soon. At the age of eleven, he could now be tested out of my program. A program he never should have been in to begin with. NaDean, Phoebe and A.J. sat together playing a card game. A.J. so tall and talkative was the natural leader here.

"No, no, Phoebe," he said, "don't bite your arm." He pulled her arm from her mouth and looked at me smiling. Maybe remembering the days when he had been so little and I had done the same for him. His voice had grown deep and I smiled back at him, remembering the first day he had been dumped on my classroom floor by the bus drivers. Wailing and screaming. How much time had passed in between those two moments!

NaDean, still breathing hard, looked up at A.J.

"Don't ever go away," she gasped, "not ever, O.K?"

"O.K.," he answered and I wondered how many people had been in and out of the lives of these kids. I had visited institutions for the mentally retarded and watched as they walked, hand in hand, caring for each other. These kids had learned the most important lesson of all. It had nothing to do with reading, math or spelling. Many of them could not even speak. But love, acceptance and understanding flowed in and around them. Without questions or explanations, they not only tolerated but, approved of each other. How much we all had to learn from them! How often words get in the way of what we really feel. How simple to think that the kids who most of us believe to know the least, know the most.

Mike Donahue was at my door now with a group of kids that are not from this school but whose faces seem strangely familiar. They look uneasy, stiff. Suddenly, I recognize a face in the crowd. It is Mark, from the Campus School. The young boy who

227

was so fond of Simone. Still witty, handsome and friendly, he has grown at least five or six inches since I've seen him two years ago.

"How's business, teach?" he asks, I feel like we have been apart for only minutes instead of years.

"Can't complain," I told him.

"Just showing the kids around the school," Mike added, "they'll all be coming here in September. Campus School is closing, you know." His eyes are roaming around my class, looking at cabinets, space, and the room size. Suddenly, I feel my stomach sinking. Mike rarely comes to my room and I know there is more on his mind than what either of us realizes at that moment.

May 1981

It was a warm, humid spring and as I gazed at the dandelions that were growing on the front lawn of Cherry Park, I mused over the dozens of chains we had made from them. Bright, yellow flowers that had graced the heads of the kids. I had shown them how to link the gold colored weeds together to form headbands. These were the flower children of the 1980's. My unconventional kids had played with exhilarating abandon in the backyard of the school, flowers swinging gracefully off their heads and necks.

My daydreaming was abruptly interrupted by one of the lunch aides from the cafeteria.

"Toni," she said, "come quick. It's NaDean." Her voice was shaky and all the color had drained from her face. I knew something was very wrong. I ran into the cafeteria but, NaDean was sitting at our lunch table with the other kids. Rocking, smiling and talking to herself. Nothing unusual for her.

The cafeteria was uncommonly quiet and as I looked around I noticed that virtually everyone was staring at my table of kids.

"Thank God she got down," one of the aides said, "I was so afraid she was going to burn herself."

"Get down from where?" I asked still watching NaDean moving in her slow, rhythmic way.

"I don't know what happened," one of the older aides blurted out, "one minute she was fine, just eating her lunch. Then she stood up on her chair, her face sort of twisted to the left and she started screaming. Then she jumped up on the serving counter, where we dish out the food."

"We didn't know how to get her down," they added, "that's when we came to get you." I looked at NaDean, her eyes were glassy and I knew she had just had another seizure.

Lately, her seizures had changed, becoming more motoric. The doctors had changed her medication and that had helped some but, these new convulsions were as unpredictable as they were scary.

I had seen them before. One minute she was fine, quiet, placid and absorbed in an activity. The next minute she would do exactly as the lunch aides had said.

Standing up on the nearest chair, her face would contort and turn to one side. Then she would take off running and screaming. Recently she had taken off running and wound up in the first grades down the hall. It must have been a bizarre scene to those small children. NaDean racing around their class while I was in pursuit.

But most of them seemed unruffled while NaDean and I went through our antics, only their teachers looked flabbergasted.

"Would you like me to come and talk to the kids about it?' I asked one of the teachers.

"It won't be necessary," she answered, "we've already explained 'those children' to our first graders." I walked back to my classroom and wondered exactly what that explanation had been. My only hope lay in the fact that these first graders would remember back to last year when we had been in their Kindergarten class. There many of them had learned, some for the first time, that individual differences were O.K.

I gathered up my small tribe of kids and together we headed back to our corner classroom. They seemed to huddle together and I knew that basically they were all they had.

Later that afternoon, the kids put on a special music show for their parents. Many of them came, including Katie's foster mother who sat proudly in the back, smiling and clapping, pride covering her face.

But the most beautiful thing I saw during the show was the look of love that Rudy gave to her mother. The look her mother returned to her was only one of love and acceptance.

June 1981

Phone calls from the Oswego County COES had never been a momentous occasion for me but the one I was walking up the school stairs to take seemed to hold a special significance. Somehow, through insight or premonition, I knew what was coming.

I picked up the receiver and held it gingerly against my ear, almost as if I didn't want to get it too close to myself.

"Toni," I heard a low voice say, "George Gramm here." I hadn't heard from the Director of Special Education in weeks and I knew he wasn't calling to wish me a pleasant summer vacation.

"Your class is leaving Cherry Park," he went on, "they need the space now that Campus School is closing."

His words filled my ears but numbness went right through my body. It seemed like a measureless amount of time passed before I was able to answer.

"Why do we have to leave?" I finally managed to ask, "I thought they wanted us back here. Isn't that why they asked us to leave Campus School?"

I heard Dr. Gramm sigh and a gasp seemed to catch in his throat.

"It's not just you," he continued, "the City School District is asking many of the special education classes to leave. The shortage of space is critical."

"But this class started here in 1973," I persisted, "they even pulled us back here from Campus School a couple of years ago when there was only six or seven weeks of school left. Why didn't they just leave the kids where they were?"

"Because then Cherry Park needed the room filled," he said, "and now they want it emptied."

I thought about his statement for moments. What were these so-called 'special children' anyway? A commodity to be used and then traded in when their value had depreciated?

"Let me talk to Mike Donahue," I said, "maybe I can reason with him. I know there are available rooms in the school."

"O.K.," he said, "just leave me out of it. You're better off handling this by yourself."

We hung up and a wave of anger washed over me for Dr. Gramm. He was willing to let me confront this problem by myself but, he would not stand next to me while I did it. As long as he was not directly involved, as long as I acted independently, I could try to rectify the situation anyway I could.

Perhaps he had his reasons for steering clear of this. If he made the school district angry by supporting us remaining in the school, he might endanger some of the rooms the other special education classes still held in the district.

The Oswego County COES handled most of the special education classes that were in operation throughout the county. The number and kinds of classes had grown incredibly. And I knew that Dr. Gramm had to rely on the public schools in the county to rent space to him. Without their assistance, many disabled children would be without an adequate classroom. It was a dilemma that I was glad I wasn't part of.

I had my own problems to contend with and that afternoon I talked to Mike Donahue in his office. He listened politely, told me he would do everything in his power to keep my kids in the school and that he would get back to me on it.

He never did get back to me and within two days brown, cardboard boxes, once again, lined the walls of my room.

It was a hot, sticky June and packing seemed more like torture than ever.

As usual, the kids helped box their belongings. If they were to be moved about again, I wanted them to have some sense of what was happening to their class. They seemed confused, disoriented and I watched them rip apart their world again and throw it in a cardboard box.

I avoided their eyes those last few days. Perhaps this was what my kids thought most kids did at the end of the school year. Pack up and leave. We had done it so often, it had become an integral part of their education. Many of the teachers came to our room in disbelief during that final week.

"Where are you going?" they asked, many of them did not know we were being asked to leave. A number of them went to Mike and asked if we could stay but, the wheels of the educational bureaucracy turned and went on without us.

The last day of the school year arrived and I let myself into the building with the custodians. It was hot and a soft, misty rain filled the air.

"All the S.O.B.'s in this school stay," one of them told me, "and the good ones have to leave." I smiled as he spoke the words to me. This particular custodian had befriended my kids and often had a kind word for them. Frequently, he brought them discarded toys or books that other teachers had thrown away. Prized treasures to my clan,

I flopped myself down in the empty, quiet classroom that I had taught in for so many years. I had seen this room go through many changes in that time. From a grotesque, pipe filled space to the ultra modern classroom that it was now.

Boxes and crates were piled on top of each other but the room seemed chameleon like to me. Changing from the old room that once was to the new room that filled my senses now.

The pipes, long since vanished with the renovation seemed clear to me. Their bright colors flashing in front of my eyes. Those pipes had been such a focal point to my kids and to me. Problems, frustrations and anxieties had been worked out while

232

they hung silently over our heads. I wanted to see their massive, unwieldy form again. But no such wish was granted to me. Unexpectedly my own kids came streaming through the door.

Looking around at their boxed class, I sensed in them a mood of uncertainty. What were all these continuous moves to different schools doing to them? Even kids without emotional problems would have a hard, if not impossible, time dealing with this.

I forced back tears but, when the buses came to collect them I cried like a baby. Some of these kids, even though I had taught many of them for years, could barely say or even knew my name. I was just the one who was there with them, through the bad as well as the good times.

The buses pulled away and I watched as they rocked their way toward home and summer vacation. I waved until they were all out of sight and then walked back to the school.

A.J's desk was still loaded with the tiny rocks and pebbles that he had collected. Their sizes, and his fears, had grown much smaller over the years. We had transported them through many classroom moves. I had taught A.J. longer than anyone. And as I stashed one of the peewee rocks in my pocket, I knew I would keep it for the rest of my life.

Cherry Park said farewell with a sheet cake that was loaded with icing. Mike handed me a miniature potted palm that was enclosed inside a terrarium. I was relieved as well as delighted when my cat ate the plant within the next few days.

The Cherry Park School still stands like a fortress on the corner of 5th and Buffalo Streets. It's modern, tinted windows shielding curious passersby from peering in. I have walked and driven by it many times since I left that warm, June day.

Summer 1981

Dan and I had moved from our cramped apartment to a large, spacious house on the West Side of town. He had recently completed his Masters degree in industrial arts and was busy looking for employment. Meanwhile, I paced the house. Waiting for the phone call that I knew would eventually come.

It was a hot July and I spent a good amount of time in the park across the street from us. Many kids came there to dunk themselves in the water sprinklers that the city turned on every summer. Their playful disposition was in direct contrast to the gloomy one that hung over me now for weeks.

Finally the call came and I took it with a sense of dreaded relief. Apprehension seemed to fill every part of me.

"We found a school for your class," Dr. Gramm told me, "the principal really wants you there. He's seen you teach before."

"Where is it?"

"Not too far from where you are now," he answered, "in the town of New Coven." I breath a sigh of relief, maybe things would work out after all.

"I want to see it," I said, "as soon as possible."

"Why don't we all go down there tomorrow," he quickly added, "you, me and the principal. He's an exceptionally nice person and he's very interested in your group of kids."

Something in Dr. Gramm's voice made me stop short. I had become adept over the years at reading things through spoken and unspoken words.

"Is it definite?" I asked.

"It's definite," he said and then paused for a few seconds, "... the room is small and it has no windows."

I spent the rest of the morning fretting over his words and finally I could stand it no longer. Dan and I drove over to the school. Tomorrow seemed like light years away.

The school stood small and neatly tucked away from the side of Route 106 that ran parallel to it. A group of teenagers played a game of touch football in the playground behind the building.

I let myself into the unlocked school and looked around. The halls were filled with desks, chairs and other classroom related paraphernalia. I knew that summer was the time when the custodians did major clean up and repair work. No one was around and I began calling out.

"Anybody home?" I yelled. Only dead silence answered me. The halls were dark and I tripped over an old globe of the world that was lying on the floor.

"What can I do for you?" a gum chewing, middle aged woman asked me. She had a broom in her hand and looked exhausted.

"I'm going to be teaching here next year," I said, "I just wanted to see my classroom."

She looked at me carefully and her chewing slowed to a series of slow, methodical grinds.

"Can't be," she said, "ain't no room left in the school. All the classrooms are filled up."

I watched her as she fiddled with a can of industrial strength cleanser, turning and twisting it in her hands.

"It's a small room," I said, "and it doesn't have windows."

She looked at me and suddenly her sour face turned into a wide smile followed by a stream of loud, uncontrollable laughter. She laughed as we walked down the dark hallway and shook her head as if amused by some private joke. Many of the doors that led to the classrooms were open and I noticed that the rooms were large and modern. Equipped with carpeting, sinks and loads of storage space. Maybe this school would be perfect. After I got the kids over their adjustment period, we could fit in here very well.

The custodian fussed over a chain of keys that she had stuffed in her pocket. Finally, after locating the right one, she opened the door and turned on the lights. My heart sunk down to the floor and she must have noticed the look on my face.

"Now you know, why I was laughing?" she said and continued chewing and smiling.

I couldn't take my eyes off the room I saw in front of me. It was half the size of the room we'd had at Cherry Park. The walls were concrete, the floors uncarpeted and a long ladder that ran from the floor to the ceiling stood like a sphinx near the rear of the room.

I leaned back against the door. My eyes wandered up to the ceiling. Pipes, thinner than the ones we had been used to at Cherry Park, snaked the top of the room

"What are those?" I asked the custodian, pointing to a long cabinet filled with books, magazines and reading materials.

"The reading teachers," she said, "he stores his things in here." I looked at the room for a moment. A storage facility for a reading teacher, complete with pipes, concrete walls, no windows and a ladder that was used for the custodians to gain access to the roof, was to be the new class for my students?

I turned and walked down the hall. I leaned against our green van and the hot sun beat down on my body, making me feel faint.

"What is it?" Dan said from inside the van. He had been waiting for me while I went in to see the school.

"The room," I gasped, "The reading teacher stores his things in there. And there are pipes on the ceiling, and no windows..."

Later that night, Dan and I sat drinking ice tea in our living room. I had quieted down but, determination and resolve had burned its way into my heart.

I sat in my rocker and moved back and forth slowly. Looking up at a picture of Sitting Bull that I had drawn for a class at the college earlier that winter. His strong face looked back at me and I tried to imagine the indignities and injustices that had been forced on indigenous people. Some of the same inequities the kids I taught were going through. Dan studied me as I rocked. The summer sun had tanned his face and he looked relaxed as he sat sipping his tea.

The walk over to the phone was a long one but, it was one I knew I had to make. I could not fight this struggle alone and I not only wanted but also, needed help.

I dialed the number that connected me with Rudy's parents. Her father had been involved in politics for years. He was well respected and I knew that his influence could help, not only his own daughter but, my other kids from spending more time in a windowless, pipe and concrete classroom.

None of the kid's parents knew we were leaving Cherry Park. Late in August they would receive a memo from the COES telling them that their child had a new school. By then it would be too late to do anything even if they wanted. Rudy's father and I had many meetings that summer at my home. Talking together I realized how little I knew about him or his wants and desires for his little girl. He and his wife had Rudy late in life and their love for her was deep.

"You know," he told me, "I've never said this to you before but, until our Rudy went to your class I didn't know what was going to become of her. So locked away in her own little world. You've done things with my daughter that even her mother and I couldn't do."

His words touched me deeply. They were words that I had needed to hear for a very long time now. Words that made so much of the hard work the kids and I had done together seem meaningful.

Her father went to the school in New Coven as I asked and came back as disgusted, if not more, than what I had been.

"No way," he told me, "there is no way my Rudy is going to that school. I wouldn't even send a dog to the room they want to put her in!"

He made an appointment with the Superintendent of Schools. The Superintendent promised him that he would visit the room himself. I knew I had boiled a pot of hot water for myself but, it was either facing the possible wrath of my own supervisor or watching the kids spending more time in an inadequate classroom.

I spent the rest of the summer in a state of gloomy anticipation for what would come the following school year. I knew that I could never teach in that class and I hoped that none of the kids would have to face those windowless walls either.

As the summer dragged on I thought frequently of the Indian proverb that I had committed to my head and heart:

The Indian takes even his dogs with him to heaven, while the paleface sends his brothers to hell.

Epilogue

As for my own small group of kids, I am happy to say that they never did go to the windowless classroom. The concern of one child's parents was enough to make several school administrators take a second look. The class that was 'definite' became, 'unacceptable.' If one set of parents can do this, imagine what an organized coalition of parents and teachers could do together. Another school was found in its place. It lay further out in the County but, most of the kids no longer have to commute hours a day just to get there.

About The Author

Antoinette Magaletta McClure received her Bachelor of Arts from Caldwell College in 1971. Her Masters in Education for Emotionally Disturbed Children was awarded to her in 1974 from Virginia Commonwealth University. She is a native of New Jersey, but has been living and teaching in upstate New York for the past twenty-eight years. Antoinette's most current educational achievement has been the inclusion in *Who's Who in American Teachers*, year 2000. She currently resides on a five-acre estate of Norway spruce trees with her husband Dan and cat Escher.

Printed in the United States
98880LV00003B/68/A